4/01

Women Writers of the 1930s

D1193456

Women Writers of the 1930s
Gender, Politics and History

Edited and with an introduction by

MAROULA JOANNOU

EDINBURGH
UNIVERSITY PRESS

© The Contributors, 1999

Edinburgh University Press,
22 George Square, Edinburgh

Typeset in Monotype Horley Old Style
by Koinonia, Bury and
printed and bound in Great Britain by MPG Books, Bodmin

A CIP record for this book is available from the British Library

ISBN 0 7486 1112 6 (paperback)

The right of the contributors to be identified as authors of this work has been
asserted in accordance with the Copyright, Designs and Patents Act 1988

This book is dedicated to Naomi Mitchison (1897–)

'As strongly as we have ever felt anything we feel that there should be no paltering with evil.' Storm Jameson, *To a Labour Party Official*

'"As a woman, I have no country. As a woman I want no country. As a woman my country is the whole world."' Virginia Woolf, *Three Guineas*

Contents

CONTENTS

Acknowledgements

E very effort has been made to contact the copyright holders of the Spanish Civil War photographs used by Elena Gualtieri, the poetry of Stevie Smith, and the cartoon reproduced in Janet Montefiore's essay. The publishers will be pleased to hear from anyone to whom copyright may belong. We are indebted to the King's Modern Archive, King's College, Cambridge University, and to the Society of Authors as the literary representatives of the estates of Rosamond Lehmann and Virginia Woolf, for permission to quote from published and unpublished materials, and to Margo Ewart for permission to quote six stanzas from the late Gavin Ewart's Poem, 'The Thirties'. The photograph on the cover of this book was originally taken for Mass-Observation and is reproduced by kind permission of the photographer, Humphrey Spender, and the Bolton Museum and Art Galleries.

The essays in this collection originated as papers which were presented to the first national conference on the literature of the 1930s organised at the University of Eastern England (then Anglia Polytechnic University), in Cambridge in November 1997. The conference was a convergence of researchers who knew of each other's writing but for whom working on the 1930s had hitherto often meant working in relative isolation. Our lives and work have subsequently been enriched by the friendships made during the production of this book and my warmest thanks are due to the contributors for the enthusiasm and scholarship which they have brought to their writing and for their individual commitment to the importance of our collective project. I hope that, like me, they will think of this book as a beginning and not an end; as one contribution to the wider enterprise of questioning, and thereby helping to reverse, the processes whereby even the authors in this book whose reputations may now appear to be the most secure

ACKNOWLEDGEMENTS

have at times in the past, in E. P. Thompson's useful phrase, been subjected to the 'condescension of posterity'.

I wish to thank everyone whose hard work made possible the conference and the book which resulted from it and particularly Jackie Jones of Edinburgh University Press for her enthusiastic advocacy of the project from its inception. John Lucas, David Margolies, Janet Montefiore, Jean Radford and Nigel Wheale all read and commented helpfully on the introduction and Pam Bowyer compiled the index. My thanks are due to Sue Gaukroger, Kate Gordon, Androula Joannou, Sana al-Khayyat, Brenda Kirsch, Gillian Maskens, Christine Petters and Maureen McWilliam for their practical and emotional support over the years and to my colleagues for living patiently with my absent-mindedness during the editing process and returning more mislaid keys and photocopying cards to their distracted owner than usual. My own research has been conducted in the Cambridge University Library which has remained a haven of peace and tranquility in spite of the recent building work, and whose staff have remained calm, courteous and helpful despite the chaos around them. I am indebted to the University of Eastern England for a very precious semester of sabbatical leave in which to attend to much unfinished business including the editorial work on this book.

Mary Joannou

1

The Woman Writer in the 1930s –
On Not Being Mrs Giles of Durham City

Maroula Joannou

In 1930 a reluctant Virginia Woolf was persuaded by her friend, Margaret Llewelyn Davies, to write an introductory letter to the accounts of their daily lives by Co-operative working women, *Life as We Have Known It*.[1] Woolf recalls a visit to the conference of the Co-operative Women's Guild in 1913 at which she found herself struggling with characteristic honesty to make sense of the 'contradictory and complex feelings which beset the middle-class visitor when forced to sit out a Congress of working women in silence'. (p. xxiv) Woolf scrupulously resists the temptation of facile identification with the conference delegates. Her emphasis is on the difference between the Co-operative women and herself rather than on their generic humanity. Feeling 'irretrievably cut off from the actors', (p. xix) she confesses that 'one could not be Mrs Giles of Durham because one's body had never stood at the wash-tub; one's hands had never wrung and scrubbed and chopped up whatever the meat may be that makes a miner's supper'. (p. xxi)

As she listened to the demands from the rostrum for reform of the divorce laws, education, the vote, higher wages and shorter hours, Woolf registered the limits to the possibilities of imaginative sympathy: 'One sat in an armchair or read a book. One saw landscapes and seascapes, perhaps Greece or Italy, where Mrs Giles or Mrs Edwards must have seen slag heaps and rows upon rows of slate-roofed houses'. (p. xxi) The differences between their respective economic circumstances determined that whereas Woolf's priorities were largely aesthetic, the working women's were substantively material; 'to expect us, whose minds, such as they are, fly free at the end of a short length of capital to tie ourselves down again to that narrow plot of acquisitiveness and

St. Louis Community College
at Meramec
Library

1

desire is impossible'. (p. xxv) Moreover, 'if every reform they demand was granted this very instant it would not touch one hair of my comfortable capitalistic head'. (p. xix)

A possible response to the request from Llewelyn Davies, which occasioned Woolf such discomfort, would have been a polite refusal. But such was her political commitment that this was impossible. This commitment was to manifest itself in various ways in the 1930s: in fiction, her magnificent anti-war polemic, *Three Guineas*, and in her essays and other discursive writings – inflected, revisited, made urgent certainly, by the spectres of Fascism and impending war as the decade unfolded, but going back much further; her links with the Co-operative working women stretching back to before the First World War. Virginia Woolf was to be in good company in attempting to rationalise and record her complicated personal responses to the contrasts between her own privilege and the deprivation she witnessed around her: many women writers embarked upon similar projects during the 1930s.

The purpose of this collection of essays is to draw attention to women writers, many of whom, as I have argued elsewhere, were like Virginia Woolf 'among the most enthusiastic creators, transmitters and publicists of the vibrant and deeply politicised literary culture of their time'.[2] But one would hardly know this when reading the standard critical commentaries on the period in which women have until relatively recently been omitted or marginalised.[3] The notion of the 1930s as a discrete historical decade with unique identifying features manifested in its literature must be recognised as problematic. Firstly, as John Lucas has recently argued, much which makes the decade unusual – for example, the radical outlook of the creative artist – can be traced back to the 1920s[4] and continues into the 1940s. Secondly, Jane Dowson has pointed out that it is specifically the periodising impulse 'in its insistence on "groups" and "movements" which has often been responsible for excluding women'[5] who do not fit into the appropriate niches. The domination of the critical discussion of the literature of the 1930s by the poetry of W. H. Auden, Stephen Spender, Christopher Isherwood, Cecil Day Lewis and Louis MacNeice has been detrimental to the reputation of many good women novelists. Moreover, women poets have often been denied the critical recognition which their work deserves by the use of the 'Audenesque' as a standard by which other poetry is judged and found to be deficient. In her essay in this volume Dowson locates the '"Audenesque" features – realism, contemporary diction, mixed public and personal rhetoric' in the poems of Sylvia Townsend Warner and Naomi Mitchison whom she argues were 'more left-wing in terms of representing democratic ideals or the voices of the socially disadvantaged than W. H. Auden'.

What marks the 1930s as a distinctive decade in British letters is the well-chronicled shift to the left on the part of many British writers. Andy Croft argues that the time of the Popular Front was a Gramscian moment, 'involving as it did a relocation of terms like democracy and patriotism, and a recognition of the central place of culture – especially of popular culture – in the battle of ideas and images, in the struggle for power'.[6] A. T. Tolley has claimed that the 'amount of left-wing journalism in the late 1930s was so overwhelming that someone of left-wing sympathies might well have been described as living in a culture as pervasively Left as the culture as a whole was pervasively Christian.'[7]

To observers at the time, radical change often seemed as inevitable as it was imminent. Many socialist intellectuals subscribed to the 'belief – half-regretful, half-exultant – the old order was doomed, that some kind of revolution ("death of the old gang") must come'[8] and they saw themselves as called to play a role in expediting it. Naomi Mitchison was speaking for them all when she remembered that 'what was so strange and striking was the feeling we all had that, if we tried hard enough, the millennium ... would come into being'.[9]

In those communities which endured destitution, hunger, sickness, humiliation, the Means Test and the dole queue, the collective memories of the 1930s as a time of unremitting despair and degradation are still often strong, 'What do you think about England', enquired Auden in *The Orators*, designating England as 'this country of ours where nobody is well?'[10] But this is not the whole picture. The standards of living of substantial sections of the population improved during this time. Extensive slum clearance and new building programmes – four million new houses were constructed between the wars – brought good, affordable housing to many families for the first time. Other signifiers of material prosperity were increasing car ownership and access to domestic appliances such as vacuum cleaners and gas cookers.

But it was the visible suffering which devastated entire communities that spoke compellingly both to the liberal conscience and to those sections of the left who saw its eradication being made possible only by revolutionary change. In the words of Storm Jameson, 'on one side Dachau, on the other the "distressed areas" with their ashamed workless men and despairing women. Not many English writers had the hardness of heart ... to hurry past, handkerchief to nose, intoning, "my concern is with art, what troubles are troubling the world are not my business"'.[11] The intensity of their identification with the disadvantaged took many intellectuals by surprise. In *The Moral Basis of Politics* Naomi Mitchison describes her dawning realisation that 'politics was not a special kind of game for skilled players, but rather a whole aspect of life. One could not draw back; one could not, as the phrase runs, "go out of politics"'.[12] Women often refused to separate their theory from their practice and were actively involved in important political initiatives against Fascism, hunger and unemployment. Storm Jameson's work on behalf of European Jews at PEN, which Joanna Labon mentions in this volume, is one good example of practical support for the victims of Fascism. For some the shift to the left was to be relatively short-lived – Rebecca West moved to the right in later life and Rosamond Lehmann once expressed admiration for Margaret Thatcher – but the strength of their left-wing commitment in the 1930s cannot be doubted.

If, as Pamela Fox has suggested in a recent ground-breaking study of the working-class novel, *Class Fictions*, feelings of class shame and the desire for self-betterment have been important factors in shaping the attitudes of working-class people – often acting as a political counterbalance to expressions of working-class militancy – [13] it may also be argued that the endorsement by middle-class intellectuals of political aims that were antithetical to the interests of their class also reflected feelings of class shame at the contrast between the comfort which they enjoyed themselves and the impoverished lives of others. Musing with some ambivalence on the hypothesised socialist society to which she was committed in principle, Naomi Mitchison surmised that 'it will be damned uncomfortable, and I shall never any more have any of the things I like, hot baths and silk clothes and quiet and leisure and a good typewriter of my own'.[14]

With the possible exception of Elizabeth von Arnim, in whose writing Alison Hennegan finds unexpected elements of dissent, the writers in the collection occupy a position on the liberal-left of the British political spectrum. But, as David Margolies argues in *Writing the Revolution*, a study of the influential journal, *Left Review*, between 1934 and 1938, even the writing of the 1930s that is self-consciously situated on the left is usually characterised by diversity in its content and form rather than by adherence to any narrow 'party line' on what constituted good writing.[15] What this collection has strenuously resisted is reproducing, albeit in an updated mode, the narrow definition of the political which pertained in the 1930s, and which Alison Hennegan observes is still that which is recognised by some who are working on the 1930s today. Instead, essayists have widened their understanding of the political to encompass a wide range of concerns including matters of race, class, nation, sexuality, personal relationships, and the uses and abuses of power.

While the literature of the period certainly acquired a more materially grounded dimension and somewhat different ethical concerns than before, the interest on aesthetic experimentation which had marked the 1920s was not simply replaced by a new interest in politics in the 1930s as is often supposed. The prose of Sylvia Townsend Warner, for example, is subtle, sinuous and aesthetically innovative; her generic inventiveness so in advance of its day that its very existence must question the usefulness of existing taxonomies. Gillian Beer writes:

> If *After the Death of Don Juan* had been published, not in 1936 but fifty years later, it would have been greeted as a magic-realist fiction; if *Mr Fortune's Maggot* had been published, not in 1928 but, likewise, fifty years later, it would be read as a post-colonial text; while *Summer Will Show* would be seen as part of the current vogue for novels that rewrite the nineteenth century, and the medieval *The Corner that Held Them* as a follower of Umberto Eco's *The Name of the Rose*. But Warner in fact wrote each of these very diverse novels long before those critical templates were in place. She composed with an exploratory verve that is quite extraordinary.

Tensions sometimes existed in this period between authors who valued artistic change more highly than political change and vice versa. As Gillian Hanscombe and Virginia Smyers have put it, 'to the political activists, artistic radicalism seems all too often traditionalist in its assumptions of the primacy of art over all the other workings of the world'.[16] But political and aesthetic innovation need not be mutually exclusive. This is exemplified in the life and work of Nancy Cunard, a prodigious political activist whose organisational flair lay behind a number of prominent campaigns. Cunard's radical publishing house, The Hours Press, which was established in Paris in the 1920s, was an important forum for Laura Riding, Ezra Pound and other writers of the avant-garde. Her editing of the anthology *Negro* is discussed here by Tory Young.

Jean Radford's essay takes issue with the manner in which history has sometimes been used to underpin the critical dichotomy between Modernism and the other writing of the 1930s. Her readings of Elizabeth Bowen and Jean Rhys emphasise the ways in which Modernist forms link to the politics of the period and the rise of anti-Semitism and

Fascism in Paris in the 1930s. Keith Williams, Steve Matthews and others have challenged the critical orthodoxy that the 1930s was an anti-Modernist decade'[17] – Pound, Eliot and Yeats continued to produce important work throughout the period. However, as Radford argues, a rather different literary history emerges if our understandings of Modernism are refashioned to take full account of the Modernist women.

First used in the sense in which we still recognise it by Laura Riding and Robert Graves in 1927,[18] the term Modernism was still relatively new in the 1930s and many women writers felt that it was of little relevance to themselves. Sylvia Townsend Warner's extraordinary ingenuity presents an exceptionally powerful challenge to the notion of Modernism as the beginning and end of literary inventiveness. As Gillian Beer puts it, the work of Warner 'abutts the Modernist: it uses surreal appositions, nonsense strides, narrative fractures and shifting scales. It is nevertheless pellucid, determined and mischievous rather than allusive and indeterminate. Its experiments are narratological rather than verbal, though the peculiar lift of her sentences produces an idiosyncratic humour.'

Modernism was not monolithic and was shaped differently in the hands of diverse men and women, and this is also true of Realism, which manifested itself in a diverse ways and reflected diverse agendas. Tony Davies suggests that 'Realism, in all its multiple incarnations, is not really a literary form or genre or movement or tradition at all but a contested space, the scene of an unfinished argument'.[19] Elizabeth Maslen argues that in the 1930s Realism 'is by no means a vehicle for cultural conservatism or a surrender to patriarchal modes of writing. It is reshaped and adapted, sometimes borrowing techniques from Modernism, always probing for satisfactory ways of conveying commitment to ideas.' It is with an understanding of how specific texts by women have constructed, mediated and represented aesthetic and other priorities and articulated various kinds of dissent in particular historical circumstances – and not preconceived ideas about the inherent virtues of particular modes of writing – that we can begin to stake out a more flexible and accommodating understanding of both Modernism and Realism in the 1930s. Valentine Cunningham is right to suggest that 'our reading of the Thirties cannot shut out Modernism and the Modernists ... our high valuation of the Modernists cannot be deployed as a simple stick to beat the red Thirties with'.[20]

This book is a response to the demand for a more informed and substantial discussion of writers on whom there is still a paucity of critical work including Naomi Mitchison and Storm Jameson. Elizabeth Maslen analyses Naomi Mitchison's use of historical fiction and Aesopian language to provide critiques of the society of her day and avoid censorship. Sylvia Vance deals with the rise of Fascism and the work of Storm Jameson, a writer whose politics are usually recognised as being crucial to her work. As Vance succinctly points out, if Woolf has acquired the status of our one 'allowed great modernist woman', Jameson has been the 'allowed political woman of the same period'. However, renewed critical interest has focused on the politics and writing of Sylvia Townsend Warner, the subject of two recent biographies,[21] who has accrued a very welcome and much higher literary profile than she has previously had.

Like all edited collections, this one is necessarily selective: there are other writers of the liberal-left, for example Winifred Holtby, who would have been included had space permitted. No attempt has been made to assimilate the writing of authors as disparate as Elizabeth von Arnim and Rebecca West to any presupposed standard of commonality. Through detailed analysis of the work of the authors selected, each essayist has attempted to address the question, 'what is radical about the writer discussed?' (Revolution in the world? and/or in the word?)

Where there has been a recent revival of critical interest in women's writing of the inter-war period which has not been preoccupied with Modernism, this has often centred on the populist conservative writers like Daphne du Maurier. One problem that must be addressed if the liberal-left women are to become better known than they are is that of the restricted availability of their writing. Although some modern editions of inter-war fiction were brought out selectively by feminist and other publishing houses during the 1970s and 1980s, many women writers have, unfortunately, once again been allowed to go out of print. Storm Jameson is one of several writers discussed in this volume whose works are not studied on academic syllabuses in higher education largely because there is little or nothing by them which can be purchased.

The importance of the radical positions occupied by the women selected for inclusion in this volume cannot be understood without an informed comprehension of the territory from which each departed. Like large sections of British society, much writing of the 1930s remained solidly conservative in its structures of feeling. This was especially true of the authors who were purchased and borrowed in large numbers from lending libraries and whose books were traditional in both content and form. This being the heyday of detective fiction, they included Agatha Christie and Dorothy L. Sayers as well as other writers of popular and middle-brow fiction: Warwick Deeping, Edgar Wallace, Richmal Crompton and P. G. Wodehouse. Indeed, the critic Alison Light has usefully invoked the notion of conservative modernity to account for the contradictions and tensions that characterise the work of writers like Ivy Compton-Burnett, and Daphne du Maurier whom she discusses in her study of femininity between the wars, *Forever England*.[22]

In a recent collection of women's writing of the First World War Suzanne Raitt and Trudi Tait have asked 'why gender has become a critical orthodoxy; why critics rarely feel the need to justify an analysis of gender, especially in writing by women, to the exclusion of many other issues'. They warn that focusing exclusively on gender can 'produce a curiously depoliticised reading of our culture, its history, and its writing'.[23] Janet Montefiore too has pointed out that an emphasis on gender may be unhelpful in reading texts like Nancy Cunard's *Negro* and Storm Jameson's *Mirror in Darkness*, works which are largely concerned with other matters.[24]

Insights into the workings of gender are not, of course, the exclusive prerogative of the woman writer: some of the more thoughtful and perceptive observations about gendered experience and identity in the writing of this time are to be found in Grassic Gibbon's important novel sequence, *A Scots Quair*. Moreover, there are limits to the usefulness of gender as an explanatory device. Few feminists would now contend that relationships of oppression and subordination are determined exclusively by gender but would point instead to a constellation of factors that might include social class, race, age, religion, as well as the two categories with which this volume is especially concerned, history and politics. Like men, women were polarised in specific ways by the historical events of the 1930s and are situated at different points in the social, political and aesthetic spectrum. In this collection Joanna Labon questions the familiar emphasis on those who went to Spain, usually but not always men, and who wrote poetry. Her discussion is focused on two women, Rebecca West and Storm Jameson, who went to Central and Eastern Europe and who wrote prose.

This was a decade in which passions about the conduct of public affairs ran extraordinarily high. Writers like Winifred Holtby, Naomi Mitchison and Sylvia Townsend Warner are clearly situated differently in relation to the pressing social and political issues of their day from others such as Edith Sitwell, Dorothy L. Sayers and Laura Riding. But the political elements in the works of the former have not always been noticed. Rosamond Lehmann, for example, is usually discussed as a writer who excels in depicting feminine sensibility. But little has been written about her anti-Fascist activities and her indefatigable efforts to raise money and support for Republican Spain. Hence the value of Wendy Pollard's essay.

Women novelists and poets have not been the only casualties produced by the extraordinary resilience of the 'Myth of the Thirties'. At its simplest, this is an account of literary history whereby 'a few young men of Great Possessions briefly exchanged Anglicanism for Soviet Communism and wrote a few bad, naive poems in praise of Stalin and Harry Pollitt'.[25] Men too – Grassic Gibbon, Hugh MacDiarmid, Jack Lindsay, David Gascoyne, James Hanley, Patrick Hamilton, Walter Brierley and Edward Upwood immediately come to mind – have been denied critical recognition by the agendas and (often unstated) critical presuppositions which have disqualified women. Bernard Bergonzi, for example, has identified the 'important formative experiences' which were shared by the key writers of the period.[26] These 'formative experiences' can be seen to have shaped the lives of Auden, Spender, MacNeice, Day Lewis and Isherwood, as well as Upward, Powell, Waugh and Henry Green. But women and working-class writers are excluded on the grounds of their sex (which puts women in a different relationship to the First World War), their class (which disqualifies the proletarian novelists whose work flowered in this period) and their education (which debars working-class men and many of the liberal-left women who did not go to university).

If an understanding of gender is crucial to an understanding of historical change, an understanding of historical change is crucial to an understanding of gender. Gender is always experienced in a specific historical situation which can be identified. How gendered identity is experienced, and how this is mediated and reflected in literature, is determined, at least in part, by the specific time in which it is lived out, by the importance of the historical moment in determining consciousness. As Gillian Beer has observed about the relationships between the characters in the novel *Mrs Dalloway* (1925), 'to be alive on the same day in London may be a deeper bond ... than any of the individual choices of love and friendship which narrative fiction ordinarily privileges'.[27]

Women in the 1930s were the first in British history to believe in any significant numbers that the struggle for equal citizenship was effectively over. Reflecting on the material aspirations voiced by the assembled women co-operators in 1913, Virginia Woolf had noted that 'in all that audience, among all those women who worked, who bore children, who scrubbed and cooked and bargained, there was not a single woman with a vote'. (p. xix) In 1928, with the extension of the franchise to all women over the age of twenty-one, the demands of the Co-operative working women for the vote on the basis were finally met. Once their acceptance had been enshrined in legislation, abstract issues of formal equality often appeared to be of little further interest. Interest in feminist ideas waned to such an extent that Janet Courtney expressed her anxiety that feminism as a political force would be extinguished in *The Adventurous Thirties: A Chapter in the Women's Movement* (1933). However, Diana Wallace draws attention to the liveliness and vigour with which the debates about the roles and responsibilities expected of men and women within the marriage contract were conducted during this time.

The most important political objectives for many women in the 1930s were the defence of democracy and the defeat of Fascism As Johanna Alberti has put it, 'the very real threat to the lives of European opponents of Fascism and their children meant that the specific threat of Fascism to women assumed secondary importance for many feminists. Those feminists who worked with refugees, or called attention to the victims of Nazism, were unequivocally opposing Fascism but could also be distracted from Fascism's specific attack on women.'[28] Women working for political change in mixed organisations during the 1930s often had an uneasy relationship to the history early twentieth-century organised feminism, which they found too redolent of yesterday's politics. Moreover, they were often resistant to feminist ideas which construed men as responsible for women's problems and not as partners in a common cause. Margot Heinemann remembered being given an unwanted present of Virginia Woolf's *A Room of One's Own* by an aunt who had supported the suffragettes. For Heinemann the book was emblematic of the ideas of an older generation from which the bright young women of her age wished to distance themselves.[29] For the Duchess of Atholl, who wanted to draw as many women as possible into active politics, any suggestion of feminist activity was a portent of separatism and all its attendant dangers. In *Women and Politics* she asks if the 'maintenance of organisations of women only, approaching political questions solely from a woman's point of view', involves 'the risk of creating a new antagonism? And is not sex antagonism even more to be feared than an antagonism based on party, or even on "class"?'[30] In her contribution to *Man, Proud Man* Storm Jameson recollects biting the ear of a policeman in Hyde Park during a

10

pre-war demonstration for the vote. This incident serves as an embarrassing prolegomenon to 'the cherished and precious independence of ours'. By the 1930s Jameson had come to believe that the modern woman was justified in taking her new-found freedoms for granted.[31]

But if issues of gender were relegated to a secondary position, they refused to go away. Margaret Lawrence's survey of the fiction of her contemporaries, *We Write as Women* (1937), was an attempt to identify the characteristics of women's writing in ways which had been suggested in Virginia Woolf's essays on women and fiction and in *A Room of One's Own*. Utopian and dystopian modes of fiction, as the essays of Keith Williams and Sylvia Vance demonstrate, proved to be particularly fruitful in the hands of liberal-left women concerned with questions of gender and sexuality. Women who worked alongside men in groups dedicated to social change were often subjected to a masculinist ethos which sometimes prompted them to question the excesses of male behaviour that they saw around them. The actions of the Fascist dictators in Europe – Hitler, Mussolini and Franco – were not infrequently interpreted as exhibitions of rampant, uncurtailed masculinity. This was a point of view shared by writers as surprisingly diverse as Winifred Holtby, Katharine Burdekin and Virginia Woolf. All were caused anguish by the incontrovertible evidence of women's support for dictatorships and the role that women played in boosting the egos of tyrannical men.

Two books entitled *Proud Man* were published during the decade. The sexual politics of the first, a work of speculative fiction by Katharine Burdekin, is the subject of Keith Williams' essay. The second, *Man, Proud Man*, a work with which Burdekin was familiar, is a disquisition on aspects of male behaviour, edited by Mabel Ulrich. The links between masculinity and Fascism, and between tyrannical behaviour in personal relationships and public life, are most memorable and originally analysed in Virginia Woolf's powerful anti-war treatise, *Three Guineas*. The three essays on Virginia Woolf, by David Bradshaw, Linden Peach and Elena Gualtieri, are variously concerned with aspects of her politics. Linden Peach argues that to read Woolf as a political novelist demands an approach posited on her cryptic use of historical and contemporary events. Elena Gualtieri discusses the relationship between photograph and text in *Three Guineas*, questioning the status of the latter as a neutral and objective account of events. Like Jean Radford, David Bradshaw is concerned with the issue of anti-Semitism. He argues that Virginia Woolfs first-hand experience of anti-Semitism in Germany, and her concern about the activities of the British Union of Fascists in her own country, 'prompted her to link two kinds of anti-Semitism in *The Years*, while at the same time stressing the rightful "place" of Jews in England' in a number of ways including 'periodic references to the "Jewish" colours blue and white.' Taken together, these essays suggest something of the importance of Virginia Woolf in any revisionary reading of the decade.[32]

Like their male counterparts, the women writers of the period are drawn almost exclusively from the upper and middle classes: Mrs Giles of Durham City, and the other working-class women whose waking hours were spent at the wash-tub, had neither the time, education nor privacy that were the prerequisites of literary success. The confidence that Elizabeth Bowen, Rosamond Lehmann, Naomi Mitchison, Virginia Woolf and others exhibited was in part the inherited moral capital of the class to which they belonged. Often referred to as English eccentrics rather than English ec-centrics (those who make a choice to reject the central ground in politics and art), these women were never, in the acutely class-conscious age in which they produced their writing, allowed to forget the privileges of their birth. In a famously splenetic review of the class dimensions of *We Have Been Warned*,[33] Queenie Leavis, unusual for a Cambridge academic of her day in that her family were orthodox Jewish, and of limited means, clearly relished the superiority over Naomi Mitchison that her modest social origins were assumed to have bestowed on her. The flamboyant, sibylline and aristocratic Edith Sitwell was the epitome of everything that was anathema to Auden and the young men in his circle. Nancy Cunard was dismissed as a rich dilettante and taunted for her upper-class origins by sections of the left long after she had severed her connections with the wealthy Cunard family. Sylvia Townsend Warner, whose Marxism, (homo-) sexual orientation and middle-class background were similar to those of Auden and his friends (her father was a master at Harrow public school), was regarded with contempt by the young Spender, who caricatured her bourgeois demeanour, 'like a vicar's wife presiding over a tea party given on a vicarage lawn as large as the whole of Republican Spain'.[34]

In a historical context in which coteries of poets frequently acted as their own best publicists, the isolation of women writers, who lacked access to supportive same-sex cultural networks, sometimes placed them at a disadvantage to men. Writing about the situation of the American women radicals in the 1930s, Tillie Olsen, Meridel le Sueur, Agnes Smedley, Grace Lumpkin and others ('lost even to the lost generation'), Elaine Showalter lays emphasis on the isolation of women on the North American left whose voices were often silenced. Many of the difficulties facing the women whom Showalter discusses were experienced by their British counterparts who were also denied recognition at the time and subsequently, 'without support either from women's groups or Communist Party networks', and 'lost to literary history and to each other'.[35] Where the creativity of British women writers was nurtured by other women, this tended to be on the basis of intimate friendship: Vita Sackville-West and Virginia Woolf, Sylvia Townsend Warner and Valentine Ackland, Winifred Holtby and Vera Brittain; or sometimes through the written correspondence that was the favoured means of communication of the time: Sylvia Townsend Warner, Vera Brittain and Virginia Woolf were all accomplished, conscientious and prolific letter-writers. Many of these women knew each other socially and, as the memoirs, diaries and auto/biographies of the period corroborate, important friendships and intellectual links between women authors existed at this time although no sense of a shared literary agenda was ever developed.

In contrast, Stephen Spender, Louis MacNeice and Cecil Day Lewis were probably never in the same room until 1948.[36] But this does not appear to have prevented each of them from enjoying the critical recognition of their fellow poets or from acquiring a positive sense of group identity which was important in boosting their individual self-esteem. This sense of group solidarity is what we can see in retrospect that the liberal-left women lacked in the 1930s, and is what they sometimes manage to intimate, albeit in an inchoate way, to the reader today that they were conscious of lacking. Much later, Sylvia Townsend Warner was to suggest that the neglect of her female contemporaries might be attributed to the fact that 'they only went off one at a time', and not in groups.[37] Like the forgotten women novelists of the 1920s who did not think of themselves as feminists at the time that they wrote, but were nevertheless pleased to see their fiction reprinted by the new feminist publishing houses half a century later, one suspects that many of the women whose work is discussed in this volume would have welcomed the recognition which has now been accorded them, albeit belatedly, but would have been bemused by agendas which are neither of their time nor making.

Notes

1. Virginia Woolf, introductory letter to Margaret Llewelyn Davies (ed.), *Life as We Have Known it by Co-operative Working Women* (London: The Hogarth Press, 1931), pp. xv–xxxix. All further references are to the first edition and page numbers are given in the main body of the text. Woolf's letter is dated May 1930.

2. Maroula Joannou, *'Ladies, Please Don't Smash these Windows': Women's Writing, Feminist Consciousness and Social Change 1918–1938* (Berg: Oxford and Providence, 1995), p. 193.

3. The only woman to be represented in Robin Skelton's classic anthology, *Poetry of the Thirties* (London: Harmondsworth, 1964), is Anne Ridler. A much later work, Jem Poster's *The Thirties Poets* (Buckingham: The Open University Press, 1993), one of the series Open Guides to Literature for students at the Open University, uses Skelton's anthology as a basis for discussion and makes no comment on its inadequacies in relation to gender. The pioneering work of Janet Montefiore and Jane Dowson in analysing women writers in *Men and Women Writers of the 1930s: The Dangerous Flood of History* (London: Routledge, 1996) and *Women's Poetry of the 1930s: A Critical Anthology* (London: Routledge, 1996) should be noted.

4. John Lucas, *The Radical Twenties* (Nottingham: Five Leaves Press, 1998). This excellent book argues that the 1920s was more radical than is often recognised.

5. Dowson, *Women's Poetry of the 1930s*, p. 3.

6. Andy Croft, *Red Letter Days: British Fiction in the 1930s* (London: Lawrence and Wishart, 1990), p. 9.

7. A. T. Tolley, *The Poetry of the Thirties* (London: Victor Gollancz, 1975), p. 27.

8. Noreen Branson and Margot Heinemann, *Britain in the Nineteen Thirties* (London: Weidenfeld and Nicolson, 1971), p. 270.

9. Naomi Mitchison, *You May Well Ask: a Memoir 1920–40* (London: Victor Gollancz, 1979), p. 205.

10. Edward Mendelson (ed.), *The English Auden: Poems, Essays and Dramatic Writings 1927–1939* (London: Faber and Faber, 1977), p. 62.

11. Storm Jameson, *Autobiography of Storm Jameson: Journey from the North*, 2 vols (London: Collins and Harvill Press, 1960–70), vol. 1, 1969, p. 293.

12. Naomi Mitchison, *The Moral Basis of Politics* (London: Constable, 1938), p. viii.

13. Pamela Fox, *Class Fictions: Shame and Resistance in the British Working Class Novel, 1890–1945* (Durham and London: The Duke University Press, 1994), p. 2.

14. Naomi Mitchison, Letter to Edward Garnett dated 8 September? 1932, quoted in Jenni Calder, *The Nine Lives of Naomi Mitchison* (London: Virago, 1997), p. 126.

15. David Margolies (ed.), *Writing the Revolution: Cultural Criticism from* Left Review (London: Pluto, 1998).

16. Gillian Hanscombe and Virginia Smyers, *Writing for their Lives: The Modernist Women 1910–1940* (London: The Women's Press, 1987), p. 12.

17. See Keith Williams and Steve Matthews (eds), *Rewriting the Thirties: Modernism and After* (London: Longman, 1997).

18. Laura Graves and Robert Bridges, *A Survey of Modernist Poetry* (London: Heinemann, 1927), p. 270. The Oxford English Dictionary gives the first usage as being later, in 1929.

19. Tony Davies, 'Unfinished Business, Realism and Working-Class Writing', in Jeremy Hawthorn (ed.), *The British Working-Class Novel in the Twentieth Century* (London: Edward Arnold, 1984), pp. 125–39, 135.

20. Valentine Cunningham, 'The Age of Anxiety and Influence; or, Tradition and the Thirties Talents', in Williams and Matthews (eds), *Rewriting the Thirties*, pp. 5–22, 21. This is a welcome change of position by Cunningham who, in *British Writers of the Thirties* (Oxford: Oxford University Press, 1988), p. 299, argued that 'Socialist Realism had a profound effect in Britain: it helped to slow down literary experiment and to smash up Modernism especially in the novel, thus pushing the novel back beyond Henry James into the arms of nineteenth-century bourgeois naturalism'.

21. Claire Harman, *Sylvia Townsend Warner: a Biography* (London: Chatto and Windus, 1989), Wendy Mulford, *This Narrow Place: Sylvia Townsend Warner: Life, Letters and Politics, 1930–1950* (London: Pandora, 1988).

22. Alison Light, *Forever England: Femininity, Literature and Conservatism Between the Wars* (London and New York: Routledge, 1991).

23. Suzanne Raitt and Trudi Tate (eds), *Women's Fiction of the Great War* (Oxford: Oxford University Press, 1997), p. 3.
24. Montefiore, *Men and Women Writers of the 1930s*, p. 2.
25. Andy Croft, unpublished paper on Randall Swingler dated November 1997.
26. Bernard Bergonzi, *Reading the Thirties: Texts and Contexts* (London: Macmillan, 1978), p. 2. Bergonzi argues that the key writers were the 'sons of the English or Anglo–Irish professional or administrative class ... very conscious of the First World War but too young to fight in it; educated at boarding schools and, in nearly all cases, at Oxford or Cambridge'.
27. Gillian Beer, 'The Body of the People in Virginia Woolf', in Sue Roe (ed.), *Women Reading Women's Writing* (Hemel Hempstead: Harvester, 1987), pp. 84–114, 85.
28. Johanna Alberti, 'British Feminists and Anti-Fascism in the 1930s', in Sybil Oldfield (ed.), *This Working-Day World: Women's Lives and Cultures in Britain 1914–45* (London: Taylor and Francis, 1994), pp. 111–123, 118.
29. Conversation with Maroula Joannou, c. 25 November 1990.
30. The Duchess of Atholl, *Women and Politics* (London: Philip Allan, 1931), p. 175.
31. Storm Jameson, 'Man the Helpmeet', in Muriel Ulrich (ed.), *Man, Proud Man: A Commentary* (London: Hamish Hamilton, 1930), pp. 105–139, 124.
32. The idea of Virginia Woolf as a consummate stylist with no interest in politics which was once a critical orthodoxy has been challenged by many feminist critics. Two good collections of essays are Mark Hussey (ed.), *Virginia Woolf and War: Fiction, Reality and Myth* (New York: Syracuse University Press, 1991) and Merry Pawlowsky (ed.), *Virginia Woolf and the Ideology of Fascism* (forthcoming).
33. Q. D. Leavis, 'Lady Novelists and the Lower Orders', *Scrutiny*, vol. 4, no. 2, September 1935, pp. 112–32.
34. Stephen Spender, *World Within World: The Autobiography of Stephen Spender* (London: Hamish Hamilton, 1951), p. 244.
35. Elaine Showalter, 'Women Writers Between the Wars', in *Columbia Literary History*, pp. 822–41, 832, 822. Cited in Gayle Greene, *Changing the Story: Feminist Fiction and the Tradition* (Bloomington: Indiana University Press, 1991), p. 40.
36. Stephen Spender, *The Thirties and After: Poetry, Politics, People 1933–75* (London: Collins/Fontana, 1978), p. 9.
37. Sylvia Townsend Warner, 'Women as Writers', the Peter le Neve Foster Lecture, *The Journal of the Royal Society of Art*, vol. 7, no. 5034, May 1959, pp. 265, 379–86.

2

The 1930s: Memory and Forgetting

Janet Montefiore

The Thirties were never only a literary memory. Inaugurated by the Wall Street Crash in October 1929 and ending with Hitler's invasion of Poland, those ten years of mass poverty, protest and imminent war have never stopped mattering in British political culture. Two histories appeared as the decade ended in 1940; so did the first influential literary retrospects: Orwell's 'Inside the Whale' and Virginia Woolf's 'The Leaning Tower'; and a book about Thirties poetry, Francis Scarfe's *Auden and After*, followed only a year later.[1] A stream of published reconstructions – social histories, political histories, literary histories, memoirs both 'straight' and fictionalised, novels, poems, television documentaries and plays, literary appraisals and reappraisals – has been flowing ever since. This paper itself, the Cambridge conference at which I gave it and the book in which it appears, themselves belong to the historiographical end of this process of collective, politicised memory.

Thinking by historical analogy is one way in which people make sense of the present, so that remembering the Thirties has been a constant, protean way of defining issues and problems in post-war Britain. Collective political memories of the 1930s have taken the form of three narratives about, respectively, heroic struggle, unheroic appeasement and secret treachery – all invoked to illuminate (and to obscure) political issues, and all influencing literary historians, often directly though sometimes negatively, as images to dissent from. The first – in this book it must come first – is the left-wing narrative of tragedy and heroism: the economic and political oppression suffered by the working class in Britain and Europe, the counter-revolutions in Germany and Spain, the struggle to preserve civil and economic rights, and the protests of brave liberals who died under arrest, like Ossietzky in Germany and Unamuno in Spain.[2] The most resonant images of that

16

narrative are perhaps those of the men of the International Brigade going to fight for the Spanish Republic, followed closely by the Hunger Marchers from Jarrow to London in 1934, 1935 and 1936, who left a permanent mark on British politics by staging their protest through a mass pilgrimage to London, an example followed by popular civil dissent in Britain ever since (unfortunately perhaps, as none of them altered the policies against which they were protesting). The anti-nuclear pilgrimages from Aldermaston to Trafalgar Square in the 1950s and 1960s, the 'Right to Work' marchers of the late 1970s campaigning under the slogan of 'No Return to the Thirties!' and in 1993 the People's March for Jobs, which took the same route from Jarrow to London that the Hunger Marchers had travelled two genera-tions before, all followed this example.

At least equally powerful in British political rhetoric is the memory of the British Government's appeasement of Hitler in the late Thirties. Unlike the examples of mass dissent remembered by the Left, the policy of 'appeasement' was not perceived by many people as dramatic until after the (almost) disastrously successful Nazi Blitzkrieg over Europe in 1940, when it became a matter of retrospective shame and anger for the British right-wing and centre. Before then, Churchill's anti-Fascist Toryism was a minority view almost as unpopular with the British Government as the Popular Front alliance of liberals and Communists, and barely represented in the British newspapers which, as Richard Cockett has shown, were loyal servants of a government that theoretically supported free speech but in practice controlled a very obedient press.[3] In the memoirs of Establishment liberals like Christopher Sykes or Rebecca West, the years 1938–40 appear as a political ice age when the national will 'locked fast in a frost' was so unwilling to question its rulers that a Tory dissenter like Robert Byron preferred the company of Communists because 'they're anti-Nazis. I feel safe with them.'[4]

Because 'appeasement' now connotes the imperilling of British prestige through a cowardly reluctance to face an enemy, it has often been invoked by politicians eager for war; thus Anthony Eden demonised Nasser as a second Hitler during the Suez crisis in 1956, while denunciations of 'appeasement' reappeared in February 1998 to justify a possible second Gulf War against Saddam Hussein. Cold War rhetoric identified the 'evil empire' of the Soviet Union with Hitler's Germany, as when a Tory Foreign Secretary used 'appease-ment' as a winning card against a Labour Party then closely associated with CND in the General Election of 1987. And the words 'Munich'

Figure 2.1 Guernica Revised. (Source: Martin Rowson, in *The Guardian*, 15 and 16 July 1995.)

and 'appeasement' have been revived by angry liberals denouncing Western politicians' passivity in the face of violent nationalism and racist mass murder, known as 'ethnic cleansing', in former Yugoslavia. Martin Rowson's cartoon 'Guernica Revised' attacking Western Europeans' failure to prevent the massacre of Bosnian Muslims by Serbians at Srebenica in July 1995 (Figure 2.1), shows the Left and Right colouring Picasso's black-and-white picture commemorating the massacre of the Spanish village Guernica by Fascist aeroplanes and machine-guns. On the Left, a uniformed International Brigader holding a red flag labelled 'The Spirit of Spain' and shouting 'Forward!' paints *Guernica* red for Communism and war; on the Right, a naked David Owen carrying a barrel labelled 'The Spirit of Munich' and shouting 'Backwards!!' paints the picture yellow for cowardice; in the centre a pinstriped politician or businessman blanks out the whole thing with a pot of 'Western whitewash'.[5]

Another potent narrative is that of the golden boys who became Communist spies in the heart of a trusting Establishment: Guy Burgess, Donald MacLean, Kim Philby, Anthony Blunt and the 'Fifth Man'. Thanks partly to John le Carré's spy stories whose villain, the raffish, bisexual Communist 'mole', Bill Haydon, is an amalgam of Kim Philby and Guy Burgess,[6] the 'Cambridge spies' became part of British political mythology where the moment of the late Thirties represents an unnoticed Fall – 'that distant afternoon,' as Auden wrote even more prophetically than he knew, 'amid rustle of frocks and stamping feet,/ They gave the prizes to the ruined boys.'[7] Although the 'Cambridge spies' had in fact nothing to do with Chamberlain's policies of appeasement, in conservative rhetoric both have coalesced into a folk memory of the Thirties as a dark time of shame, cowardice, treachery and disgrace, all blamed on Communism.

These political mythologies have inspired novels as well as spy stories. Women have hardly featured here, except in Lillian Hellmann's story 'Julia' in *Pentimento* (1973, filmed by Fred Zimmermann, 1977), whose beautiful heroine trains with Freud in Vienna, becomes an undercover anti-Fascist activist (once persuading the author/narrator to help smuggle out some vital documents), and is tortured, mutilated and finally murdered by the Nazis.[8] Unusually, 'Julia' represents its anti-Fascist heroine as unequivocally heroic; other novelists mostly write about personal and political betrayals committed by barely dis-guised historical figures. The poignant ironies of Kazuo Ishiguro's *The Remains of the Day* (1990), whose country-house setting recalls Lord Halifax's seat at Cliveden, centre of the appeasement lobby, arise from the characters' dedication to ideals not perceived as treacherously inhuman until too late. John Banville's novel *The Untouchable* (1996), whose villain combines homosexuality, art criticism and spying for Russia, is even more transparently based on the life of Anthony Blunt; and David Leavitt's novel *While England Sleeps* (1993) followed Stephen Spender's memoir of his relationship with Tony Hyndman, the ex-guardsman, in *World Within World* so closely that Spender sued to have it censored (it is no longer available in Britain).

Literary-critical accounts of the radicalising of the British intelligentsia during the 1930s have likewise been coloured by political memories. Lillian Hellmann's fictional canonisation of Julia the anti-Fascist martyr has its scholarly equivalent in the small but vigorous (if hitherto somewhat sexist) tradition of left-wing histories of the Thirties, produced mostly by groups of radical critics in the late 1970s. Orwell's account of Thirties literature as the regrettable dabbling in politics of deluded intellectuals headed by Auden, Spender & Co. dominated the popular mainstream histories of the period, notably Julian Symons' *The Thirties* (1960) and Valentine Cunningham's *British Writers of the 1930s* (1988),[9] whose jeering contempt for left-wing writers accords with the political orthodoxy presciently summed up by Claud Cockburn:

> Pretty soon every schoolboy will think he knows all about that time, certified as having been full of starry-eyed do-gooders with pink illusions which, when darkness came at noon, blew up in their faces and turned them a bright blue or else a drab neutral grey.[10]

This obviously alludes to the contributors to *The God that Failed* (1950), notably Stephen Spender representing his young self as a wide-eyed innocent manipulated by unscrupulous Reds, and Arthur Koestler, author of the classic *Darkness at Noon* (1940), whose ironic verdict on his past – 'the shadow of barbed wire lies across the condemned playground of memory' – subtly turns Audenesque rhetoric against itself.[11] (Donald Davie wondering what 'world of difference' might have occurred if the British Fascists had succeeded 'or if I/ Had canvassed harder for the Peace Pledge Union', suggests a milder version of this irony.)[12] That dismissive critical consensus began to change with Samuel Hynes' *The Auden Generation*, whose launch in 1976 was marked by an exhibition of the lives, letters and manuscripts of Auden, Isherwood, Upward and Spender, at the National Portrait Gallery in London. Hynes emphasised the traditional Auden-centred

version of Thirties writers, but suggested a more sophisticated paradigm: the 'parable art' of men caught between public events and
private dreams, a model followed in other sympathetic liberal accounts
by Bernard Bergonzi, Frank Kermode and the undeservedly neglected
James Gindin. The canonical Auden Generation writers have now
acquired considerable retrospective glamour, nicely captured by the
poet Gavin Ewart in *The Thirties*:

> Ah, did you once see Spender plain,
> And tow-haired awkward Auden?
> In days when politics meant Spain?
> And Art Paul Nash and Bawden?

> When Christopher was an Issyvoo
> And Eliot primly clerical,
> When Joyce and Pound knew a thing or two
> (And Edith Sitwell hysterical)?

> When great Virginia was a Woolf
> And Wyndham Lewis a lion,
> And C. S. Lewis had Beowulf
> And Betjeman Mount Zion?

> Did you see Layard in a chair
> Sitting there and talking?
> Lys with Elizabeth Bergner hair
> And Connolly fatly walking?

> And smooth John Lehmann, eagle-tall
> With the good looks of an eagle?
> An editor – one of the best of all
> (But his sex-life was illegal).

> And Blunt and Burgess and the boys
> Who haunted their vicinity,
> The intellectuals with poise
> In Apostolic Trinity?[13]

In all these representations of the Thirties, women are conspicuous by
their absence. (True, Ewart does include a few, but he indicates that it is
Auden, Issyvoo & Co. who really count.) The political folk memories
described above – cloth-capped Hunger Marchers, the International
Brigade, Neville Chamberlain at Munich – are all male; even Cockburn's
jibe about textbook orthodoxies presupposes knowledge as a masculine

21

domain. Although from the mid-1970s onwards both feminist criticism and the revival of mid-century women's writing through the Virago Classics series were establishing an intellectual presence to be reckoned with, no book about the Thirties paid serious attention to women until Andy Croft's *Red Letter Days* (1990). My own recent *Men and Women Writers of the 1930s* (1996) lists twenty-three women writers who published important work between 1930 and 1939;[14] I should have included Elizabeth Daryush, Stella Gibbons, Rose Macaulay, Ruth Pitter, Mary Renault, Laura Riding, Vita Sackville-West (possibly), Dorothy L. Sayers (certainly) and E. J. Scovell. That makes over 30 names of which barely any are mentioned, much less discussed, in the standard literary textbooks.

To say that women were ignored because of sexual prejudice does not in itself explain just why – or rather, how – that prejudice could produce such a near-complete intellectual apartheid exercised by liberals (and Marxists) who ought to have known better. The principal reason lies, I think, in the lingering notion of women as private creatures living apart from the public sphere inhabited by male politicians and intellectuals. The young Auden Generation writers assumed their own dominance in the realm of public writing, and their male contemporaries likewise tended to equate women with private life, as when Anthony West in 1939 attacked women novelists for their alleged 'infatuation with the personal equation'.[15] A related assumption subtly structures Edgell Rickword's brilliant satire *To the Wife of any Non-Intervention Statesman*, although Rickword was himself no misogynist. The poem deliberately connects the feminine with the private:

> Lest a final crime condones
> Fresh massacres with British loans
> Should not its sponsor be outlawed
> From power, position, bed and board?
> Should not a thinking wife contemn
> The sneaking hand that held the pen
> And with a flourish signed the deed
> Whence all these hearts and bodies bleed?
> Would not his fingers freeze the breast
> Where the young life should feed and rest?

It might seem odd that this fiery speech is directed at a relatively powerless woman in her 'boudoir's private shade'.[16] Why address the wife instead of the husband whose policies have such bloody public consequences? Partly because an upper-class woman was a convenient soft target for the Thirties Left – a man might talk back, but a silent woman is satisfactorily vulnerable. Thus the woodcuts illustrating the poem's first appearance in *Left Review* (Figure 2.2) show a silly-looking woman in bed with a rat (i.e., the Statesman), then covering her ears against a man (i.e., the poet) shouting furiously at her against a background of guns, falling buildings and a bomber plane, the rat now gnawing at a severed hand. (The final picture, not reproduced here, shows him nibbling at her prone body.) More subtly, the Wife's relatively powerless role also enables Rickword to direct his words through her at the indifferent mass of private citizens, speaking at once publicly and intimately to rouse them – perhaps – into imaginative sympathy and public protest (though those illustrations probably restricted his audience to already-converted *Left Review* readers).[17]

Other left-wing writers tended similarly to represent women as private creatures, inhabitants of the kitchen or back yard if poor or, if wealthy, the bedroom or at best the department store.[18] Post-war critics reproduced these assumptions unquestioningly because they either shared them (like Julian Symons) or simply failed to notice them (like Samuel Hynes). Hence the paradox that Stephen Spender's self-absorbed poem *Vienna* (1934) gets considerable attention from Hynes and Cunningham who ignore Naomi Mitchison's *Vienna Diary*, written in March 1934 to record the effects of Dollfuss' right-wing coup and rushed into print by Gollancz in the same year.[19]

A like silence has effaced the memories of Storm Jameson and Nancy Cunard, two of the most active and influential anti-Fascist intellectuals. President of the English PEN Club from 1938 to 1945, Storm Jameson used her influence to help many European refugee writers; she was an energetic activist, author and co-author of pamphlets, and member of innumerable committees ('Writers in Defence of Freedom, Writers' Committee of the Anti-War Council, Congress of Writers for the Defence of Culture, Writers' Section of the World Council against Fascism ... I forget the names').[20] She recorded the struggles of British and European liberalism in the Thirties in vivid naturalist novels, notably the *Mirror in Darkness* sequence (1934–36) and the prophetic *In the Second Year* (1935), about British politics, the biting, poignant vignettes of Vienna, Prague and Budapest in *Europe to Let* (1940), followed by *Before the Crossing* (1946) and *The Black Laurel* (1947) and finally her classic memoir *Journey from the North* (1969, 1970).

Nancy Cunard, writer and publisher, campaigned against racism (she was a passionate advocate of the black 'Scotsboro boys' who were

TO THE WIFE OF ANY NON-INTERVENTION STATESMAN

By Edgell Rickword

PERMIT ME, MADAM, to invade,
Briefly, your boudoir's pleasant shade:
Invasion, though, is rather strong,
I volunteered, and came along.
So please don't yell, or make a scene,
Or ring for James to—intervene.
I'm here entirely for the good
Of you and yours, it's understood.
No ballyhoo, what I've to say
May stand you in good stead one day.

I have to broach a matter that
Less downright folk might boggle at,
But none need blush because we try
To analyse the marriage tie.

The voice that breathed o'er Eden laid
Some precepts down to be obeyed:
To seek in marriage mutual trust
Much more than sentiment or lust:
To base our passion on esteem
And build a home for love's young dream.
With this in mind, I'll state a case
Of interest to the human race.

Suppose a husband yarns in bed,
Of plans that fill his lofty head,
Think what should be a wife's reaction
If he turned out the tool of faction,
Who put across the crooked schemes
Of statemen sunk in backward dreams;

24

Whose suave compliance sealed the fate
Of thousands left to Franco's hate—
(Those very Basques whose fathers drowned
To keep our food-ships safe and sound,
Sweeping for mines in furious seas),
Our Fleet stood by, but ill at ease:
Restive, our sailors watched the shore
Whilst hundreds drowned who'd starved before,
Victims of Franco's sham blockade—
Though in the way of honest trade
Potato Jones and his brave lass
Had proved this husband knave or ass.

Suppose he argues: Though I swerve
From honour's course, yet peace is served?

Euzkadi's mines supply the ore
To feed the Nazi dogs of war:
Guernika's thermite rain transpires:
In doom on Oxford's dreaming spires:
In Hitler's frantic mental haze
Already Hull and Cardiff blaze,
And Paul's grey dome rocks to the blast
Of air-torpedoes screaming past.
From small beginnings mighty ends,
From calling rebel generals friends,
From being taught at public schools
To think the common people fools,
Spain bleeds, and England wildly gambles
To bribe the butcher in the shambles.

Traitor and fool's a combination
To lower wifely estimation,
Although there's not an Act in force
Making it grounds for a divorce:

Figure 2.2 To the Wife of any Non-Intervention Statesman. (Source: Edgell Rickword, in *Left Review*, vol. 3, no. 3, March 1938, pp. 834, 836.

'framed' for alleged rape), edited the classic pioneering *Negro Anthology* in 1934, devised and published the questionnaire *Authors Take Sides on the Spanish War*, published six pamphlet poems for Spain including Auden's *Spain 1937*, worked during the war with the Free French and published an anthology of Resistance poems, *Poems for France* (1944).[21] Jameson's writings are unmentioned by mainstream historians unless one counts Samuel Hynes citing her 1937 essay 'Documents' as a critical framework for male realists;[22] Nancy Cunard only appears – distorted – in Martin Green's *Children of the Sun* (1975), a crude, lightweight book which 'explains' its chosen writers by slotting them into stereotypes. Green represents Nancy Cunard as 'in real life enacting the "Columbine" *femme fatale*' and as being, like Brian Howard, a 'socialite [with] left-wing views and a recklessly ... self-destructive pattern of behaviour'. He ignores her record as an inspired and efficient publisher, editor and journalist, apart from a discussion of *Negro Anthology* so vague and inaccurate that he can never have bothered to read it.[23]

Given this pervasive exclusion of women from the dominant accounts of the Thirties, the question is how to redraw the literary maps a little more accurately. Of course, no historian would now aspire to write history 'as it really was', but we can at least correct some errors of omission. This is not simply a matter of mentioning previously ignored names; it also means both questioning the paradigms by which the history of the Thirties has been defined, and attempting the more difficult task of creating new ones. This is not and cannot be a job for just one person: the work of rediscovering the past has to be collective (as in this book). The revival of women writers is already under way; it was inaugurated by Alison Light's pioneering *Forever England* (1992), an influential reading of the literature of the 1930s in terms of an apparently paradoxical concept of conservative modernity. Through subtle readings of its chosen women writers, this book revalued what is conventionally thought of as the 'private' world of women's lives and writings, showing how the values of a feminised domesticity first interacted with the 'public' realm and then entered the self-definitions and perceptions of English public thought, as in the liberal pacifism of Jan Struther's 'Mrs Miniver'. (So when Orwell in 1941 defined the chief characteristics of English culture as privateness, gentleness and respect for law,[24] he unconsciously showed the influence of 'feminine' domestic values a piquant thought for feminists.) Attending to genre rather than theme, Jane Dowson has given long-overdue attention to women poets in her recent anthology *Women Poets of the 1930s* (1995).

Much new work has been done on women's complicated, often but not always dissenting, relationship to war and militarism in the twentieth century: notably Maroula Jouannou's recent *'Ladies, Please Don't Smash these Windows': Women's Writing, Feminist Consciousness and Social Change 1918–38* (1995), which surveys, among other things, the links between pacifist politics and women's writing, and Gill Plain's subtle psychoanalytic readings of public mourning in *Women Writers and the Second World War* (1996). Here again, academic work has followed political memory. Well before feminist scholars and critics had started to resurrect Virginia Woolf's feminist pacifism, the women of Greenham Common were invoking *Three Guineas* as they engaged in civil disobedience against nuclear missiles. Thus one anti-nuclear poster (1982) captioned a photograph of a baffled policeman standing over a prone female protester netted in her own spider-web of ropes with the quotation, 'As a woman I have no country. As a woman I want no country. As a woman my country is the whole world.'[25]

My own interest in the Thirties focuses both on the notion, briefly sketched above, of public and political narratives as forms of collective memory, a concept first defined by the French sociologist Maurice Halbwachs,[26] and on the problem of defining the relation between individual experience and collective representation. This project includes looking at the gendering of collective memory (which should not mean denying the importance of memories shared by men and women alike, even if the sexes often have a different 'take' on them). It also problematises the frontiers of Thirties or even inter-war writing, because once one starts seeing the texts of the Thirties as a literature of memory rather than witness, one has to start looking backwards at least to the First World War (memories of which profoundly affected the writers of the Thirties) and beyond that to the pre-war era, often remembered in the Thirties as paradise lost, as well as forwards to the post-war years when so many retrospects of the Thirties were produced.

There are many unnoticed links between well-known liberal women writers, namely Rebecca West, Storm Jameson, Vera Brittain, Winifred Holtby and Naomi Mitchison in the Thirties. These did not form a clique like the Auden Generation writers, but nevertheless had close intellectual, political and sometimes personal ties. All were left-wing liberals but none was a Communist; all wrote as feminists, except perhaps Storm Jameson (a liberal humanist for whom 'brotherhood' was 'God, the Son and the Holy Ghost of my creed');[27] and all embraced internationalist pacifism during the 1930s (though only Brittain stuck to this after 1940). Vera Brittain and Winifred Holtby were active campaigners and speakers for the League of Nations.[28] Storm Jameson was one of the first sponsors of the Peace Pledge Union in 1936;[29] Vera Brittain soon followed her and became a lifelong member. Naomi Mitchison and Rebecca West publicly identified themselves as pacifists in a 1936 letter (also signed by Sylvia Townsend Warner) to the liberal feminist weekly *Time and Tide*,[30] to which all contributed: Rebecca West belonged to its inner circle, and Holtby became a director at the invitation of Lady Rhondda, the owner and editor, though Brittain wrote relatively little for it because Lady Rhondda disliked her as a rival for Holtby's attention and later denounced her as unpatriotic to British Intelligence in 1940.[31] All wrote polemical novels using fairly old-fashioned realist narrative modes, though Rebecca West and Storm Jameson were deeply stirred by high Modernist art (the former to praise, the latter to revulsion from its anti-humanism); each admired the great French novelists whose influence appears in the clarity and economy of their own best fictions.[32] All inhabited different districts of London in the 1930s: Storm Jameson in St John's Wood, Rebecca West in Regents Park, Naomi Mitchison in Hammersmith, and Vera Brittain and Winifred Holtby in Chelsea (though Holtby divided her time between London and Yorkshire). Naomi Mitchison, who seems to have known most of literary London, was friendly with Storm Jameson, knew Rebecca West and met Vera Brittain at parties.[33] Vera Brittain's own friendship with Winifred Holtby is well documented, both by Brittain herself and more recently by the feminist historians Jean Kennard and Marion Shaw; she also knew Rebecca West and her husband Henry Andrews well enough to appoint him her children's guardian in her 1941 will.[34] Winifred Holtby admired Naomi Mitchison, heading her list of the six most important novels of 1931 in *The Bookseller* with Mitchison's *The Corn King and the Spring Queen*, 'a great English novel' which she put, surprisingly, above Woolf's *The Waves*.[35]

Storm Jameson's relationships with these women were spiky. She made friends with Brittain from 1927, wrote a glowing review of *Testament of Youth* in 1933 and compared her own memoir *No Time Like the Present* (1932) to the voice of 'the Baptist crying in the wilderness to announce the coming' of the *Testament*. The two remained intellectually and politically close until political differences in 1940 broke up the friendship; Jameson burnt Brittain's letters to her (many of which, however, survive because Brittain kept carbon copies) and she avoids mentioning either Brittain or her own pacifist activism in

Journey from the North.[36] How close her friendship was with Naomi Mitchison is hard to say. Her scathing reminiscence of the 'well-to-do novelist [who] said at a dinner-party that one advantage of doing socialist propaganda was the chance it offered to get inside workers' houses – "to get the background right"'[37] sounds ominously like Dione, in Mitchison's *We Have Been Warned* (1935), patronisingly visiting a Labour voter in her shabby kitchen. This scene was noticed in a devastating *Scrutiny* review of Mitchison by Q. D. Leavis, who was later a lifelong friend of Storm Jameson (and who in the same review praised 'Miss Jameson's *The Mirror in Darkness*' as a corrective counter-example of 'what can be done by observing and composing with nothing more showy than stubborn honesty, humility and the sensitiveness that goes with solidity of character').[38] Storm Jameson also knew and disliked Rebecca West; her post-war writing unkindly emphasises the other woman's 'yellow sagging jowls', noted both in the 1970 memoir and in the novel *A Cup of Tea for Mr Thorgill* (1957), which caricatures her as Retta Spencer-Savage, a celebrated but second-rate writer using the pseudonym 'Athene', who has achieved eminence by shrewdly capitalising on her early illicit affair with a 'famous man of letters'.[39]

I don't want to suggest that this sketch of the social and intellectual links between a few middle-class women writers is or should be *the* paradigm of revisionary Thirties history – not least because it is liable to suggest more and closer ties between the women than actually existed. Both Naomi Mitchison and Rebecca West drew ideas from male traditions and writers, while Storm Jameson's autobiography records many more conversations and friendships with men – journalists and diplomats, and literati – than with women. And feminising the record is not of itself going to solve the problem of forgetting (I am aware of mentioning no working-class writers, hardly any Europeans and only one American). But given the prevailing silence about women writers, it seems useful to attempt a partial reconstruction of women's history – what, following Gavin Ewart, I might call *The Thirties (Feminist Version)*:

> Ah! did you see Virginia plain
> And Laura riding language,
> When authors took sides over Spain
> And peasants took the damage?
>
> Did you see Vera's *Testament*
> And Winifred's *South Riding*,

And Rebecca West on what history meant
And all of them *Time and Tide*-ing?

When lovely Rosamond Lehmann came
To Naomi's Boat Race parties
(Though Q. D. Leavis savaged them
As well-off female smarties),

And PEN was run by Storm *und Drang*,
And *Scrutiny* thought it tawdry
That *Dusty Answer* made a bang
And Oxford nights were gaudy?

Did you see Stevie Smith in shorts
Leading her dark chimera,
And Freya setting starkly forth
With mule and Arab bearer?

And Sylvia breathing smoke and wit
From unexpected angles
And Nancy swiping Her Ladyship
With African ivory bangles?

All gone from us, except their books
That deathless second-best.
(Yes, but the shop-girls, typists, cooks,
Do we forget the rest?)

Notes

1. See Malcolm Muggeridge, *The Thirties* (London: Hamish Hamilton, 1940); Robert Graves and Alan Hodge, *The Long Week-End* (London: Faber, 1940); Francis Scarfe, *Auden and After: The Liberation of Poetry 1930–41* (London: Routledge and Kegan Paul, 1941). Orwell's 'Inside the Whale' was the title essay of a collection published by Victor Gollancz in March 1940. Virginia Woolf's 'The Leaning Tower' was first given as a WEA lecture on 27 April 1940 and was published in *Folios of New Writing*, November 1940.
2. See Hubert Butler, *The Children of Drancy* (Mullingar, Ireland: Lilliput Press, 1988), pp. 182–5 for a fine account of Carl von Ossietzky who died in Estermegen concentration camp in 1936 (p. 182). For Unamuno's protest against Franco and subsequent death under house arrest, see Hugh Thomas, *A History of the Spanish War* (1961; Harmondsworth: Penguin, 1974, pp. 443–4).
3. See Richard Cockett, *Twilight of Truth: Chamberlain, Appeasement and the Manipulation of the Press* (London: Weidenfeld and Nicholson, 1989) for a full account of the British Government's control of Fleet Street.
4. Rebecca West, *Black Lamb and Grey Falcon* (London: Macmillan, 1942), 2 vols, vol. 2, p. 511; Christopher Sykes, *Four Studies in Loyalty* (London: Collins, 1946), p. 172.
5. Martin Rowson, 'Guernica Revised', *The Guardian*, 15 July and 16 July 1995 ('Outlook' section), p. 24. Immediately below, Ed Vulliamy, asking 'For whom does the bell toll?', criticises the European Left for failing to support democracy against Fascism. Robert Fisk similarly attacked the Foreign Office for repeating the betrayal of democracy at Munich in *The Independent*, 7 February 1994, p. 15.

6. John le Carré, *Tinker, Tailor, Soldier, Spy* (London: Hodder and Stoughton, 1974).
7. W. H. Auden, *Poems* (London: Faber, 1930; 2nd edn 1933), no. XXI, p. 88.
8. Lillian Hellmann, *Pentimento* (London: Little, Brown, 1973). The fictional 'Julia' was based on the psychoanalyst Muriel Gardiner who trained with Freud and later became an under-cover anti-Fascist, but, unlike Hellmann's heroine, survived into the 1980s, writing about these experiences in *Code Name Mary: Memoirs of an American Woman in the Austrian Underground* (New Haven, CT: Yale, 1983).
9. See Richard Crossman, *The God that Failed: Six Studies in Communism* (London: Hamish Hamilton, 1950), Julian Symons, *The Thirties: A Dream Revolved* (London: Cresset 1960), Valentine Cunningham, *British Writers of the Thirties* (Oxford: Oxford University Press, 1988); Samuel Hynes, *The Auden Generation* (London: Faber 1976); Bernard Bergonzi, *Reading the Thirties* (London: Macmillan, 1979), Frank Kermode, *History and Value* (Oxford: Oxford University Press, 1988), James Gindin, *British Novelists of the 1930s* (London: Macmillan, 1992); Keith Williams and Steven Matthews (eds), *The Thirties: Modernism and Writing* (London: Longman, 1997). For radical histories, see John Lucas (ed.), *The 1930s: A Challenge to Orthodoxy* (Brighton: Harvester, 1978), Francis Barker *et al.* (eds), *1936: The Sociology of Literature*, 2 vols (Colchester: University of Essex, 1979), Jon Clark *et al.* (eds), *Culture and Crisis in Britain in the 1930s* (London: Lawrence and Wishart, 1979); Frank Gloversmith, *Class, Culture and Social Change* (Brighton: Harvester, 1980); Andy Croft, *Red Letter Days* (London: Lawrence and Wishart, 1990). For a fuller account of Thirties historiography see my *Men and Women Writers of the 1930s* (London: Routledge, 1996), pp. 11–18, 220–21.
10. Claud Cockburn, *I, Claud ...* (London: Penguin, 1967), p. 187.
11. Koestler, *The God that Failed*, p. 64, echoing Cyril Connolly's *The Condemned Playground* (London: Routledge, 1945), whose title echoes Auden: 'The children/ At play on the fuming alkali-tip/ Or by the flooded football field, know it,/ This is the dragon's day, the devourer's.' (Auden, *Poems*, 1933, no. XVI, p. 65).
12. Donald Davie, 'Barnsley and District', *Events and Wisdoms* (London: Routledge, 1965), p. 33.
13. Gavin Ewart, 'The Thirties', *85 poems* (London: Hutchinson, 1993), pp. 39–40.
14. See Montefiore, *Men and Women Writers of the 1930s*, p. 21.
15. Anthony West, *New Statesman and Nation*, August 1939. Quoted by Jill Benton in *Naomi Mitchison: A Biography* (London: Pandora, 1990), p. 113.
16. Edgell Rickword, 'To the Wife of any Non-Intervention Statesman', *Left Review*, vol. 3, no. 3, March 1938, pp. 834, 836.
17. For a full account of the issues raised by Rickword's poem, see my discussion in pp. 104–5 of 'Vamps and Victims' (ch. 3 of *Men and Women Writers of the 1930s*), Alan Munton's response in 'Sexism and Spain', *PN Review* 119 [24], 3, January–February 1998, pp. 28–33, and myself 'On reading Edgell Rickword', *PNR* 120 [24], 4, March–April 1998, pp. 37–40.
18. See Montefiore, *Men and Women Writers of the 1930s*, pp. 81–112.
19. For Spender's *Vienna*, see Hynes, *The Auden Generation*, pp. 144–51; Cunningham, *British Writers of the Thirties*, pp. 34, 43, 157, 275, 380. Neither mentions Mitchison's *Vienna Diary* (London: Victor Gollancz, 1934).
20. Storm Jameson, *Autobiography of Storm Jameson: Journey from the North*, 2 vols, (London: Collins and Harvill Press, 1969–70), vol. 1, 1969, p. 292.
21. Nancy Cunard (ed.), *Poems for France* (London: La France Libre, 1944).
22. Hynes, *The Auden Generation*, pp. 270–73.
23. See Martin Green, *Children of the Sun* (London: Constable, 1975), pp. 57, 292. He calls *Negro* a '900-page book' (it has 854), instances Harold Acton as a typical contributor, approving his 'genuine response to black music and black dancing' (it had 150 contributors, mostly black; Acton's piece is actually about Alexander Pushkin), and ludicrously attributes to this pro-Communist compilation of politics, history and sociology 'a politics that shades fast into aesthetics and erotics' (pp. 330–31).
24. See Orwell, *The Lion and the Unicorn* (London: Secker and Warburg, 1941), reprinted in Sonia Orwell and Ian Angus (eds), *Collected Essays, Journalism and Letters*, vol. 2, *My Country Right or Left* (London: Secker and Warburg, 1967), pp. 59, 60, 62.
25. Virginia Woolf, *Three Guineas* (London: Hogarth, 1938; reprinted 1991), p. 125.
26. See pp. 9–11 of my *Men and Women Writers of the 1930s* for a discussion of the significance of Halbwachs on collective memory.

27. Jameson, *Journey from the North*, vol. 2, p. 312.
28. See Brittain, *Testament of Youth* (1933; London: Virago/Fontana reprint, 1979), pp. 539–43, 553–60, 568–73; also Muggeridge, *The Thirties: 1930–1940* (London: Fontana reprint, 1971), p. 138.
29. On Storm Jameson and the PPU, see Paul Berry and Mark Bostridge, *Vera Brittain: A Life* (London: Chatto and Windus, 1995), p. 363.
30. Jill Benton, in Berry and Bostridge, *Vera Brittain: A Life*, p. 113.
31. For Winifred Holtby's directorship of *Time and Tide*, see Berry and Bostridge, *Vera Brittain: A Life*, p. 227; for Vera Brittain's frosty relationship with Lady Rhondda, see pp. 221, 227, 277–8, 393.
32. See Rebecca West, *The Strange Necessity* (London: Macmillan, 1928) and Jameson, *Journey from the North*, vol. 1, pp. 116, 117, 196, 238–9, 244–5.
33. See Jameson, *Journey from the North*, vol. 1, p. 287, mentioning the flat she took 'for three years' from 1932; Naomi Mitchison, *You May Well Ask* (London: Victor Gollancz, 1966), pp. 21, 57–61 (on her Hammersmith house) and pp. 95–158 and 169, and *Among You Taking Notes* (London: Victor Gollancz, 1985) p. 114 for her literary friendships, also Benton, in Berry and Bostridge, *Vera Brittain: A Life*, pp. 34, 114, 122); Carl Rollyson, *Rebecca West* (London: Hodder and Stoughton, 1996), p. 123; Berry and Bostridge, *Vera Brittain: A Life*, pp. 242–3, on her home at No. 5, Glebe Place, Chelsea.
34. For Brittain's acquaintance with Naomi Mitchison and Rebecca West, see Berry and Bostridge, *Vera Brittain: A Life*, pp. 249, 270–71, 288; and with Henry Andrews, p. 416. For detailed discussion of her friendship with Holtby, see also Jean Kennard, *Vera Brittain and Winifred Holtby: A Working Partnership* (Hanover: University Press of New England, 1989) and Marion Shaw, 'A Noble Relationship: Friendship, Biography and Autobiography in the Writings of Vera Brittain and Winifred Holtby', in Vita Fortunati and Gabriella Morisco (eds), *The Representation of the Self in Women's Autobiography* (Bologna: University of Bologna Press, 1991).
35. See Benton, *Vera Brittain: A Life*, p. 69.
36. Berry and Bostridge, *Vera Brittain: A Life*, pp. 360–63, 414–18. Beth Foxwell kindly told me about Brittain's friendship with Storm Jameson, and lent me copies of her 1940 letters to Jameson which are preserved in the library of MacMasters University, Ontario.
37. Jameson, *Journey from the North*, vol. 1, p. 297; but she may possibly have been alluding to Amabel Williams-Ellis, another 'well-off novelist' whose novel *To Tell the Truth* (1933) was slated by Q. D. Leavis in the *Scrutiny* review discussed below (see fn. 40).
38. See Q. D. Leavis, 'Lady Novelists and the Lower Orders', *Scrutiny*, vol. 4, no. 2, pp. 112, 114: one of several bitter tendentious but sharp critiques of contemporary women novelists, which would repay closer attention; also Jameson, *Journey from the North*, vol. 1, pp. 201, 297; vol. 2, pp. 234–6 on her friendship with Q. D. Leavis.
39. Jameson, *Journey from the North*, vol. 2, p. 252; *A Cup of Tea for Mr Thorgill* (London: Macmillan, 1957), p. 13.

3

Late Modernism and the Politics of History

Jean Radford

> As the Marxist critic Georg Lukács has charged, modernism despairs of human history, abandons the idea of linear historical development, falls back upon notions of a universal *condition humaine* or a rhythm of eternal recurrence ... Irving Howe[1]

Lukács' early characterisation of Modernism as a-historical, formalist and subjectivist, despite repeated challenges, has had an enduring legacy with effects on the periodisation, canon and reading of Modernist writing.[2] One of the concerns of this essay is to challenge the ways in which 'history', or the lack of it, has been used to characterise Modernism and to underpin the critical dichotomy between Modernism and the writing of the 1930s. For, as Valentine Cunningham argues, 'the traditional knee-jerk division between Modernism and the Thirties' can be sustained only by caricatures of both.[3] One of the chief props to this division is the literary-historical periodisation of Modernism itself, specifically the claim, stated most forcefully by Terry Eagleton, that Modernism ended on or about 1930:

> There was of course an English Modernism, but it was mostly a foreign implantation. Joyce and Beckett left Ireland for Europe, by-passing the imperialist homeland for the cradle of the avant-garde. Lawrence spurned England likewise; Pound passed through; Eliot arrived to import Europe into it. The Modernist moment occurred, but in peculiarly ephemeral, marginalized and reactionary form ... By the 1930s, with Auden and Orwell, realism was firmly back in the saddle.[4]

The examples here – of both Modernism and realism – are exclusively male. Richardson, Woolf, Bowen and Rhys, the English-language writers that I am most concerned with, do not feature in this list although they produced some of their most important writing in the 1930s. And, if for no other reason, their omission makes this account of literary history highly suspect. (Eagleton, it must be said, elsewhere forcefully challenges the very opposition invoked here, stressing the point that the realism or Modernism of a text does not depend on its intrinsic qualities but on the effects produced within a specific conjuncture.)[5]

In our specific conjuncture, with current attempts to rewrite the history of the Thirties and recent debates in historiography, it is now possible to move beyond the subjective/objective, consciousness/ history oppositions which for far too long dominated discussions of Modernism. Keith Williams and Steven Matthews in *Rewriting the Thirties: Modernism and After* (1997) claim that there is an urgent need 'to challenge the persistent aftermyth of the Thirties as a homogeneous anti-Modernist decade' in order to redraw outdated cultural maps of the time.[6] One of the ways of doing this, I would argue, is to look more closely at the ways in which personal and collective histories are registered in Modernist narratives of the Thirties. Although there are some excellent studies of the major male Modernists' relation to history, with the exception of Virginia Woolf very little attention has as yet been given to this question in the work of women Modernists. I want to argue that the question of history is as significant in the work of Elizabeth Bowen or Jean Rhys as, in a different way, it is in the work of Sylvia Townsend Warner or Rebecca West. For just as there is, clearly, more than one way of representing history and historical processes, there may be more than one conception of history in question.

Lukács' fulminations against the Modernists' lack of history, echoed by Howe and other critics, depend on a Hegelian view of the historical. History is conceived as a totality, as universal, and as an inexorable, dialectical progression toward the future. Thus as Lukács says in *The Historical Novel*, written in 1936–7, 'The past will show the way mankind has gone and the direction in which it is moving'.[7] This teleological view of history is precisely what Walter Benjamin in his *Theses on the Philosophy of History* (1940) felt impelled to reject. Benjamin, drawing not on Hegel but on Nietzsche's critique of nineteenth-century historicism in *The Uses and Abuses of History for Life* (cited in the *Theses*), launches a critique of both teleological and relativist historicisms defined, roughly, as:

1. any philosophy of history which posits an end or telos – a teleology of reconcilement in historical time, and
2. any historicism which seeks to interpret phenomena solely in relation to the period in which they occur.[8]

At the philosophical level, his objection to both these forms of historicism is that they refuse to consider the present except as a transitional moment en route to the future, and thus deny the constitutive role of the present in the construction/understanding of the past, the present becoming what he calls 'empty homogeneous time'. Adorno makes this point in a different way when he says: 'Historicism slanders its own principle, the force of history.'[9] For Benjamin, as for Adorno, there was no dialectical 'law' of history or nature which functioned independently of men's actions and which could guarantee progress toward a rational, classless society.

At the political level, Benjamin's *Theses* make an impassioned case for the rewriting of history from the perspective of the defeated, the victims not the victors of history. Although the rise of Fascism in Europe informs the *Theses*, Benjamin was not himself 'writing' such a history but writing about the need for a new concept of history since, as Rolf Tiedemann puts it, 'He could no longer be convinced that every historical event derives from another by necessity and that all events together constitute a progressive motion.'[10] Historicism and a belief in the inevitability of progress, Benjamin argues, favour the ruling class and disarm and disable those who would oppose them. This argument is set out in the seventh of the *Theses* which culminates in the well-known passage on civilisation and barbarism:

> All rulers are the heirs of those who conquered before them. Hence, empathy with the victor invariably benefits the rulers. Historical materialists know what that means. Whoever has emerged victorious participates to this day in the triumphal procession in which the present rulers step over those who are lying prostrate. According to traditional practice, the spoils are carried along in the procession. They are called cultural treasures ... [which] owe their existence not only to the great minds and talents who have created them, but also to the anonymous toil of their contemporaries. There is no document of civilisation which is not at the same time a document of barbarism. (p. 258)

Benjamin saw the notion of 'Progress' as in part responsible for the current historical situation in Europe: the failure of Social Democracy to prevent the rise of Fascism. 'Nothing has corrupted the German working class so much as the belief that *it* was moving with the current', he goes on to say. (p. 260) As Tiedemann points out, Benjamin's *Theses* are written in response to a political situation which seemed increasingly hopeless; this is the point of his reading of Klee's painting of the *Angelus Novus* where the angel of history, caught in 'this storm ... [which] we call progress', sees the chain of events as 'one single catastrophe, which keeps piling wreckage upon wreckage'. (p. 259) The *Theses* present the search for an alternative concept of history which would fan the 'spark of hope' from the past into the present. Benjamin's concept of history thus includes an idea of 'afterwardness' (Nachtraglichkeit), as he says at the end of the *Theses*:

> No fact that is a cause is for that reason historical. It became historical posthumously, as it were, through events that may be separated from it by thousands of years. A historian who takes this as his point of departure stops telling the sequence of events like the beads of a rosary. Instead, he grasps the constellation which his own era has formed with a definite earlier one. (p. 265)

The *Theses* 'On the Concept of History' call not only for a new reading of the past but for a transformation of the present. For only if the unrealised possibilities of the past ('the route not taken' in Eliot's phrase) can be activated, brought into a new 'constellation' with the present, can a new future be brought into being. It is this concept of history which I wish to draw on in what follows.

Benjamin's propositions arise from a specific historical experience – Gershom Scholem claims indeed that the *Theses* represent Benjamin's 'awakening from the shock of the Hitler–Stalin pact' – but they are relevant, I want to suggest, to a number of Modernist narratives written in the 1930s.[11] These narrative dislocations can be read, not as a 'negation of history' as Lukács maintains but, as with Benjamin, a resistance to a particular view of history – as linear, progressive.[12] (A resistance produced for many by the First World War and confirmed by events following 1933.) For one of the ways in which the question of history is written into these texts is by refusing to totalise, by posing the narrativisation of the past as a problem, so that the reader, like the participant in history, must piece together his or her own fragmentary and contradictory grasp of events. Continually positing and undermining particular ways of understanding, making and remaking stories about themselves, the characters' struggles to make sense of their memories stage questions of history and historicism as urgently, if differently, as any realist novel of the period. If, as Le Goff claims, 'Memory is the raw material of history',[13] then the ways in which memories are narrativised relate to the process whereby histories are produced.

The narrativisation of history is the theme of Woolf's last, post-humously published novel *Between the Acts* (1941). As Judith L. Johnson and others have argued, *Between the Acts* is a major example of the Modernist challenge to the notion of a continuous, ameliorative cultural history.[14] Miss La Trobe's historical pageant, performed at a village fete in the summer of 1939, offers an interrogation of that version of English history which traces its descent from the Greek, to the Roman, through the Norman to the British Empire. This triumphalist history is staged here as a construction, a story line whose authority is subverted as characters forget their lines, the audience interpolate their comments, and the natural world disrupts the human – when the gramophone fails and cows add their voices to those of the script. The final scenes of the play representing the present, in which the actors hold up mirrors to reflect the images of the spectators, emphasise their involvement in the present and stress the question of individual and collective agency in the making of history. For, as Catherine Wiley points out, one of the radical problems posed in the novel is how we can intervene in history as the repetition of war and conquest, and how, in the summer of 1939, the audience might stop history from repeating itself as war.[15] The 'interrupted structure' of the pageant parodically replays scenes from the past not as an inevitable sequence of cause and effect but as discontinuous, man-made and open to intervention. As Wiley concludes, 'Despite her own despair, Woolf holds out the hope that when the documents of civilisation are rewritten by those whom history has acted upon, those documents will not also be records of barbarism'.[16]

Woolf's novel is perhaps one of the most brilliant meditations on history in Thirties Modernism but it was not by any means the only one. Jean Rhys' *Good Morning Midnight* (1939) might also be called, in Benjamin's phrase, a 'history of the defeated' since the memories of the ageing alcoholic, Sasha Jensen, are primarily those of defeat: the death of her child, the failure of a marriage, a series of jobs lost, betrayals and humiliations endured. Set in Paris, cross-cutting between the present – 'late October 1937' – and a past which extends backwards to the early 1920s, this first-person novel assembles a sequence of memories, of events which seem, like the beads of a rosary, to tell a relentless (historicist) story of decline and fall. Yet the novel also offers a counter-history to her catalogue of victimisations: memories in which she recognises, like Pompey in Stevie Smith's *Over the Frontier*, her own capacity for cruelty but also more positive moments of agency, protest and solidarity with others: with 'the girl who does all the dirty work and gets paid very little for it'[17] and with Serge Rubin, the Russian Jew whose painting she buys. Her repeated identification with class, gender and racialised others in the novel is extended, via a quotation from Oscar Wilde (GMM, p. 115), to include the despised and rejected of all Paris.

During her stay in Paris, Sasha spends much of her time in a small hotel room, a room which for her embodies her past history, the sequence of events which has led inexorably to the present:

> This damned room – it's saturated with the past. ... It's all the rooms I've ever slept in, all the streets I've ever walked in. Now the whole thing moves in an ordered, undulating procession past my eyes. Rooms, streets, streets, rooms ... (GMM, p. 91)

Imprisoned in the room as she feels entrapped by her history, both the room and the streets of Paris are presented as a kind of spatialised history, where the historical and temporal are presented in spatial imagery – 'materialised history' in Bakhtin's terms.[18] Rhys' treatment of her setting contains a doubled set of references. It is the Paris of 1920s expatriate fiction, centred on the bars and cafés of Montparnasse, but it also appears as the increasingly xenophobic Paris of the Thirties, full of Russian and Jewish immigrants (GMM, p. 136) where Parisians curse 'foreigners', and exiles from Franco's Spain haggle for identity papers. It is moreover the stage for the World Exhibition (opened in May 1937) where Picasso first exhibited *Guernica* and where the pavilions of Germany and the USSR faced each other under the illuminated Star of Peace. Visited by Sasha and Rene toward the end of the novel, the Star of Peace and its 'rainbow lights on the water' is used to represent Sasha's hopes for the future, for peace rather than war, and for an escape from the determinism of her own past. (GMM, p. 137) A recent book on Rhys calls the novel 'one of the great anti-Fascist novels of the 1930s'.[19] Although I would not want to make that argument, it is a significant move against formalist or *ad feminam* readings of Rhys' writing, allowing one to resituate *Good Morning, Midnight* among the political and historical texts of the 1930s.

The closure of the novel, with its parodic echo of Joyce's *Ulysses* (Sasha's 'Yes-Yes-Yes ...'), does not resolve the different narrative possibilities. Is Sasha's final act (sex with the stranger from the next room) another act of self-abasement, continuous with the history of her as victim? Or, is it an attempt bring the counter-history into a new constellation with the present, to change at a more significant level than the new clothes and hair-style, by acting out the possibility of solidarity and love between strangers? Sasha's words leave the question open: 'I look straight into his eyes and despise another poor devil of a human being for the last time. For the last time ...' (GMM, p. 159)

The ironical ellipsis suggests that there may be no 'last time' and no final interpretation; like past events, *this* present one will take its meaning from future events and its future readers.

The relation of the present and the past, memory and history are also central issues in Elizabeth Bowen's *The House in Paris* (1935). The novel is divided into three parts named: 'The Present', 'The Past', 'The Present'. The narrative of a single day in the present is inter-rupted, split open by a long flashback which describes Karen Michaelis' brief affair with Max Ebhart which produced the nine-year-old Leopold, who, in the present, waits to meet the mother whom he has not met since his adoption as a baby. The narrative organisation has multiple effects but in terms of my argument here, it serves to disrupt linear progression, and the reader's experience of the 'plot' events – as a sequence of cause and effect – is dislocated. 'The Past' in this novel is not simply that which causes/gives meaning to the present; the present is also what gives meaning to, and causes the past to come into being as narrative. Temporality is represented not as a one-way system of past to present to future but, as in Benjamin's *Theses*, as a more complex interactional process. Although Bergson may be an influence, as in Rhys, Richardson and other Modernists, it is contemporary film techniques that Bowen invokes as parallels for her historiographical method:

> You suppose the spools of negatives that are memory (from moments when the whole being was, unknown, exposed) devel-oped without being cut for a false reason: entire letters, dialogues which, once spoken, remain spoken forever being unwound from the dark, word by word.[20]

However, *The House in Paris* is not just a Modernist parable about time, it is also a novel *of its time*, a historical novel which reflects upon England and Europe between the wars and on the political history of Paris since 1789. And it is this reading I want, briefly, to outline next.

V. S. Pritchett claimed that the novelist in this period had become 'the historian of a crisis in a civilisation':

Without knowing it, often by responding with his private sensibility only, the novelist has slipped into the role of unofficial historian. He has become the historian of the crisis in a civilisation, whether he writes politically (as Koestler has done), as a religious man like Graham Greene, or with the obliquity of those dispossessed poets, Henry Green and Miss Elizabeth Bowen.[21]

The links between Paris, violence and revolution are introduced early in the novel through the eyes of the child: 'Henrietta had heard how much blood had been shed in Paris'. (HP, p. 22) The text of *The House in Paris* is studded with literary allusions but also with 'oblique' political and historical references – to Napoleon, Shylock, Weininger, Dreyfus, the Stavisky scandals and to Anatole France, the pro-Dreyfus writer whose funeral procession through Paris in 1924 Sasha Jensen watches in *Good Morning, Midnight*. (GMM, p. 15) Bowen names the street in which Madame Fisher's *pension* stands after the character in Anatole France's popular novel *Le Crime de Sylvestre Bonnard* (1881) – a street which, significantly, remains unstained by Max Ebhart's blood. Her heroine, Karen Michaelis, seems to be named after the Danish feminist whose novel *The Dangerous Age* had been a bestseller before the First World War.

The love affair between Max Ebhart, the son of an English Jewish father and French mother, living in Paris, and Karen Michaelis, the daughter of an upper-middle-class English family living in Regent's Park, is presented in Part 2 of the novel entitled 'The Past'. Their relation is difficult not merely because each is engaged to another person and they live in different places (not inconsiderable problems in themselves!) but because of the cultural differences between them. They speak different languages, literally and metaphorically:

> Their worlds were so much unlike that no experience had the same value for both of them. They could remember nothing that they could speak of, and memory is to love what the saucer is to the cup ... (HP, p. 143)

Their recourse is to speak of history: 'His view of the past was political, hers dramatic, but now they were free of themselves they were of one mind.' The passage goes on:

> Side by side in the emptying restaurant, they surrounded themselves with wars, treaties, persecutions, strategic marriages, campaigns, reforms, successions and violent deaths. (HP, p. 143)

In the Boulogne restaurant, history seems to offer a way out for these two but in another sense, the novel seems to suggest, they are actually surrounded by 'wars, treaties, persecutions', etc. and not simply as topics of conversation. In *The Age of Extremes* Eric Hobsbawm, now an *official* historian, one might say, characterises the between-the-wars period as 'The Fall of Liberalism' and identifies within it three main features:

1. The fall of democratic governments in Germany, Italy and Spain into different forms of dictatorship.
2. That European populations were subject to mass forms of migration, making questions of 'homelessness', belonging, refuge and asylum into subjects of daily news.
3. The emergence of new forms of anti-Semitism.[22]

All three features – the weakness of liberalism, migration and anti-Semitism – are textualised in *The House in Paris*. Karen's family (the Michaelises) and her fiancé's family (the Forrestiers) represent the English liberal tradition after the First World War and the novel offers a detailed critique of this class at both the familial and the political levels:

> The Michaelis lived like a family in a pre-war novel in one of the tall, cream houses in Chester Terrace, Regent's Park. Their relatives and old friends, as nice as they were themselves, were rooted in the same soil. Her parents saw little reason to renew their ideas, which had lately been ahead of their time and were still not out of date. Karen had grown up in a world of grace and intelligence, in which the Boer War, the War and other fatigues and disasters had been so many opportunities to behave well. The Michaelis's goodness of heart had a wide field: they were not only good to the poor but kind to the common, tolerant of the intolerant. (HP, p. 70)

The satirical presentation of Karen's family and class together with the references to 'revolution' throughout the middle section, allude not merely to Karen's private revolt against her family values but to a broader 'crisis in civilisation', as V. S. Pritchett calls it. 'Revolution', in my reading, refers not just to the nationalist 'revolutions' like that which burned down the family house of her uncle Colonel Bent in Ireland, nor simply to the revolution of 1917 which in Russia attempted to destroy the privileges of the class to which Karen belongs, but to the threatened and actualised revolutions in Germany, Spain and Italy. (As Hobsbawm says, revolutions can occur from the Right as well as the Left.)

It is these historical points which give significance to the identity of Karen's 'significant other'. The description of Max as 'French-English-Jewish' (HP, p. 89) echoes that given of his son whom Henrietta sees ten years later: 'He had a nervous manner. She saw a dark-eyed, very slight little boy who looked *either* French *or* Jewish ... (HP, p. 27) Under Jewish law, neither Max Ebhart nor Leopold Grant-Moody is Jewish. They are what Zygmunt Bauman in *Modernity and Ambivalence* calls 'undecidables', those who are 'in-between' categories of national or religious identities: here neither Christian nor Jewish, French nor English but *'either* French *or* Jewish'. The year in which *The House in Paris* was published was the year in which the Nazi Government in Germany introduced the Nuremberg Laws which defined the Jew in a more inclusionary sense – as anyone with a Jewish grandparent.[23] All such persons were in 1935 legally deprived of German citizenship, made 'homeless' within the German homeland. Although in the early 1920s France had welcomed immigration, as unemployment grew, so did xenophobia and by 1934 the French Government introduced a series of restrictions on naturalisation and employment, while on the streets the slogan *'France pour les Français'* was used not only against new immigrants but against older assimilated communities.

Thus one might say, as Phyllis Lassner has, that Leopold's 'nervousness' is not merely the result of heredity or upbringing; he has something to be nervous about.[24] In a similar way, I would argue that Max Ebhart's situation in Paris – 'My lack of a home, of any place to return to, had not only deprived me, it chagrined me constantly' (HP, p. 163) – is not merely an individual predicament; it represents the situation of many Jews in Europe after 1933. Max's Jewish identity, which makes him unassimilable in France, also brings home the weakness of English liberalism. Face to face with this Jewish other, the 'grace and intelligence' and 'tolerance' of Karen's family give way to stereotypes (Max is 'womanish', and 'No Jew is unastute'), (HP, p. 176) exposing the particularism within their supposedly universalist liberal values. Mrs Michaelis' genteel anti-Semitism is complicitous with the more virulent anti-Semitic discourses in circulation during the 1930s, and while her techniques of silence and surveillance with Karen ('Nothing was said ... Nothing was to be said ...') (HP, p. 172) serve to link her with the Grant-Moodys' treatment of Leopold, they can also be read to refer to the failure of her family and class to speak to or about events they wish to ignore. Their silence links with the 'sinister silence' of the British Establishment about events in Germany, noted by Leonard Woolf in his autobiography.[25]

As I have argued elsewhere, *The House in Paris* engages, very explicitly, with the claims of the other not just as an ontological category but as an ethical issue in a specific historical period.[26] It places the question of the other diagnostically, as it were, as a symptom of the 'Fall of Liberalism', and as the failure of the French Republic to meet its obligations to those whom the Republicanism of 1789 had promised to house. The house in Paris, where Max Ebhart cuts his wrists rather than accept Madame Fisher's definition of him (as the same as her), turns out to be indeed a *pension* not a 'home' to French-Jewish Max and he dies with melodramatic but appropriate symbolism in an 'alley between the two studio walls'. (HP, p. 183)

Victor Gollancz, the publisher of *The House in Paris*, told Bowen that it was:

> One of not more than half a dozen contemporary novels that I have really enjoyed during the last ten years. I wonder if you realise how un-English it is? It will be appreciated most by Maxes, Frenchmen and Jews.[27]

As Bowen's contemporary, Gollancz had little difficulty in seeing the novel's relevance to the history and politics of the 1930s. Since that time, it has primarily been read either as 'textbook Modernism' (in Jameson's phrase), or as a novel of childhood, a romance, or in terms of Bowen's position as an Anglo-Irish writer. Bowen herself was diffident about defining her politics. When asked to define the writer's relation to society she responded:

> My books *are* my relation to society. Why should people come and ask me what the nature of this relation is? It seems to me that it is the other people, the readers, who should know.[28]

Although Benjamin was not a reader of either Bowen or Rhys, as a German Jew who from 1933–40 lived and worked in Paris, he might well, like Victor Gollancz, have appreciated their novels about Paris. For us, present-day readers, reading these fictions in conjunction with Benjamin's *Theses on the Concept of History* allows us to retrieve the historical dimension embodied in Modernist narrative forms and may even – in Benjamin's words – enable us to grasp the 'constellation' which it makes with our own era.

Notes

1. Irving Howe, 'The Culture of Modernism', in *The Decline of the New* (London: Victor Gollancz, 1971), pp. 7–8.
2. Georg Lukács, 'The Ideology of Modernism', in *The Meaning of Contemporary Realism* (tr. John and Necke Mander, London: Merlin Press, 1962), pp. 17–46.
3. Valentine Cunningham, 'The Age of Anxiety and Influence; or, Tradition and the Thirties Talents', in Keith Williams and Steven Matthews, *Rewriting the Thirties: Modernism and After* (London and New York: Longman, 1997), p. 5.
4. Terry Eagleton, *Walter Benjamin: or Towards a Revolutionary Criticism* (London: Verso, 1981), p. 95.
5. Eagleton, *Walter Benjamin*, pp. 88, 89.
6. Williams and Matthews, *Rewriting the Thirties*, p. 1. For an overview of recent debates on historiography see *History and Theory, Studies in the Philosophy of History*, vol. 36, no. 4, December 1997.
7. Georg Lukács, *The Historical Novel* (1936; tr. Hannah and Stanley Mitchell, London: Merlin Press, 1962), p. 271.
8. See Walter Benjamin, 'Theses on the Philosophy of History', tr. in *Illuminations* (London: Fontana, 1970), pp. 257, 262–3. All subsequent citations are given by page reference from this edition. See also Gillian Rose, *The Melancholy Science: An Introduction to the Thoughts of Theodor W. Adorno* (London: Macmillan, 1978), from whom these definitions are adapted.
9. Theodor W. Adorno, cited in Rose, *The Melancholy Science*, p. 146.
10. Rolf Tiedemann, 'Historical Materialism or Political Messianism? An Interpretation of the Theses "On the Concept of History"', *The Philosophical Forum*, vol. 15, no. 1–2, Fall–Winter 1983–4, pp. 71–104.
11. Cited in Tiedemann, 'Historical Materialism or Political Messianism?', p. 192.
12. Lukács, *The Meaning of Contemporary Realism*, p. 21.
13. Jacques Le Goff, *History and Memory* (1977; tr. Steven Rendall and Elizabeth Claman, New York: Columbia University Press, 1992), p. xi.
14. Judith L. Johnson, 'The Remedial Flaw: Revisioning Cultural History in *Between the Acts*', in Jane Marcus (ed.), *Virginia Woolf and Bloomsbury* (London: Macmillan, 1987), pp. 253–78; Patricia Klindienst Joplin, 'The Authority of Illusion: Feminism and Fascism in Virginia Woolf's *Between the Acts*', *South Central Review*, vol. 6, 1989, pp. 88–104; Catherine Wiley, 'Making History Unrepeatable in Virginia Woolf's *Between the Acts*', *Clio*, vol. 25, 1995, pp. 3–20.
15. Wiley, 'Making History Unrepeatable', p. 4.
16. Wiley, 'Making History Unrepeatable', p. 20.
17. Jean Rhys, *Good Morning Midnight*, p. 87. All citations are given by page reference from the Penguin edition (Harmondsworth, 1969), with the initials GMM.
18. Mikhail Bakhtin, *The Dialogic Imagination*, tr. and ed. Caryl Emerson and Michael Holquist (Austin, Texas: University of Texas Press, 1981), p. 247.
19. Helen Carr, *Jean Rhys* (Plymouth: Northcote House, 1996), p. 20. Although the politics of the novel are anti-authoritarian and anti-nationalist, it could be argued that the identification with outsiders is too generalised and unstable to be called anti-Fascist, since the *ressentiment* of the outsider could be (and often was) enlisted by Fascist as well as anti-Fascist movements.
20. Elizabeth Bowen, *The House in Paris*, p. 68. All citations are given by page reference from the Penguin edition (Harmondsworth, 1976), with the initials HP.
21. V. S. Pritchett, 'The Future of Fiction', in John Lehmann (ed.), *New Writing and Daylight*, vol. 7 (John Lehmann, 1946), p. 77.
22. Eric Hobsbawm, *The Age of Extremes* (London: Michael Joseph, 1994), p. 109ff.
23. Under the Nuremberg Laws, the Reich Citizenship Act stated that 'A citizen of the Reich is that subject only who is of German or kindred blood'; under the Law for the Protection of German Blood and German Honour, marriages and extra-marital relations between Jews and German citizens were forbidden. (Geoff Layton, *Germany: The Third Reich 1933–45* (London: Hodder and Stoughton, 1992), p. 89.)
24. Phyllis Lassner, 'The Coming of World War II and Bowen's Fated "Others"', conference paper presented at 'Elizabeth Bowen: London, Ireland, Modernism', December 1996. See also Phyllis Lassner, *British Women Writers of World War II* (London: Macmillan Press, 1998).

25. Leonard Woolf, *Downhill All the Way*, cited in Wendy Mulford, *This Narrow Place: Sylvia Townsend Warner and Valentine Ackland* (London, Sydney and Wellington: Pandora, 1988), p. 57.

26. Jean Radford, 'Face-to-Face with Levinas: The House in Paris', in Manuel Barbeito de Varela (ed.), *Modernism and Modernity* (Santiago: University of Santiago Press, forthcoming).

27. Cited in Victoria Glendinning, *Elizabeth Bowen: Portrait of a Writer* (London: Weidenfeld and Nicolson, 1977), p. 97.

28. Elizabeth Bowen, *Why Do I Write? An Exchange of Views Between Elizabeth Bowen, Graham Green and V. S. Pritchett* (London: Marshall, 1948), p. 23.

4

Women Poets and the Political Voice

Jane Dowson

The following discussion of Sylvia Townsend Warner, Valentine
Ackland, Naomi Mitchison, Nancy Cunard and Stevie Smith is
intended to address the lingering misconception that women's poetry
is of little significance in the field of Thirties poetry because it is not
political or, if it is politically engaged, it is merely a cultural record.
For example, reviewers of *Women's Poetry of the 1930s*[1] have tended to
notice the poets' lives more than the poems and to regard the political
poetry as of historical but not literary interest:

> In the area of the great concerns of the Thirties – the Civil War
> in Spain, poverty, impending war – the poems seem weakest and
> the ghosts of their male counterparts strongest ... Young men
> have always been better at grasping public rhetoric than women
> ... there are no serious rivals to Auden and MacNeice in the
> realm of public affairs, but it does remind us that, even if the
> boys did outrun the pack and sing the loudest anthems, women
> such as [Stevie] Smith and [Frances] Cornford were in the space,
> but tranquilly off in the outfield somewhere humming an entirely
> different tune.[2]

> These women's political and social involvement matches and often
> exceeds the much trumpeted 'engagement' of the writing men ...
> [but] the poems are generally disappointing.[3]

The problem with these conclusions is that they continue to assign
women to the sidelines in relation to a conceptually dominant public
type of poetry. Also, because Thirties poetry is understood to be motivated by left-wing politics, they perpetuate the myths that women tend
to be conservative and politically uninterested. As Cora Kaplan
observes, these myths need contesting because 'the emphasis on

women's imagination relating to the private realm can be understood as the control of high language which is a crucial part of the power of dominant groups, and ... the refusal of access to public language is one of the major forms of the oppression of women.'[4] Additionally, while maps of the Thirties poetry are dominated by the liberal writing of the Auden group, the extent and significance of the more strenuously left-wing writing by both men and women are still not recognised.

During the 1930s there was a reluctance to acknowledge the radical politics of women because they challenged the nostalgic notions of femininity which were propagated between the wars. Stephen Spender was famously sarcastic about the '*lady* communist' Sylvia Townsend Warner.[5] Women's involvements in war, class and gender politics have also been subsequently undermined by biographers, editors and literary critics. For example, most of Sylvia Townsend Warner's journal entries during her most politically active years, 1932–49, were excised from her *Diaries* and the political correspondence cut from her letters.[6] Another reason why women's political poems have been largely unrecognised as such is that they been measured by the 'Audenesque' and found wanting: 'Not even Dowson's younger writers seem aware of Modernism ... a few have noticed Auden'[7] or 'To say that women produced some fine and much interesting poetry during the Thirties is not, of course, to claim that their works constitute a mine of forgotten or undiscovered gems which outshine the poems of Auden and Co.'[8] In fact, the poems of Warner and Mitchison, for example, are characterised by Audenesque features – realism; contemporary diction; mixed public and personal rhetoric – and they were more left-wing in terms of representing democratic ideals or the voices of the socially disadvantaged than W. H. Auden. Their poems particularly register the contemporary debates over whether direct polemic was the aesthetic or anaesthetic of art.[9] Looking back on these debates, Julian Symons said, 'the technical problem that faced these poets was that of expressing revolutionary sentiments, which was something "new" in English poetry, in some appropriately "new" language.'[10] Form was, however, a particularly complicated issue for women who needed to gain credentials as poets by demonstrating proficiency in high literary forms and metres which have wrongly given the impression of political conservatism, although nothing in the 1930s was as stylistically radical as the Twenties avant-garde. As David Perkins observes, however, the retrospective fetishisation of formal experimentation has given it 'an unwarranted moral glamour' which it did not have at the time, and according to D. E. S. Maxwell, 'much of what was prized as formal innovation was in fact unusual mainly in its sentiments.'[11] Maxwell also observes that some of the most interesting poems are the 'categorically propagandist poems' where 'Party zeal well outruns aesthetic decorum'.[12]

Kathleen Raine's long poem *Fata Morgana*, which was published in *New Verse* and several anthologies, registers the writing-versus-action tension which dogged many writers. She was conscious of her distance from the action of the Spanish Civil War to which she felt compelled, as a poet, to respond:

> While they were on the march to their desires
> Through painful brilliance of Iberian day
> These arguing remained by their homefires
> Still living in the old, unhealthy way.
> …
>
> Books, idle books, and hours, unfruitful hours,
> Weigh on my genius and lay waste my will,
> While heavenly wings are without power to raise
> Me from beneath the stone with which they kill.
> …
>
> But I, who have no words, nor heart, nor name,
> Can still suppose how it would feel to march
> Guided by stars along the roads of Spain
> Because of what I learn, but cannot teach.[13]

Throughout the poem Raine oscillates 'between the writer's individual struggle to become a poet and her imaginative involvement with Spain.'[14] Raine's poems were often published during the 1930s and Geoffrey Grigson published more of hers than of Auden's in *New Verse* although – and no doubt because – she was not politically motivated; if anything, she identified with Conservative ideals.

For Valentine Ackland, Sylvia Townsend Warner, Naomi Mitchison, Nancy Cunard and Stevie Smith, the relation between propaganda and art was not just a cerebral diversion but a critical one. They were aware of the Modernist demands of 'impersonality' and also that poetry could represent the plight of the oppressed and dispossessed. Sylvia Townsend Warner reconciled the tension between being a writer and an active social reformer in her 'discovery that the pen could be used as a sword'.[15] Warner and Ackland were driven by the urgency to 'combat Fascism as Intellectual enemy No 1.[16] They belonged to the Left Book Club although they found that *Left Review* was inappropriately dominated by poets 'from Oxbridge or Chelsea or Bloomsbury', but it was an outlet for their poems, fiction and journalism.[17] In 1935 they joined the Communist Party and went to the Congress of Writers in Paris, which was also attended by Winifred Holtby, Storm Jameson and Naomi Mitchison. In 1939 they joined the Third American Writers Congress in New York, to consider the loss of democracy in Europe, and Warner became an executive committee member of the Association of Writers for Intellectual Liberty. In 1936 she was present as a British delegate to the International Peace Congress in Brussels, organised by the Communist Party, and in 1937 at the Congress of the International Association in Defence of Culture in Madrid and Valencia. The Association aimed for an international exchange of literature and to fight against war, Fascism and 'everything that menaces culture.'[18] During the Spanish Civil War they gave assistance to the Red Cross Unit in Barcelona. On returning to England, Valentine Ackland worked voluntarily at Tythrop House, near Thame, a home for Spanish refugee children, and reviewed books on the war. Warner 'wrote as much as anybody did about the war'[19] and her poems and anti-Fascist articles were published in *Time and Tide* and *Left Review*. These, along with her letters and notebooks, record her admiration for the Spanish people. As Barbara Brothers observes, however, 'in the narrative of Spanish Civil War writing, women become an emblem, bibliographic entry, or footnote'.[20] Additionally, war writing is suspect because ideology is assumed to supersede aesthetic concerns:

> Political commitment ... is proclaimed by the academic, critical establishment, worshipers of the idol of Modernism, to be the antithesis of literary value. Like the adjective 'woman', political effaces the category 'writer' to which the adjectives are applied ... Literary histories of the Spanish Civil War proclaim themselves as part social history – the literature not real literature – and part literary history.[21]

For all writers, the Spanish Civil War clearly posed both the opportunity and the difficulty of negotiating between polemic and art. One way of appreciating the imaginative aspect of the poetry – which distinguishes it from propaganda or autobiography – is to compare it with journalism and essays, such as Sylvia Townsend Warner's article 'Barcelona', written for *Left Review* after her first visit to help the Republican Medical Services.[22] Warner's best poems combine her skill as a narrator and observer. *El Heroe*[23] depicts the death of the unknown soldier with stark realism and a painterly eye; interestingly, one stanza was omitted from the typescript which Warner prepared for *Collected Poems*:

And the western sky was flushed
With the setting sun when a shot
Rang out, and he fell to the ground
With a bullet through his head.[24]

As Brothers puts it, Warner's poems 'do not romanticise or sentimentalise the soldier'.[25] Her poems are written in the context of suffering and unheroic conditions that the First World War poets pictured for those on the homefront. In *Port Bou* she relates the smells, tastes and sounds of Spain for those who had not been there; at the end of the poem, however, she moves from the descriptive to the didactic with a rousing call for 'those who fight for Spain!'[26] In her lecture 'Women as Writers' Warner explained the importance of 'immediacy', which meant freedom from the author's 'anxious presence'.[27] In *Journey to Barcelona* she succeeds in achieving this 'immediacy' through a first-hand narrative: the pallid landscape and the dwellings 'like hempen shrouds' mirror the lifelessness of the peasants who are under the shadow of death, 'Pale is that country, like a country of bone'. As in *Port Bou*, the last line is a summons for the communist cause: 'Rain for the red cloud, come to Spain.[28]

Waiting at Cerbere combines the eye of the journalist and poet:

And on the hillside
That is the colour of peasant's bread,
Is the rectangular
White village of the dead.[29]

As Barbara Brothers states, 'after her visits to Spain, Warner used the Spanish landscape to express the stark inner reality of life for the peasants and soldiers.'[30] *Benicasim* pulls together her observations in other poems, such as images of waiting, stillness, heat, salt air, the rugged landscape and the numbed inhabitants. These poems are what Sally Alexander observes as typical wartime writing in their 'immediate and often urgent description'.[31] Typically, surface events such as blood, silence, horror and retreating refugees are merely recorded and the complex nature of the struggle is left uninvestigated.

The two most militant poems, *Red Front* and *In This Midwinter*, both printed in *Left Review* in 1935,[32] are not included in Warner's *Collected Poems* or *Selected Poems* because they seemed to be 'shouted ... through a megaphone'.[33] Claire Harman records that *Red Front* was 'read as a declamation in Battersea late in 1935 and again in Whitechapel in 1936 (Sylvia was not able to attend)' and that 'with its worker-memorable chorus in common time, [the poem] harks back to the Great War'.[34] In *Red Front* Warner also draws upon the associations of the French Revolution to cultivate the horror of the bloodshed in Spain. Wendy Mulford described it as a 'choric, dramatic piece, but not particularly successful', perhaps because of its archaic vocabulary like 'mire' and 'blight' or because of its rousing refrain:

> Comrade, are you mired enough,
> Sad enough, tired enough –
> Hush! – to march with us tonight
> Through the mist and through the blight?
> Can the knitted heart sustain
> The long Northeaster of In Vain,
> The whining, whining wind unbinding? –
> Red! Red![35]

As Barbara Brothers puts it, the direct call to action 'offends the sensibilities of poetry readers taught to disdain didacticism … Yet the history and experience evoked by the surface details, her imagery and allusions, evoke the suffering and deprivation of the poor whom those in power in the government and in the church use to serve themselves'.[36] *In This Midwinter* is also strident but more lyrical, described by Mulford as 'a Marxist carol'.[37] As Sally Alexander observes in *Women's Voices of the Spanish Civil War*, women were more intent on democracy than feminism although Margot Heinemann recalled that these were linked because Fascism meant 'war, the abolition of civil liberties and the return of women to the status of second class citizens and to child-bearing as their exclusive social useful function.'[38]

The voices of the Republican supporters in Valentine Ackland's war poems are of indeterminate gender. *Winter*, published in *Left Review* in 1936, represents her conscious search for a voice within regular metres. It seems like an attempt to invoke support for the Spanish Republicans without forgoing lyricism:

> Then the word moves in us and we stir in our bed,
> Clotted together in misery, hungry and time-besotted,
> The drag of time on our hands and on nerves the nag,
> Then we whisper together and the word we say is red.[39]

Ackland found it difficult to harness her political engagement to her preferred lyrical modes. Carol Rumens applauds her concern for aesthetics over party politics: 'Even when writing about the coming revolution in the approved manner, Ackland is concerned to hammer out a new kind of verse as well as a statement'.[40] *Instructions for England* is, however, unashamed polemic.[41]

Like Sylvia Townsend Warner and Valentine Ackland, Nancy Cunard funnelled much of her political anger into journalism, but her poem *To Eat To-day* is a striking depiction of a Spanish peasant family ravaged by the Civil War. The strong rhythms, shocking images and dramatic dialogue construct a kind of filmic realism but Cunard cannot resist the didactic note in addressing the Fascists, 'is the mark worth the bomb?'[42] Initially, she went to Spain as a journalist but became engaged by the Republican cause, 'Spain took hold of me entirely'.[43] She instigated the letter from Paris addressed 'To the Writers and Poets of England, Scotland, Ireland and Wales', requesting statements of their position regarding the Spanish Civil War. The replies were published by *Left Review*, in 1937, as 'Authors Take Sides on the Spanish War'[44] and sold a good three thousand copies. She travelled to America, Moscow and Geneva between 1930 and 1935 to fight for the cause of the dispossessed; in 1936 she went to help the Republicans in Spain and in 1939 to give aid to the Spanish refugees as well as continuing to write articles on Spain for *The Manchester Guardian*. On her second visit to Barcelona, she was appalled to find 'hunger everywhere' and started a food campaign through *The Manchester Guardian*, *The News Chronicle* and *The Daily Herald*.[45] Through her political activities Nancy Cunard became a good friend of Sylvia Townsend Warner. She worked for the League of Nations and provided money towards a mobile exhibition which would raise awareness about the victims of the Spanish war. She also reopened her Hours Press in order to print poems on the war. At the end of the Civil War she assisted refugees in southern France and obtained the release of the Spanish poet Caesar Arconada, who, with others, lived in her home in Réanville. In a letter to Nan Green in 1963 she wrote, 'I have so many poems written on Spain that I wonder if they, in their different years, during and after, could not be done up into a volume.'[46] The volume was never completed.

Nancy Cunard's unusual *Sonnet in Five Languages* is printed with her explanatory notes in Valentine Cunningham's *The Penguin Book of Spanish Civil War Verse*.[47] The anthology also reproduces some of her translations, such as Pablo Neruda's *Almeria*, which provided another outlet for her hostility to the upper class:

> Ambassadors, ministers, guests in abominable assembly,
> Aristocrats, landowners, writers labelled *neutrality*,

Ladies of tea-room and of divan ease –
A dish of destruction, befouled with the blood of the poor[48]

Cunningham also includes Warner's translations such as José Herrera
Petere's *El día que no vendrá* which commemorates the fall of Madrid:

Day of meal, day of masses,
Day of cannon, day of churchbells,
Day of shrines and day of bullets,
Strewn with fresh blood and with blossom –
Such the day the Fascists looked for
On that morrow of that nightfall
When they took Madrid.[49]

The rhythmic beat and strong rhetoric may have influenced her own
poems like *Red Front*. Valentine Ackland's translation of Louis Aragon's
Waltz was published in *Left Review* but is not included in *The Penguin
Book of Spanish Civil War Verse*.[50] These translations by Cunard,
Warner and Ackland indicate where they found like-minded poetry of
commitment and epitomise the way in which they assumed a male
poet's identity or assumed a gender-neutral voice in writing war poems.

Considerations of gendered identity also seem to be suspended in
addressing class politics in Britain. Valentine Ackland's subjects in
Communist Poem are genderless comrades.[51] Warner assumes the
persona of a rebellious male civilian in *Some Make This Answer*, published in *Left Review*, February 1936; her vehement opposition to
bureaucratic fudging of unjust systems is dramatised into a rhetorical
monologue. *Song for a Street Song* also explores collective rather than
individual experiences in the break-up of local communities caused by
war. Although her diction is stilted in places, she was obviously developing a more natural voice which was at its most free in the Spanish
Civil War poems. Her difficulty in negotiating the interface of the
didactic and lyrical is further illuminated by the easier lyricism of her
love poems which are unencumbered by the impulse for propaganda.[52]

The poetry and journalism of Ackland, Warner and Cunard register
the social concern of many women whose politics have often been
ironed out in subsequent records. Sally Alexander found that 'women's
participation in anti-fascist movements has been largely suppressed',[53]
yet as Brothers indicates, 'why Warner and others like her were against
the British government is clear from the pages of *Left Review*. Over
and over again those writers in the 1930s who, like Warner, joined the
Communist party repeated their ideals – "democratic liberty, anti-

Fascism, and peace.'"[54] Ackland wrote a series of articles entitled 'Country Dealings' which exposed the deprived conditions of the rural poor, and Sylvia Townsend Warner's concern for their exploitation is dramatised in her satirical narrative poem *Opus 7* (1931). During the 1930s Nancy Cunard became mythologised as a rebel for her 'almost frenetic involvement in social and political affairs'.[55] Her articles appeared in *Left Review* and the publication of her bold treatise *Black Man and White Ladyship* (1931) was a controversial attack on the prejudices of the British aristocracy. *Negro: An Anthology* (1934) was an eight-hundred-page 'record of the struggles and achievements, the persecutions and the revolts against them, of the Negro people.'[56]

Naomi Mitchison and Winifred Holtby were, as Branson and Heinemann record in their social history of the Thirties, among the anti-Fascist writers involved in *Left Review*.[57] Naomi Mitchison aimed to promote socialist and feminist ideals through her writing and through the women's, peace and labour movements. She joined the Labour Party in 1930 and stood as Labour candidate for the Scottish Universities parliamentary seat in 1935. In 1934 she went to Vienna to provide aid to the social democrats after the killings and violations of civil liberties by the Austrian government. The poet Margaret Cole and her husband Douglas were among the 'labourite' friends of the Mitchisons. Jill Benton describes the Mitchisons' home in Hammersmith during the 1920s and 1930s as a 'class melting pot', where their working-class neighbours mixed with their social circle of politicians and artists.[58] Mitchison's *To Some Young Communists from an Older Socialist*, printed in *New Verse*, January 1933, registers her interest in building bridges between communism and socialism. The rift between her radical socialism and the intellectual socialism of the younger generation is strikingly similar to the Old and New Labour factions of the 1990s:

> Tolerance and irony were the things we once hated.
> Now there is nothing but that – you've cornered, corralled the rest.
> Look, our car's luggage of high violent hopes is only socks and
>   vests:
> Kick them away, careless, marching, you and your mates.
>
> We who were young once in that war time, we are now not young
>   but apart,
> Living with photos of friends, dead at Ypres or Menin,
> Remembering little of lies or truth perhaps defended;
> We were hit then in the head, but now, hopeless, in the heart.[59]

It is, of course, a direct reply to her friend Auden's *A Communist to Others* and imitates his blend of personal and public speech. Her long poem *The Alban Goes Out* is an allegorical narrative about the lives of sea fishermen and a shorter poem, *Eviction in the Hebrides*, printed in *Left Review* in 1937,[60] expresses her vehement anti-colonialism.

Stevie Smith refers to Naomi Mitchison's politics in a letter to Denis Johnson in 1937: 'more talkie from Naomi Mitchison, and she's got world problems on the brain too ... but if she thinks she is going to rope me in to the Haldane-communismus gang she is mistaken.'[61] Stevie Smith would have been more opposed to what she called the 'groupismus' of party politics than to Mitchison's socialist principles. Her two novels, *Novel on Yellow Wallpaper* (1936) and *Over the Frontier* (1938), deal with war but she tends to focus on cosmic evils as a microcosm of an individual's social identity. The major enemy for her was totalitarianism of either left or right: totalitarianism meant state control and organised religion, which were to be feared for producing cultural mediocrity – a condition she dramatises in the poem, *Sterilisation* (1937). Through mimicry and conflation of high and popular cultural discourses, she undermines the grand narratives of Literature, Science, History and the Church. At the same time she registers her objection to the culture of 'the masses' because it threatened individualism: 'And soon all our minds will be flat as a pancake,/ With no room for genius, exaltation or heartache'.[62] Stevie Smith was a prolific poet during the 1930s but could not get published until David Garnett risked printing some of her poems in the *New Statesman* in 1936. There was sufficient response to these to persuade Jonathan Cape to publish two volumes, *A Good Time Was Had by All* (1937) and *Tender Only to One* (1938). In addition to these, eighteen out of the sixty-two uncollected poems in *Me Again* (1981) were dated in the 1930s.

Like other Thirties poets, Stevie Smith wrote about the new developments on the edge of towns and cities, but unlike them she is more critical of social snobbery than of the stereotyped uniformity of suburbia. In *The Suburban Classes* she exposes the manipulation of those who play upon the proverbial conformity of the lower-middle-class mind:

> There is far too much of the suburban classes
> Spiritually not geographically speaking. They're asses.
> Menacing the greatness of our beloved England, they lie
> Propagating their kind in an eightroomed stye.
> Now I have a plan which I will enfold
> (There's this to be said for them, they do as they're told)

Then tell them their country's in mortal peril
They believed it before and again will not cavil
Put it in caption form firm and slick
If they see it in print it is bound to stick:[63]

Her treatment of the working class similarly does not patronise but gives dignity to the unsung heroes of prosaic routines, as sketched in *Alfred the Great*.[64]

A comment in *The Year's Poetry* of 1938 discerned a 'smell of light verse around', but although Smith's poetry may be 'light' in Auden's sense of aiming for a community of shared assumptions between the poet and the audience, it is not light-hearted verse.[65] It is easy to dismiss as sheer play her challenge to British imperialism in the four-lined *Happy Dogs of England*[66] where she parodies the nationalistic hymn tune *O happy band of pilgrims* – typically using a common cultural form –, offsets it with demotic prose and turns a sacred text into a nursery rhyme. She does not retreat into playful aesthetics and was absolutely serious in her hostility to the hierarchical structures of the Church and State. She unsettles their status by satirising their authority figures in vitriolic portraits like *The Bishops of the Church of England* and *Lord Mope*.[67] *Souvenir de Monsieur Poop* is similarly one of several assaults at the literary establishment which made it difficult for her to get her poems published and properly reviewed:

I am the self-appointed guardian of English Literature,
I believe tremendously in the significance of age;
I believe that a writer is wise at 50,
Ten years wiser at 60, at 70 a sage.
I believe that juniors are lively, to be encouraged with discretion
    and snubbed,
I believe also that they are bouncing, communistic, ill mannered
    and, of course, young.
But I never define what I mean by youth
Because the word undefined is more useful for general purposes
    of abuse.

...

But then I am an old fogey.
I always write more in sorrow than in anger.
I am, after all, devoted to Shakespeare, Milton,
And, coming to our own times,
Of course
Housman.[68]

Her poems can be read according to Ian Gregson's version of post-modern dialogic which is the tendency to 'arbitrate between strangeness and familiarity', in terms of Mikhail Bakhtin's carnivalesque which 'brings together, unifies, weds and combines the sacred with the profane, the lofty with the low, the great with the insignificant, the wise with the stupid.'[69]

Ultimately, Stevie Smith's politics are to be found in her disregard for all the discourses of power; by disrupting familiar syntactical or formal structures, she challenges their associated assumptions and cultural authority. Her irreverence towards those whose status was conventionally unquestioned stretches to war heroes in poems like *Private Means is Dead (originally entitled 'Chaps')* and *The Lads of the Village*.[70] In the latter poem she is undermining the poetry of war (and implicitly those who market and consume it) for aestheticising pain rather than war *per se*, but its daring during a period where war sensitivities were still acute should be appreciated:

> Oh sing no more: Away with folly of commanders.
> This will not make a better song upon the field of Flanders,
> Or upon any field of experience where pain makes patterns the
> poet slanders.

Here, the nonchalant air of anti-realism is a typical defence against going over the line. The authority of her writing derives from this persistent transgression of conventional frontiers.[71] As Martin Pumphrey observes, 'through the voices of her fantasy characters, her poems repeatedly investigate the difficulties of negotiating between inner desires and outer restraint (and contemplate the allure and danger of resistance and transgression)'.[72] In her investigations of desire and social taboos, she frequently drew upon the new language of psychology, most directly in poems with titles like *Egocentric* and *Analysand*, and also in her characteristic poems on death such as *Goodnight* and *When I Awake*.

There is little room here to look at the woman-centred poetry which tackled gender politics, usually indirectly. For Stevie Smith, feminism and socialism, never articulated as such, were parallel impulses rooted in a liberal temperament which sided with the underdog. Although she does not directly speak in the language of feminist protest, satires like *Major Macroo* depict women as casualties of men's freedom to choose:[73]

> Major Hawkaby Cole Macroo
> Chose very wisely

A patient Griselda of a wife with a heart of gold
That never beat for a soul but him
Himself and his slightest whim.
...

He'd several boyfriends
And she thought it was nice for him to have them,
And she loved him and felt that he needed her and waited
And waited and never became exasperated
...

Such men as these, such selfish cruel men
Hurting what most they love what most loves them,
Never make mistake when it comes to choosing a woman
To cherish them and be neglected and not think it inhuman.[74]

Her treatment of organised feminism, however, was characteristically dialectical:

Dear Female heart, I am sorry for you,
You must suffer, that is all that you can do.
But if you like, in common with the rest of the human race,
You may also look most absurd with a miserable face.[75]

Naomi Mitchison, on the other hand, was an active feminist who tried to connect her socialist and feminist ideologies. During the 1920s she had helped to found the North Kensington clinic which undertook birth control and abortions. She belonged to the Women's National League; she lectured for the World Sexual Reform League which was aimed at educated career women; she published an essay 'Breaking Up the Home' which criticised the nuclear family as incompatible with work for women. Mitchison was commissioned by Faber to write *Comments on Birth Control* in 1930, and published *We Have Been Warned*, a novel 'about my own times' (1933), *The Moral Basis of Politics* (1938), *The Blood of the Martyrs* (1939), a modern political parable, and *The Kingdom of Heaven* (1939). During the 1930s, Mitchison, like others, became disillusioned with the Communism which she had witnessed in Russia and the London-based Socialism, partly because of their indifference towards women's emancipation.[76] The impulse for freedom which strained against the reins of convention is the subtext of many of her poems. She and her husband practised an open marriage but *Dick and Colin at the Salmon Nets*, printed in *Time and Tide*, 25 February 1933, suggests that the traditional roles which separate men and women are inevitable:

> Must we be apart always, you watching the salmon nets, you in
> the rain,
> Thinking of love or politics or what I don't know,
> While I stay in with the children and books, and never again
> Haul with the men on the fish nets,[77]

It echoes Mitchison's assertion in 1930 that feminism's battles had not been won: 'Apparently, all the feminist battles are gained, or almost all. Actually nothing is settled, and the question of baby or not baby is at the bottom of almost everything.'[78] Many poems record women's sense of possible change alongside their individual experience of stagnation. Arnold Rattenbury quotes Sylvia Townsend Warner writing to Nancy Cunard in 1944 on the subject of the progress of civilisation:

> The great civil war, Nancy, that will come and must come before the world can begin to grow up, will be fought out on this terrain of man and woman, and we must storm and hold Cape Turk before we talk of social injustice.[79]

This analysis of women's poems has been directed at the arguments that women were either 'out on the backfields singing an entirely different tune' or 'shouting through a megaphone' in their poems. They were participating in the movements and discourses concerning war, class and gender, and their poems negotiate the line between political and aesthetic concerns which characterise much Thirties poetry. The stylistic diversity of their poems represents the stylistic diversity of all poetry in the 1930s; it also illustrates the impossibility of aligning political and stylistic radicalism. Sylvia Townsend Warner's prosody has been called 'traditionalism'[80] and yet she was one of the most politically active of all Thirties poets whereas Laura Riding, who was the most adventurous stylistically, 'dispense[ing] with literary conventionalities and poetic idiom', was the most politically conservative.[81] With Henry Kemp, Robert Graves and others she issued *The Left Heresy in Literature and Life*, which advertised itself as 'a virile indictment, by distinguished poets, of left wing sectarianism and its intrusion in literature, psychology, politics etc.'[82] Stevie Smith was not a political activist but her textual subversions went further than those of other poets and were an aspect of her humanist egalitarianism. The common commitment to democracy, which was strengthened by the rise of Fascism, is, however, reflected in all these poets' conscious experiments with colloquial speech and their representations of injustice.

Notes

1. Jane Dowson (ed.), *Women's Poetry of the 1930s: A Critical Anthology* (London: Routledge, 1996).
2. Kate Clanchy, 'Loud hailers and currant rolls', review of Dowson, *Women's Poetry of the 1930s, The Independent,* 3 February 1996.
3. William Fiennes, 'Beyond the Locker Room', review of Dowson, *Women's Poetry of the 1930s, Times Literary Supplement,* 1 March 1996.
4. Cora Kaplan, 'Language and Gender' in Deborah Cameron (ed.), *The Feminist Critique of Language* (London: Routledge, 1990) pp. 57–69, 58.
5. Barbara Brothers, 'Writing Against the Grain: Sylvia Townsend Warner and the Spanish Civil War', in Mary Lynn Broe and Angela Ingram (eds), *Women's Writing in Exile* (Chapel Hill: University of Carolina Press, 1989), pp. 350–66, 362.
6. Arnold Rattenbury, 'Literature, Lying and Sober Truth', in John Lucas (ed.), *Writing and Radicalism* (Harlow: Longman, 1996), pp. 201–44.
7. Carol Rumens, 'Smitchwelby', review of Dowson, *Women's Poetry of the 1930s, Poetry Review,* vol. 85, no. 4, Winter 95/6, pp. 23–4.
8. Janet Montefiore, *Men and Women Writers of the 1930s: The Dangerous Flood of History* (London: Routledge, 1996), p. 115.
9. See, for example, Edgell Rickword, 'Art and Propaganda', *Left Review,* vol. 1, no. 2, November 1934, p. 44 and Julian Symons, *The Thirties: A Dream Revolved* (London: Faber, 1975).
10. Symons, *The Thirties,* p. 25.
11. D. E. S. Maxwell, *Poetry of the Thirties* (London: Routledge & Kegan, 1969), p. 460.
12. Maxwell, *Poetry of the Thirties,* p. 460.
13. Kathleen Raine, from 'Fata Morgana', *New Verse,* no. 25, May 1937, pp. 7–9.
14. Adrian Caesar, *Dividing Lines: Poetry, Class and Ideology in the 1930s* (Manchester: Manchester University Press, 1991), pp. 138–9.
15. Sylvia Townsend Warner, 'The Way by Which I Have Come', *The Countryman,* vol. xix, no. 2, 1939, pp. 472–86, 475.
16. Valentine Ackland, 'Writers in Madrid', in Sally Alexander and Jim Fyrth (eds), *Women's Voices from the Spanish Civil War* (London: Lawrence & Wishart, 1991), p. 292.
17. Noreen Branson and Margot Heinemann, *Britain in the Nineteen Thirties* (St Albans: Panther, 1973), p. 299.
18. 'Declaration of the Association of Writers in Defence of Culture', *Left Review,* vol. 1 no. 11, August 1935, p. 462.
19. Valentine Cunningham (ed.), *Spanish Front: Writers on the Civil War* (New York: Oxford University Press, 1986), xxxii.
20. Brothers, 'Writing Against the Grain', p. 350.
21. Brothers 'Writing Against the Grain', p 350.
22. Sylvia Townsend Warner, 'Barcelona', *Left Review,* vol. 2, December 1936, p. 812.
23. Sylvia Townsend Warner, 'El Heroe', in Dowson, *Women's Poetry of the 1930s,* pp. 153–4.
24. Sylvia Townsend Warner in Claire Harman (ed.), *Collected Poems* (Manchester: Carcanet, 1982), p. 276.
25. Brothers, 'Writing Against the Grain', p. 358.
26. Sylvia Townsend Warner, 'Port Bou' in Dowson, *Women's Poetry of the 1930s,* p. 154.
27. Sylvia Townsend Warner, 'Women as Writers', in Harman, *Collected Poems,* pp. 265–74.
28. Sylvia Townsend Warner, 'Journey to Barcelona', in Dowson, *Women's Poetry of the 1930s,* p. 155.
29. Sylvia Townsend Warner, 'Waiting at Cerbere', in Harman, *Collected Poems,* p. 36.
30. Brothers, 'Writing Against the Grain', p. 358.
31. Alexander and Fyrth, *Women's Voices from the Spanish Civil War,* p. 17.
32. Sylvia Townsend Warner, 'Red Front', *Left Review,* vol. 1, April 1935, 255–6.
33. Harman, *Collected Poems,* xxii.
34. Claire Harman, *Sylvia Townsend Warner: A Biography* (London: Chatto & Windus; London: Minerva, 1985), p. 147.
35. Sylvia Townsend Warner, 'Red Front', in Brothers, 'Writing Against the Grain', pp. 363–6.
36. Brothers, 'Writing Against the Grain', p. 358.
37. Sylvia Townsend Warner, 'In This Midwinter', *Left Review,* vol. 1, June 1935, p. 101.

38. Margot Heinemann, in Alexander and Fyrth, *Women's Voices from the Spanish Civil War*, p. 14.
39. Valentine Ackland, 'Winter', *Left Review*, vol. 2., March 1936; Dowson, *Women's Poetry of the 1930s*, p. 32.
40. Carol Rumens, 'Smithchwelby', review of Dowson, *Women's Poetry of the 1930s*, *Poetry Review*, vol. 85, no. 4, Winter 95/6, 23–4.
41. Valentine Ackland, 'Instructions for England', in Dowson, *Women's Poetry of the 1930s*, p. 33.
42. Nancy Cunard, 'To Eat To-day', in Dowson, *Women's Poetry of the 1930s*, p. 53.
43. Foreword, Samuel Putnam (ed.), *Nancy Cunard: Brave Poet, Indomitable Rebel 1896–1965* (Philadelphia: Chilton Book Company, 1968).
44. See Valentine Cunningham, Introduction to *The Penguin Book of Spanish Civil War Verse* (Harmondsworth: Penguin, 1980), p. 50.
45. See 'The Refugees at Perpignan, Miss Cunard's Appeal', in Putnam, *Nancy Cunard*, p. 196.
46. Putnam, *Nancy Cunard*, pp. 173–4.
47. Cunningham, *The Penguin Book of Spanish Civil War*.
48. Nancy Cunard, tr. of Neruda, 'Almería', in Cunningham, *The Penguin Book of Spanish Civil War*, pp. 379–80.
49. José Herrera Petere, 'El día que no vendrá', tr. Warner, in Cunningham, *The Penguin Book of Spanish Civil War*, pp. 291–3.
50. Louis Aragon, 'Waltz', *Left Review*, vol. 1, October 1934, pp. 3–5.
51. Valentine Ackland, 'Communist Poem, 1935', *Left Review*, vol. 1, July 1935, p. 430; Dowson, *Women's Poetry of the 1930s*, p. 35.
52. For the poems and further discussion see the sections on Ackland and Warner in Dowson, *Women's Poetry of the 1930s*.
53. Alexander and Fyrth, *Women's Voices from the Spanish Civil War*, p. 21.
54. Brothers, 'Writing Against the Grain', p. 359.
55. Hugh Ford, in Putnam, *Nancy Cunard*, p. 37.
56. Nancy Cunard, Introduction to Nancy Cunard (ed.), *Negro: An Anthology* (London: Wishart & Co.; New York: Frederick Ungar Publishing Co., 1934; reprint 1970).
57. Branson and Heinemann, *Britain in the Nineteen Thirties*, pp. 298–9.
58. Jill Benton, *Naomi Mitchison: A Biography* (London: Pandora, 1990), pp. 38–9.
59. Naomi Mitchison, 'To Some Young Communists from an Older Socialist', in Dowson, *Women's Poetry of the 1930s*, pp. 76–7.
60. Naomi Mitchison, 'Eviction in the Hebrides', *Left Review*, vol. 3, no. 1, February 1937, p. 20.
61. Stevie Smith, Letter to Denis Johnson, 10 June 1937, in Stevie Smith, *Me Again: The Uncollected Writings of Stevie Smith* (London: Virago, 1981), p. 259.
62. Stevie Smith, 'Sterilisation', in Dowson, *Women's Poetry of the 1930s*.
63. Stevie Smith, 'The Suburban Classes', in *Stevie Smith: Collected Poems* (London: Allen Lane, 1975), p. 26.
64. Stevie Smith, 'Alfred the Great', in *Stevie Smith: Collected Poems*, p. 19.
65. Denys Kilham Roberts and Geoffrey Grigson (eds), Preface to *The Year's Poetry 1938* (London: John Lane, The Bodley Head, 1938), p. 7.
66. Stevie Smith in Hermione Lee (ed.), *Stevie Smith: A Selection* (London: Faber, 1983), p. 65.
67. Stevie Smith, 'The Bishops of the Church of England' and 'Lord Mope', in *Stevie Smith: Collected Poems*, pp. 58, 96.
68. Stevie Smith, 'Souvenir de Monsieur Poop', in *Stevie Smith: Collected Poems*, p. 137–8.
69. Mikhail Bakhtin, 1984, in Ian Gregson, *Contemporary Poetry and Postmodernism: Dialogue and Estrangement* (Basingstoke: Macmillan, 1996), p. 9.
70. Stevie Smith, 'Private Means is Dead', in *Stevie Smith: Collected Poems*, p. 74; 'The Lads of the Village', in *Stevie Smith: Collected Poems*, p. 142.
71. Stevie Smith, 'Egocentric', in *Stevie Smith: Collected Poems*, p. 18; 'Analysand', in *Stevie Smith: Collected Poems*, p. 54; Goodnight', *Me Again*, 1981, p. 245; 'When I awake', *Me Again*, 1981, p. 232.
72. Martin Pumphrey, 'Play, Fantasy and Strange Laughter: Stevie Smith's Uncomfortable Poetry', *Critical Quarterly*, vol. 28, no. 3, Autumn 1986, pp. 85–96, 87.
73. See, for example, Stevie Smith, 'Octopus' and 'The Word', in Dowson, *Women's Poetry of the 1930s*, pp. 148, 147.

74. Stevie Smith, 'Major Macroo', in *Stevie Smith: Collected Poems*, p. 72.
75. Stevie Smith, 'Dear Female Heart', in *Stevie Smith: Collected Poems*, p. 130.
76. See Benton's discussion of Naomi Mitchison's 'The Moral Basis of Politics' (1938) in Benton, *Naomi Mitchison*, pp. 111–15.
77. Naomi Mitchison, 'Dick and Colin at the Salmon Nets', in Dowson, *Women's Poetry of the 1930s*, p. 81.
78. Naomi Mitchison, *All Change Here*, 1930, p. 52; See Benton, *Naomi Mitchison*, p. 72.
79. Sylvia Townsend Warner, 1944, in Lucas, *Writing and Radicalism*, p. 232.
80. Montefiore, *Men and Women Writers of the 1930s*, p. 133.
81. Laura Riding, *The Poems of Laura Riding* (Manchester: Carcanet, 1980), p. 12.
82. Advert for *The Left Heresy in Literature and Life*, Laura Riding, Henry Kemp, Robert Graves and others in *Twentieth Century Verse*, June/July 1939, p. 57.

5

Revising the Marriage Plot in Women's Fiction of the 1930s

Diana Wallace

In *British Writers of the Thirties* Valentine Cunningham comments on the 'misogyny' which was 'rife in the writing of this period'.[1] He suggests that:

> Even the determinedly womanising and married found it hard to steer their texts clear of the prevailing hostility to women and marriage ... A whole generation of writers refused to countenance the normal family in their work, as they refused in their lives to acquire wives and become fathers.[2]

While Cunningham's comments may hold true for the small group of public-school-educated (and often homosexual) male writers – Auden, Isherwood, Spender *et al.* – who have dominated critical accounts of the period, the picture is very different for women writers. The writers discussed by Cunningham reject marriage, but there is a group of novels by women in the 1930s which use the marriage plot specifically to explore how marriage might be refashioned to accommodate women's increasing expectations in sexual, political and professional life. Written by novelists including Vera Brittain, Rebecca West, Naomi Mitchison, F. Tennyson Jesse, E. H. Young, Dorothy L. Sayers, Margaret Kennedy and Storm Jameson, who themselves frequently combined a professional life with marriage, some of these novels are remarkably positive about its possibilities.

Several studies have drawn attention to the conservative ideology of domesticity which characterised the inter-war period, especially the 1930s.[3] A focus on marriage in fiction might seem, at first glance, part of the backlash against feminism which sent women, in Deirdre Beddoe's phrase, 'back to home and duty'.[4] What I want to do here is to place these novels in the context of the debates about marriage which were conducted throughout the 1930s. In that context, a context which the critical focus on 'MacSpaunday' has obscured, these women's novels can be seen as direct, and sometimes radical, interventions in the sexual politics of the day.

The marriage plot was, of course, far from new. The Edwardian 'marriage problem novels' have been examined by Jane Eldridge Miller, who situates them within specific social and legal changes.[5] Moving on to women's inter-war fiction, Maroula Joannou has shown how the 'topic of spinsterhood recurs in the 1920s with a frequency and insistence that can only be understood in its historical specificity', particularly in relation to the two million 'surplus women' of this period.[6] 'The meaning of spinsterhood', Joannou suggests, 'became a site of contestation between those who wished to objectify the spinster and others who saw her as a person with needs, desires and potential of her own'.[7]

In the 1930s the emphasis shifts so that it is the meaning of marriage which is the central site of contestation in the group of women's novels I want to discuss. Again, this shift has to be understood in its historical context. By the 1930s the population imbalance was evening out and statistically more people were getting married than before the war.[8] As Martin Pugh shows, the 1930s 'marked the start of a significant long-term trend towards marriage'.[9] On the other hand, there was both concern expressed at the rising number of divorces following the Matrimonial Causes Bill of 1923, and a campaign for a further liberalised divorce law. The latter culminated in A. P. Herbert's Matrimonial Causes Bill in 1937, which made it possible for both sexes to obtain a divorce on the grounds of desertion, cruelty or insanity.

Radical thinkers such as Bertrand and Dora Russell and Naomi Mitchison argued for, and experimented in, 'free love' and open marriages. In *Marriage and Morals*, for example, Bertrand Russell argued for 'trial marriages', which could be easily dissolved if childless, and suggested that adultery should not be grounds for divorce. He also predicted that the increasing role of the State in childcare could lead eventually to the elimination of the role of the father in family life.[10]

There is a sense that there is, as a six-part series in *The Listener* in 1931 put it, a 'Present Crisis in Marriage' throughout the 1930s. This series, based on radio talks given by Professor Bronislaw Malinowski and Dr Robert Briffault, signalled the subject as 'one of the most debatable questions of our time'.[11] Another series of talks orchestrated by Sir William Beveridge in 1932 was entitled 'Changes in Family

Life' and used a 'Family Form' sent out to listeners to gather information on those changes.[12]

The key elements responsible for the 'crisis' in marriage and the
changing nature of family life were the emancipation of women and
the increasing spread of birth control. Contraception not only released
married women from repeated pregnancies and made combining
marriage and a career more feasible (although until 1935 the marriage
bar forced married women teachers and civil servants to give up work),
it also made sex outside marriage less risky. Neither the spread of birth
control nor the new Freudian-inspired emphasis on women's 'right' to
sexual fulfilment, however, can be seen as unproblematic. Concern
about the falling birth rate meant that contraception was presented
mainly as a way for married women to space their children. Moreover,
as Margaret Jackson has shown, the explicit rationale of the flux of
inter-war marriage manuals was 'the prevention and cure of sexual
"maladjustment" in marriage', precisely because it was seen as 'a
threat to the institution of marriage, and thus to the social order
itself'.[13]

The debates around marriage were conducted in the press and on
the radio. Vera Brittain's writings on marriage, for example, appeared
in a range of publications from the *Evening News* to *Time and Tide*. By
1939, Jan Struther's conservative 'Mrs Miniver' is noting a newspaper
article on the 'well-worn subject of marriage'.[14] Her own musings on
the 'private marriage vows' made by herself and her husband to avoid
'turning into Siamese twins' are themselves a contribution to this
ongoing reshaping of marriage.[15]

The reprints of wireless talks in *The Listener* in the 1930s provide a
particularly fascinating insight into the popularisation of these debates,
as well the range of discourses within which they were discussed:
anthropology, psychology, philosophy, economics, education, law, medicine and religion. The six-part debate between Bronislaw Malinowski
(author of influential studies of the Trobriand islanders) and Robert
Briffault in 1931 discussed anthropological studies of polygamy,
monogamy, and 'group marriage', as well as the contemporaneous
loosening of marriage laws in Socialist Russia and the prohibition of
divorce in Italy. While Briffault located the 'matrimonial unrest' in
Britain in women's dissatisfaction with traditional marriage,[16] Malinowski was more sanguine, arguing that marriage would survive, partly
because it safeguarded women's interests. Indeed, as a debate in 1935
between the novelists E. Arnot Robertson and Rose Macauley, entitled
'Are Women Bored with Emancipation?' suggested, not all women

were in favour of being 'emancipated'. Robertson argued that women were turning to marriage because they were 'bored' with the vote and their jobs, a view Macauley strongly disputed.[17] The issue of sex outside marriage was a particularly heated one. A conservative view was taken by the Rev. Hugh Martin in 'Marriage and Some Alternatives'.[18] His assertion that sex must not take place outside marriage because of the risk of contraceptive failure, and the fact that the secrecy of such arrangements frequently led to tragedy, sparked off a series of letters both for and against his views.

Articles also provided advice on making a marriage work, often (like that in the marriage manuals) based on popularised psychoanalysis. 'The Psychology of Marriage' by 'A Doctor'[19] and 'Marriage' by 'A Practising Medical Psychologist'[20] both discussed the practical difficulties of adjusting to a spouse. Both pieces emphasised that each spouse has a different but equal and complementary function. Increasingly, marriage was envisaged as companionship between equal partners. As an acetylene welder put it on his 'Family Form': 'Woman has forged ahead so much in sport, industry, social and political life that no man, young or old, need hesitate at saying that a woman is his friend and pal'.[21] However, as a debate entitled 'Marriage on the Dole' shows, high unemployment in the 1930s created a particular problem for men without the funds to finance married life.[22]

It is debates of this kind which are reflected in women's novels, both 'popular' and 'literary'. The context I have outlined here provides a way of beginning to reassess the work of E. H. Young, a fine novelist whose work has much in common with that of Rosamond Lehmann in its anti-romantic analysis of class and gender. Two of Young's novels – The Curate's Wife and Celia[23] – focus directly on the sexual politics of marriage. Young explores especially the disjunction between women's expectations and the reality of married life. The Curate's Wife is an account of the first few months of the marriage between Dahlia Rendall and the curate, Cecil Sproat. Young tracks the power negotiations necessary between a couple who are different in class, religion, morality and attractiveness, and who differ in the strength of their love. The plot is negligible, a matter of the 'small grievances' which rock the precarious stability of married life, but Young makes it clear that the stakes are high, especially for the ordinary woman for whom, as Dahlia comes to recognise, 'marriage can be a career, too'.[24]

Celia deals with the disillusionment of middle age when that 'career' has gone wrong, and it is especially interesting for its restrained but candid portrayal of sexual failure within marriage, a failure due to a deep-seated emotional incompatibility which no marriage manuals can resolve. Celia, witness to the unfulfilled marriages of her relatives, is finally confronted with the shortcomings of her own marriage, due at least in part to her idealised attachment to the idea that she is in love with someone else. The ending offers no 'miraculous' falling in love with her husband, merely an understanding that 'like the others they would just go on and ... it was not a bad thing to do'.[25] This is a blow to the illusions peddled by popular novels which featured, as Winifred Holtby put it in an earlier anti-romance novel, 'beautiful girls who get married or married women who fall in love with their husbands'.[26]

These novelists, then, reveal the very real risks of marriage for women: boredom, frustration, self-delusion, loss of self and even, at an extreme, adultery, abortion and death. These fears are moulded into a Gothic shape in Daphne du Maurier's *Rebecca*.[27] In the historical context of the 1930s when a divorced or widowed man was three times as likely to remarry as his female counterpart,[28] *Rebecca* may be read as an expression of the specific anxieties experienced by the second wives of this period.

F. Tennyson Jesse's *A Pin to See the Peepshow* is a *Madame Bovary*-esque study of female adultery based on the Bywaters-Thompson murder case.[29] The protagonist Julia, a lower-middle-class, poorly educated girl also marries an older widower, mainly to escape from home. She has an adulterous affair, and, when her lover kills her husband, both are hanged for murder. Julia's defence is hampered by the fact that her counsel will not let her admit that her cryptic letters refer to an abortion because 'An English jury might think an illegal operation quite as bad as adultery – and adultery, apparently, was quite as bad as murder!'[30] Tennyson Jesse's novel explores the economic and social differentials which, before the 1937 Bill, made divorce for women of Julia's class 'as unknown and difficult a luxury as a private aeroplane'.[31] The difficulties of getting a divorce are also underscored in Storm Jameson's semi-autobiographical *Mirror in Darkness* trilogy. In *Company Parade* Jameson anatomises the effects of marriage to an improvident man.[32] Hervey Russell has to leave her son in Yorkshire in order to earn the money to support him, making the point that married women frequently *had* to work in order to support dependants.

Margaret Kennedy's *Together and Apart*, as her daughter recalled, was inspired by 'what amounted to an epidemic of divorce among [Kennedy's] acquaintance'.[33] The novel examines the disastrous effects of the divorce of Alex and Betsy Canning, precipitated not so much by

Alex's desultory adultery as by Betsy's half-formed feeling that she has been 'cheated' of 'real happiness'.[34] Both partners make subsequent, less satisfactory marriages, and their son's involvement in a hit-and-run accident is directly attributed to the family breakdown. The novel reflects not only contemporary concern about the rising divorce rate but also the 'moral panic' 'about an alleged increase in juvenile delinquency, which was attributed to "broken homes"' which Jackson has noted.[35]

One of the most prolonged treatments of the marriage theme may be observed in the detective novels of Dorothy L. Sayers. The six-year courtship of Lord Peter Wimsey and Harriet Vane, from *Strong Poison* in 1930 to *Busman's Honeymoon* in 1937, can be read as a meditation on marriage and its possibilities for the educated woman, and as a plea for women to be able to continue the work they do best after marriage.[36] As Susan Leonardi notes, Sayers transforms Wimsey from 'detective hero to flawed human being' in order to make him an appropriate husband for Harriet.[37] The turning point for Harriet in *Gaudy Night* is the moment at which she realises that Wimsey conceives of marriage in terms of equality, which makes him, as she puts it, 'not a man but a miracle'.[38] A final short story, 'Talboys', offers a glimpse of their marriage seven years on with Harriet dextrously juggling the deadline for an impending book and her responsibilities to her husband and children.[39] This suggests that the experiment in equality has been successful.

A more radical exploration of marriage is provided in Naomi Mitchison's *We Have Been Warned* which depicts the attempts of a Socialist couple, Tom and Dione Galton, to conduct an open marriage inspired by the Communist marriages they see in Russia.[40] While both Beveridge and Malinowski refer to the 'Russian Theory' of marriage as an extreme possibility,[41] Mitchison was able to draw on what she had witnessed in Russia, as well as on her own experimental open marriage. In *We Have Been Warned*, Tom, a Labour candidate, has a sexual relationship with a Russian girl, which Dione encourages. But Dione fails to carry out her intention of having sex with Donald Maclean, a Scottish Communist, because, despite feeling that a good 'Socialist woman' would be sexually generous, she is in love with her husband.[42] Mitchison balances the personal and emotional costs of this action against the political ideal, and suggests that it is more difficult for women to separate the personal and political, partly because of their biological role as mothers. In a key passage Dione decides that she must not have any more children:

Unless the revolution came in time, before she was too old. She mustn't think that either: it was romanticising; it was making personal and little something that was so big and so real that she couldn't think about it properly. What Tom called Realistically.[43]

It was Mitchison's 'purely emotional' response to 'theories' which Edwin Muir damned in his review of the novel, writing that 'the story is so sentimentalised that it is an object lesson in how not to write about serious things'.[44] What Muir misses, however, is Mitchison's concern with the intersection of sexual and party politics, and with marriage as a key site for that intersection. Tellingly, Mitchison had problems finding a publisher for We Have Been Warned because it included not only references to contraceptives, but also an account of an abortion being performed in Russia where such operations were legal.

Two of the most extensive treatments of the marriage plot – Vera Brittain's Honourable Estate and Rebecca West's The Thinking Reed – were both published in 1936. This was the year in which the abdication of Edward VIII provided a public example of the importance of the 'marriage question' and the stigma attached to divorce. While both novels centralise the issue of marriage (indeed, each is dedicated to the writer's husband), they represent two very different types of writing. Brittain's text is explicit polemic in the realist tradition while West's complex exploration of gender difference has its roots in Modernist experimentation.

Despite the fact that both are better known in terms of their earlier relationships – Brittain as a woman who lost her fiancé in the First World War and West as an unmarried mother following her ten-year affair with H. G. Wells – both women made marriages which, although problematic in personal terms, became key structuring elements in their writing. Brittain married the political scientist George Gordon Catlin in 1925, and West married the banker Henry Maxwell Andrews in 1930.

Brittain's marriage was what she called 'semi-detached'.[45] She and Catlin lived apart every other six months, with Catlin working in America, while Brittain and their children lived in England where, with the support of her friend Winifred Holtby, she could continue her writing. As Brittain wrote, such 'semi-detached marriages' solved the problem women faced of choosing between a career and the 'sacrifice of marriage, motherhood and all her emotional needs', or marriage and 'intellectual starvation and monotony'.[46] Brittain regarded her own marriage as an important example to others and her ideal has been seen by Martin Pugh as her 'greatest contribution to feminism'.[47]

Honourable Estate is an attempt to trace the evolution of the 'honourable estate' of matrimony from what Brittain elsewhere called the 'master–servant relationship of most nineteenth-century marriages' to the twentieth-century model of 'companionship between equals'.[48] Despite stylistic differences, it can be compared to Virginia Woolf's similar tracking of historical shifts in *The Years*, and with Vita Sackville-West's *All Passion Spent*, with its condemnation of the way that traditional marriage suppressed female individuality.[49]

Brittain first presents two 'nineteenth-century' style marriages – those of Janet and Thomas Rutherston, and of Stephen and Jessie Alleyndene – and uses them to argue for education for women, and for women to have the freedom to continue working after marriage. Perhaps more radically, she uses the disastrous marriage of the young, uneducated Janet to Thomas Rutherston, an older clergyman, to put the case for sex education, birth control and women doctors to attend childbirth – all key issues in contemporaneous feminist campaigns. Brittain makes it clear that women must have the right to refuse sex within marriage. Janet is forced into premature motherhood by her husband, induces a miscarriage to avoid a second baby, and finally leaves Thomas and her son in order to work for the suffrage cause. The novel also provides an argument for the provisions for divorce made in the 1937 Matrimonial Causes Bill. In the case of the Rutherstons' marriage, cruelty, desertion and insanity (Thomas becomes insane) are all involved.

The third part of the novel deals with the marriage of the children of these two marriages, Ruth Alleyndene and Denis Rutherston (who were based on Brittain and her husband). Here Brittain offers a blueprint for the new kind of marriage, premised on 'companionship between equals' and where the wife continues her career, in Ruth's case as an MP. The Oxford-educated Ruth sums up Brittain's ideas when she tells Denis: 'Don't you see that it is just because I *am* better qualified than your mother and still able to go on with my work, that I care for the twins [their children] so much'.[50] As Brittain sees it, education and a career are valuable not least because they make a woman a better wife and mother.

However much Brittain believes that the institution of marriage needs reform, it is clear that she wants to retain certain aspects of it, particularly the ideal of monogamy. *Honourable Estate* can be read as an illustration of Brittain's earlier pamphlet *Halcyon: Or the Future of Monogamy*, which was in part a reply to Dora Russell's *Hypatia: Or Women and Knowledge*.[51] The aspect of Russell's book which had caused most outrage – the *Sunday Express* called it 'pernicious rubbish'[52] – was her suggestion that both sexes were naturally polygamous and her advocacy of 'free love'. Brittain, in reply, frames *Halcyon* as a defence of monogamy as benefiting both sexes: 'No other relationship appears so well fitted to leave the mind free from the fret of sexual urge by adequately satisfying the demands of the body without giving to them that undue degree of attention which renders sex an incubus rather than an inspiration to mankind'.[53] Thus, in *Honourable Estate* it is only once she is married and has had children that Ruth can get on with her work.

Brittain's work is premised on the assumption that marriage can be made to work if women are given legal and social equality. Rebecca West's *The Thinking Reed*, on the other hand, can be seen as an attempt, to paraphrase the title of one of Luce Irigaray's books, to 'think the difference' between the sexes.[54] Just as Irigaray suggests in *An Ethics of Sexual Difference* that sexual difference is 'one of the major philosophical issues, if not the issue of our age ... which could be our "salvation" if we thought it through',[55] so West writes in *The Thinking Reed*: 'It struck [Isabelle] that the difference between men and women is the rock on which civilisation will split before it can reach any goal that could justify its expenditure of effort'.[56]

The Thinking Reed is a revision of Henry James's *The Portrait of a Lady*.[57] While West admired James's characterisation of Isabel Archer, she suggested provocatively that 'the conduct invented for Isabel is so inconsistent and so suggestive of the nincompoop, and so clearly proceeding from a brain whose ethical world was but a chaos, that it is a mistake to subject the book to the white light of a second reading'.[58] West's own Isabelle, a rich American widow living in France, has a 'competent, steely mind' and likes 'to bring everything that happened to her under the clarifying power of the intellect'.[59] Above all, Isabelle desires order and pattern in her life, but, because she is woman, she is forced to act in 'feminine' ways – as if she were irrational, illogical and uncontrolled – in order to negotiate her relationships with men. Thus, while West sets out to explore the 'difference' between the sexes, she destabilises the binary oppositions – logical/illogical, rational/irrational, controlled/emotional and so on – traditionally associated with 'masculinity' and 'femininity'.

Like James's Isabel, West's Isabelle marries a man she does not love. The industrialist Marc Sallafranque is grotesquely ugly, but he is also a 'naturally good' man[60] and Isabelle is delighted to find herself growing to love him. West uses as a figure for their initially successful marriage and as a 'symbol of domesticity'[61] the image of a ormolu candelabra in their salon which has 'four eaglets ... winging their way to the four quarters of the globe, but held back by stiff yet gracious bands'.[62] This positive image of wildness domesticated into elegant order echoes a key metaphor in James's novel. Discussing his marriage to Isabel Archer, Gilbert Osmond tells her former suitor that he and his wife are 'as united ... as the candlestick and the snuffers'.[63] Osmond, clearly, has attempted to 'snuff' out his wife's individuality.

The more equal marriage of Marc and Isabelle still runs up against the 'rock' of sexual difference. In an unpleasant scene in a casino, Isabelle is forced to falsely accuse Marc of infidelity in order to prevent him gambling and losing his factory. To rescue him, she has to allow her body to 'become an instrument of violence and disorder'[64] and, as a result, has a miscarriage. Here Marc stands for what West saw as the male 'will to death', the principles of chaos and destruction, which she opposes to a female-identified 'will to life', associated with order and nurturance.

This is not an essentialist analysis of sexual difference which simply inverts the current order. In *Black Lamb and Grey Falcon* West makes a distinction between male and female in terms of 'lunacy' and 'idiocy':

> Idiocy [a word which she reminds us comes from the Greek word meaning private person] is the female defect: intent on their private lives, women follow their fate through a darkness deep as that cast by malformed cells in the brain. It is no worse than the male defect, which is lunacy: they are so obsessed by public affairs that they see the world as by moonlight, which shows the outline of every object but not the details indicative of their nature.[65]

The social constructions of both 'masculinity' and 'femininity', then, are dangerously debilitating.

Isabelle's final return to Marc after her initial decision to divorce him, is problematic. 'All men are my enemies', she thinks, and although she suggests that 'making love is important [because] it is a reconciliation between all such enemies', she follows this with the bleak thought, 'Had you not better learn to put up with men, since there is no third sex here on earth?'[66] Isabelle's return may be a form of wish-fulfilment on West's part. Victoria Glendinning records that, having married Henry Andrews without being in love with him, West did come to love him and said 'that the first five years of her married life – the years in which [*The Thinking Reed*] was taking shape – were the happiest of her life'.[67] The portrayal of their marriage as a happy, balanced partnership is an important structuring element in *Black Lamb and Grey Falcon*, but, as Janet Montefiore has shown, West's private diaries tell a rather different story of infidelity and frustration.[68]

It is possible to generate a more positive reading of the novel's ending. In their final conversation, both Isabelle and Marc admit that they believe the other to be their 'superior'.[69] This invokes another key debate of the 1930s: the question of how married couples make decisions if they are equal partners. Citing an old saying about marriage that, if two people ride the same horse, one must ride behind, Sir William Beveridge argued that modern marriage is 'more like two people riding abreast on the same horse ... It's more companionable than the old way, but it's more complicated, and must at times be rather confusing to the horse'.[70] This is the problem Isabelle pinpoints when she tells Marc, 'You could not have two people running a department in your works, each thinking the other was the head'.[71]

Marc's reply is the key to West's thinking on marriage here. He tells Isabelle that, 'none of us can see our own faces. The faces we see in mirrors are not our own ... You think that the self you see in my face is superior to yourself, just because you can't see your own face ... Neither of us ever shows a true face except to the other. That is why we are important to each other.'[72] Marc's argument is that each partner offers the other a reflection of themself as 'other'. In *An Ethics of Sexual Difference* Irigaray uses the figure of the 'couple' to theorise precisely such a possible relationship between the sexes. Margaret Whitford glosses her thinking as an ideal where 'Each sex would be an "other" for the other sex'.[73] West's text, then, maps a shift away from a conceptualisation of gender difference within marriage as a hierarchy, to a genuine alterity.

There are obvious problems with using marriage as a trope for 'thinking the difference' between the sexes, not least because its heterosexual bias allows no space for alternatives. Not all women's novels of the 1930s see marriage as reclaimable. Sylvia Townsend Warner's *Summer Will Show*, for example, provides a scathing analysis of the economic inequality of nineteenth-century marriage from which her protagonist Sophia Willoughby escapes to a passionate relationship with another woman.[74] However, what I have suggested here is that these women's novels, with their reworkings of the marriage plot, look both more interesting and more complex in the historical context of the 1930s marriage debates. Placing them in that context will allow us both to reassess some of these neglected novelists and to redraw our critical map of the 1930s.

Notes

1. Valentine Cunningham, *British Writers of the Thirties* (Oxford and New York, Oxford University Press, 1988), p. 151.
2. Cunningham, *British Writers of the Thirties*, p. 152.
3. See Martin Pugh, *Women and the Women's Movement in Britain: 1914–1959* (London: Macmillan, 1992); Jane Lewis, *Women in England 1870–1950: Sexual Divisions and Social Change* (Brighton: Wheatsheaf; Bloomington: Indiana University Press, 1984); Deirdre Beddoe, *Back to Home and Duty; Women Between the Wars 1918–1939* (London: Pandora, 1989); Alison Light, *Forever England: Femininity, Literature and Conservatism Between the Wars* (London and New York: Routledge, 1991).
4. Beddoe, *Back to Home and Duty*.
5. Jane Eldridge Miller, *Rebel Women: Feminism, Modernism and the Edwardian Novel* (London: Virago, 1994).
6. Maroula Joannou, *'Ladies, Please Don't Smash These Windows': Women's Writing, Feminist Consciousness and Social Change 1918–1938* (Oxford: Berg, 1995), p. 77.
7. Joannou, *'Ladies, Please Don't Smash These Windows'*, p. 78.
8. *Census figures (in thousands)*

Date	Total	Male	Female
England and Wales			
1911	36,070	17,446	18,625
1921	37,887	18,075	19,811
1931	39,952	19,133	20,819

Source: B. R. Mitchell, *International Historical Statistics: Europe 1750–1988* (New York: Stockton Press; Basingstoke: Macmillan, 1992), p. 8.

First marriage rates among women (per 1,000 population over 16)

1921–25	55.2
1926–30	54.8
1931–35	57.3
1936–40	73.3

Source: A. H. Halsey (ed.), *British Social Trends Since 1900* (Basingstoke: Macmillan, 1988), p. 73.
9. Pugh, *Women and the Women's Movement*, p. 222.
10. Bertrand Russell, *Marriage and Morals* (London: George Allen and Unwin, 1929).
11. *The Listener*, vol. V, no. 104, 7 January 1931, pp. 7–8.
12. Later published in book form as: Sir William Beveridge, *Changes in Family Life* (London: George Allen and Unwin, 1932).
13. Margaret Jackson, *The Real Facts of Life: Feminism and the Politics of Sexuality c. 1850–1940* (London and Bristol, PA: Taylor and Francis, 1994), p. 160.
14. Jan Struther, *Mrs Miniver* (London: Chatto and Windus, 1939), p. 108.
15. Struther, *Mrs Miniver*, p. 111.
16. *The Listener*, vol. V, no. 105, 14 January 1931, p. 51.
17. *The Listener*, vol. XIV, no. 357, 13 November 1935, pp. 841–5.
18. *The Listener*, vol. XIII, no. 327, 17 April 1935, pp. 665–6.
19. *The Listener*, vol. XVI, no. 403, 30 September 1936, p. 633–4.
20. *The Listener*, vol. XVIII, no. 549, 27 October 1937, p. 916.
21. Beveridge, *Changes in Family Life*, p. 133.
22. *The Listener*, vol. XV, no. 366, 15 January 1936, pp. 102–4.
23. E. H. Young, *The Curate's Wife* (London: Jonathan Cape, 1934); *Celia* (1937; London: Virago, 1990).
24. Young, *The Curate's Wife*, p. 333.
25. Young, *Celia*, p. 414.
26. Winifred Holtby, *The Crowded Street* (1924; London: Virago, 1981), p. 219.
27. Daphne du Maurier, *Rebecca* (1938; London: Pan, 1975).
28. Lewis, *Women in England*, p. 4.
29. F. Tennyson Jesse, *A Pin to See the Peepshow* (1934; London: Virago, 1979).
30. Tennyson Jesse, *A Pin to See the Peepshow*, p. 355.
31. Tennyson Jesse, *A Pin to See the Peepshow*, p. 85.
32. Storm Jameson, *Company Parade* (1934; London: Virago, 1982).

33. Margaret Kennedy, *Together and Apart* (1936; London: Virago, 1981), p. viii.
34. Kennedy, *Together and Apart*, p. 25.
35. Jackson, *Real Facts of Life*, p. 160.
36. Dorothy L. Sayers, *Strong Poison* (1930; London: Hodder and Stoughton, 1989); *Busman's Honeymoon* (1937; London: Hodder and Stoughton, 1988).
37. Susan Leonardi, *Dangerous by Degrees: Women at Oxford and the Somerville College Novelists* (New Brunswick and London: Rutgers University Press, 1989), p. 100.
38. Dorothy L. Sayers, *Gaudy Night* (1935; London: Hodder and Stoughton, 1963), p. 209.
39. Dorothy L. Sayers, 'Talboys' in *Striding Folly* (London: Hodder and Stoughton, 1972).
40. Naomi Mitchison, *We Have Been Warned* (London: Constable, 1935).
41. Beveridge, *Changes in Family Life*, p. 109.
42. Mitchison, *We Have Been Warned*, p. 252.
43. Mitchison, *We Have Been Warned*, pp. 3–4.
44. *The Listener*, vol. XIII, no. 330, 8 May 1935, p. 814.
45. Paul Berry and Alan Bishop (eds), *Testament of a Generation: The Journalism of Vera Brittain and Winifred Holtby* (London: Virago, 1985), pp. 130–32.
46. Berry and Bishop, *Testament of a Generation*, p. 130.
47. Pugh, *Women and the Women's Movement*, p. 262.
48. Vera Brittain, *Lady into Woman: A History of Women from Victoria to Elizabeth II* (London: Andrew Daker, 1953), p. 170.
49. Virginia Woolf, *The Years* (1937; Harmondsworth: Penguin, 1968); Vita Sackville-West, *All Passion Spent* (1931; London: Virago, 1983).
50. Vera Brittain, *Honourable Estate* (London: Victor Gollancz, 1936), p. 550.
51. Vera Brittain, *Halcyon: Or the Future of Monogamy* (London: Kegan Paul, Trench, Trubner, 1929); Dora Russell, *Hypatia: Or Women and Knowledge* (London: Kegan Paul, Trench, Trubner, 1925).
52. *Sunday Express*, 12 July 1925, p. 3.
53. Brittain, *Halcyon*, pp. 90–91.
54. Luce Irigaray, *Thinking the Difference: For a Peaceful Revolution*, tr. Karin Montin (London: Athlone, 1994).
55. Luce Irigaray, *An Ethics of Sexual Difference*, tr. Carolyn Burke and Gillian C. Gill (London: Athlone, 1993), p. 5.
56. Rebecca West, *The Thinking Reed* (1936; London: Virago, 1984), p. 431.
57. Henry James, *The Portrait of a Lady* (1881; Harmondsworth: Penguin, 1966).
58. Rebecca West, *Henry James* (London: Nisbet, 1916), p. 69.
59. West, *The Thinking Reed*, p. 4.
60. West, *The Thinking Reed*, p. 408.
61. West, *The Thinking Reed*, p. 362.
62. West, *The Thinking Reed*, p. 142.
63. James, *The Portrait of a Lady*, p. 505.
64. West, *The Thinking Reed*, p. 305.
65. Rebecca West, *Black Lamb and Grey Falcon*, 2 vols (London: Macmillan, 1942), vol. 1, p. 3.
66. West, *The Thinking Reed*, p. 420.
67. Victoria Glendinning, *Rebecca West* (1987; London: Macmillan, 1988), p. 150.
68. Janet Montefiore, *Men and Women Writers of the 1930s: The Dangerous Flood of History* (London and New York: Routledge, 1996), pp. 209–15.
69. West, *The Thinking Reed*, p. 413.
70. Beveridge, *Changes in Family Life*, p. 105.
71. West, *The Thinking Reed*, p. 414.
72. West, *The Thinking Reed*, pp. 414–5.
73. Margaret Whitford (ed.), *The Irigaray Reader* (Oxford: Blackwell, 1991), p. 25.
74. Sylvia Townsend Warner, *Summer Will Show* (1936; London: Virago, 1987).

6

Sylvia Townsend Warner: 'The Centrifugal Kick'

Gillian Beer

Sylvia Townsend Warner is rare among writers of the 1930s in producing work at once sceptical about belief and wholehearted in its relish of the possible. The Utopian reach of her fictions of the 1930s is, over and over again, undermined sardonically from within. Her narratives never rest content with their initial project; instead, the eye of the reader is obliged to pan across fields and back alleys obliterated by the opening vision. The eye and mind are led to focus on people socially and psychologically excluded at the outset, to accept the impossibility of hopes provoked, old tales recognised and thwarted.

Warner's first novel, *Lolly Willowes* (1926), written in the mid-Twenties and an immediate bestseller, is, uniquely among her works, about successful escape. The spinster heroine leaves behind the demands of her family and achieves independence in a solitary country life as a witch, striking a happy and unpunished bargain with the devil. Before the publication of Woolf's *A Room of One's Own* and *Orlando*, Warner imagines a different way for female self-discovery. Warner nonchalantly topples the whole Faustian edifice of the devil's bargain: masculine knowledge may be achieved only at the cost of death but female knowledge, it seems, can triumph as independent life.

The total fantasy gratification of this first novel was never repeated in her work, nor indeed was its commercial success. *The True Heart* (1929), a version of the Cupid and Psyche myth, struggles awkwardly with innocence and ends with the acceptance of a yoked life. In her other novels of the late Twenties and Thirties, escape is investigated rather than celebrated. The hoped-for alterity – of island life in *Mr Fortune's Maggot* (1927), of revolution in *Summer Will Show* (1936), of Spain in *After the Death of Don Juan* (1938) – is bared to view, with all its catastrophic losses. These sound like sombre tales, but they shine too.

Before I go further, let me sketch something of Sylvia Townsend Warner's career and life. These may throw light on how we ordinarily characterise Modernism and how that characterisation may need to be opened out in order to think afresh about the 1930s. Of course, there is no need to turn writers into Modernists to justify them, nor can the Modernist project encompass all kinds of creativity. Indeed, in the early Thirties few writers knew that they were, or were not, Modernists. Harold Nicolson wrote, as it were, alongside James Joyce and indeed acted as his champion. Modernism at the time referred also to movements in theology and quantum mechanics, as well as to new genetic understandings of evolutionary theory.

Like Ivy Compton Burnett and Henry Green, Stevie Smith, David Jones and the Powys brothers, Sylvia Townsend Warner's work abutts the Modernist: it uses surreal appositions, nonsense strides, narrative fractures and shifting scales. It is nevertheless pellucid, determined and mischievous rather than allusive and indeterminate. Its experiments are narratological rather than verbal, though the peculiar lift of her sentences produces an idiosyncratic humour. John Updike reviewing one of her later collections of short stories, *A Stranger with a Bag* (1966), wrote admiringly: 'She has the spiritual digestion of a goat. Her stories tend to convince us in process and baffle us in conclusion; they are not rounded with meaning but lift jaggedly toward new, unseen, developments.'[1]

The novels are also experiments in *affect*, for these works at once baffle *and possess* the reader. Douce, whimsical and shifting seamlessly across verbal registers, they suddenly expose us to appalling suffering that cannot be set aside. Calamity is simply there, and to be practised. It is shared with the characters. Sometimes it closes up again into comedy.

The charged dismay experienced in *Mr Fortune's Maggot*, or *Summer Will Show*, or, above all, in *After the Death of Don Juan*, depends upon the readerly desire she provokes: the desire to read on, certainly, but also to move closer inside the text than it quite permits. As Levinas puts it: 'an exterior vision – of a total exteriority, like the exteriority in rhythm ... is the true vision of the novelist.'[2] Empathy is encouraged and then deflected. The process of her novels induces attachment at once sophisticated and infantile. Joy is unforeseen, suddenly present. As she writes of a disastrous life-story in *Summer Will Show*: 'Candour gave a quality almost like blitheness to the story'.[3]

In 1929, having just been reading I. A. Richards's *Practical Criticism*, Warner noted in her diary two lists side by side, one headed 'I am prejudiced: against', the other 'in favour of'. The topic was kinds of poetry and was related to her own ambitions as a poet. But the dead-pan account gives some forward glimpses as well into the methods she developed in her fiction, both novels and short stories:

> I am prejudiced:
> against poems that/ are in *vers libre*
> express soul-states and interior rumpuses
> talk much about love, unless sub-acidly
> go on for a long time
> are verbally rich
>
> sonnets, if petrarchan
>
> end on a soul-stirring note
> ask questions and exclaim
> describe

The parallel list runs:

> I am prejudiced:
> in favour of poems/ that are
> formally tight in thought and construction
> evoke frames of mind, mention death
> contain conceits, and intellectual stresses
> look neat
> use few images, especially visual
> contain references to christian faith and mythology
> end cynically
> appear very self-controlled
> state[4]

'State' not 'describe': despite the plainness of 'state', a closer form of identification is induced between writer and reader than through description. She rejects Richards's discrimination between 'accepting emotionally, rejecting intellectually' when reading a Donne sonnet.

> I think the process is more of an identification. The reader must for the space of that sonnet *become* the writer: for this accounts for much subtler digestions, matters of tone.[5]

Digestion, with its processes of absorption, transformation and expulsion, well fits the intimacy and internality her writing also demands of the reader. And 'tone' here for her, as a musician, is no cliché but an awakened metaphor. Her writing occupies the inner ear like a voice, with a wide and various range of intonation and pitch. But she never suggests we become her *characters*, rather that we inhabit the sinuous discourse of the *writer* who approaches, makes and sometimes vitiates these apparitions, so close to the human. Paradoxically, through this lean distance, her fictions have the power to move profoundly.

The attachments, political and personal, of Sylvia Townsend Warner chime with a number of other Thirties writers like W. H. Auden. She was for several years a committed Communist Party member; she went to Spain at the start of the Spanish Civil War (among the party was Stephen Spender: they heartily loathed each other); from 1930 onwards she lived in a life partnership, at times extremely troubled but devoted, with a woman, her lover Valentine Ackland.

At the start of the Thirties Warner was herself in her mid-thirties, having been born in 1893; she lived until 1978. The first half of her life seems quite out of kilter with the life she later lived with Valentine and with her own socialist concerns. In mid-life she shifted both gender and class attachments; yet there are continuities, particularly in her competence as a professional woman in two careers (as musicologist and writer) and in her capacity for sustained friendship. Warner's father was a housemaster at Harrow and she grew up at the school, always on its edge, educated by private tuition, much of it from her father. From the age of nineteen she was for seventeen years the lover of Percy Buck, an older and married musicologist who had been her music teacher since her mid-teens. Though her attachment to him was not exclusive, it shaped her profoundly, both professionally and personally and, I would argue, in the temper of her writing. The long secrecy of their affair seems to have been a means of imagining multiple lives, making space for contradictory experiences that could lie almost autonomously alongside each other. It also hampered her; she found control through writing down with droll detachment and livid insight the shocks between herself and Buck.

For example: her lover (whom she always calls Teague) returns from several months in Africa and lets himself into her flat with the laundry; she has been thinking about ending the long affair and in her mind has chimed the start of the shooting season with the return of Teague:

> October 1. Teague came to tea. He got himself into the house with the wash, and when I came on him in the hall he appeared so perfectly life-size that I began to feel that I had been in Africa, not he. How are you? he said. Rather dirty, said I, too surprised

to be anything but immediate. I should have added that during a great part of his absence I had been perfectly clean. The pheasant-shooting effect was perfectly unnoticed in the greater shock of discovering how massively intimacy can just sweep one on as before. And there was the reflecting piano-top accepting the umbrella, calm as a glacier; and it was only when he said Kiss me, that absence, his share of it, roared in my ears for a moment.[6]

The economy here is extraordinary. It seizes the shock of return: the lover 'perfectly life-size'; the umbrella for the umpteenth time placed and reflected on the piano, the menace of glacier-slow change caught by the act of observing its repose; the roaring abyss of absence; help-lessness and relief in the grip of intimacy's repeat. The writing is forthright, light, humorous and devastating. This is private writing (part of its pleasure is, of course, that it is secret also from Teague), but she is able to transfer those same qualities into texts meant for eyes other than her own. And she feels wry pleasure when Percy Buck does not thoroughly appreciate her new public life as fiction-writer and poet.

Her early career was as a composer (she later destroyed almost all her own music) and musicologist. She was one of the five editors of *Tudor Church Music*, the ambitious ten-volume project which, over twelve years from 1918 on, established and published the corpus of sacred music that has been one of the foundation stones of the Early Music movement in Britain. Working almost entirely from manuscript part-books, the editors brought into currency the work of Taverner, Thomas Tallis, Robert White, William Byrd, Orlando Gibbons and Thomas Tomkins among others. Sylvia Townsend Warner was con-siderably the youngest among the editors and the only woman. She was also decisively anti-clerical in opinion and opposed to all forms of religious belief. Still, she could not keep altogether away from it in her fiction, so deeply tinctured was her imagination by her long habitation among the staves of church music. And she relished the paradoxes of religion, devoting herself to the growing unbelief of Mr Fortune, her missionary character, and to the worldliness and fear within convent life over two centuries in *The Corner That Held Them* (1948). She is fundamentally sceptical, indeed, in all matters of belief, often to comic effect. In May 1928 she remarks in her *Diary*:

During the morning I thought about thought, and decided it would really be easier to believe in the divinity of Christ than in twice two making four. Somehow the very frequency of twice two etc. seems to invalidate it as a concept.[7]

Her training as a transcriber of music and her gifts as a musician move into the pacing and timbre of her writing: she has a particularly acute ear for the nuanced hesitations of dialogue; the narrative presence of her work relies often on the unvoiced rests between sentences for its effect, and she also draws freely on musical experience in describing emotional states – or everyday scenes: 'the raspberries go on and on like Schubert' she tosses off in a letter. Engaging directly with the hands of individual scribes in sixteenth-century manuscripts also taught her intimacy with unknown people across a long historical span:

> The patient organist
> Who scrolled this clef;
> The boy who drew him horned
> On Gibbons in F;
> Singers and hearers all
> Are dumb and deaf[8]

Despite their long-ago deaths, she hears, as she edits, the same music in her head as they did in theirs:

> At the bass entry on *mortem Domine* I was cast into such a rapture of knowing the man's mind that I was ready to count all the damnations of scholarship as nought for the sake of that one passage alone. O William, my dear, I said. And William chow woke up, not knowing the William I addressed had been bones for three hundred years.[9]

That intimacy with the absent other (here, perhaps, William Byrd), a feeling for the mind and body lost, yet still present, persists throughout her fiction.

From the Thirties on, her main source of income was from the *New Yorker* for which she wrote short stories for many years. As a result, she became – has remained – better known in the United States than in Britain. Throughout her life from the mid-1920s she wrote and published technically dextrous poetry, some of it oddly Georgian in vocabulary and word order, some mordant and gripping. In recent years several of her novels have been republished by Virago, and selected letters and diaries have become available, largely so far through the work of Claire Harman. Warner was one of the most wonderful letter writers of the twentieth century in English; much of the correspondence was addressed to people far away whom she had only rarely met, and partly for that reason the letters admit each reader to an intimacy immediate and uncurtailed.

Perhaps the thing that now most stands out about her novelistic career in terms of genre is its prescience. If *After the Death of Don Juan* had been published, not in 1936 but fifty years later, it would have been greeted as a magic-realist fiction; if *Mr Fortune's Maggot* had been published, not in 1928 but, likewise, fifty years later, it would be read as a post-colonial text; while *Summer Will Show* would be seen as part of the current vogue for novels that rewrite the nineteenth century, and the medieval *The Corner that Held Them* as a follower of Umberto Eco's *The Name of the Rose*. But Warner in fact wrote each of these very diverse novels long before those critical templates were in place. She composed with an exploratory verve that is quite extraordinary.

That narrative confidence, even recklessness, never blurs the intransigent clarity of her language. Embedded in that language is a storyteller's voice, droll, discomfitting, serene and implacable. But the storyteller, too, is subject to revisionary judgment as her career goes on. In *Summer Will Show* Minna makes her living as a storyteller, embroidering and recounting her picaresque life: the child surviving the pogrom, the refugee, the courtesan, the revolutionary. Warner had no such terrible and romantic personal background to recount, but the relation between apparent improvisation and revision in her work produces an effect of communal intimacy often more like that which Benjamin attributes to the storyteller in his 1936 essay of that name than to that of the novelist. The telling is ruthless. The reader flinches but is sustained by the unexpected sequencing of her narratives, which gives an affect of improvisation, of freedom for the reader, even while the characters are pinched.

In 1928 Warner met a young German publisher who turned out to have been a prisoner of war in a hospital in Dartford while she was working down the road in a munitions factory in 1915. In a surge of intimacy 'as though we had not seen each other for years and there was a great deal to tell' they talked the war through.

> His theory of the war: that it is like a work of art, unstayable, obeying its own laws, a masterpiece to itself; and live men and dead men and courage and rancour all powerless but to one purpose: to be constructive units in that work of art.[10]

At the time in her diary she seems contented by this codification. By the time she came to write *Summer Will Show* and *After the Death of Don Juan* a few years later, she set against that kind of Futurist patterning the muddle and stench of human participants in armed struggle which springs up unorganised out of class tension. In both these novels dire conflict is the product of justified class hatred. In both of them, too, the arc of the narrative concern shifts gradually and inexorably across from one group of characters to another.

In *Summer Will Show* the shift takes place within the life of Sophia Willoughby, haughty mistress of a fine estate, mother of two beloved children and wife of the unsatisfactory Frederick who at the novel's start is dallying in Paris with a mistress whom Sophia scorns by repute as 'a byword, half actress, half strumpet; a Jewess; a nonsensical creature bedizened with airs of prophecy, who trailed across Europe with a tag-rag of poets, revolutionaries, musicians and circus-riders snuffing at her heels'.[11] In a series of leisurely disasters Sophia is denuded: the children die, in deathbed scenes as extreme and more abstemious than those of the Victorian novels in whose period this is set; she is humiliated in sex and class by the limekiln man whose plague has unwittingly brought about the children's deaths; she seeks her husband and is worsted by him, losing all her wealth. She meets Minna, the scorned mistress, and life begins again for her, a new life emboldened and enriched by Minna's own past life told to her as story and rendered stringent by sharing the revolutionary struggle of Paris in 1848. Sophia remains constant in person, still austere, but free and rejoicing in her mutual love with Minna. So far, so romantic. But Warner refuses to let the personal dominate the political entirely. She wrote the novel through the Thirties from 1931 to publication in 1936. Not only does she incorporate terrible scenes of a pogrom against the Jews, told by Minna from her old childhood, but she ends with a turn that challenges her own past work and looks forward relentlessly, too.

The last scenes of the novel show the muddle, the spattered blood and bone of the barricades, the senseless ignominy of unsuccessful uprising. But more than that they take up a figure from the start of the book, the lovely black bastard child Pascal, child of a male relative from whose colonial estates, it is suggested, some of Sophia's wealth (as does any British reader's) inevitably flows. Sophia first delights in Pascal, then ships him off to a terrible school remote from her home when he becomes a nuisance. He finds her again in Paris, seeking her love and support; but he is now a considerably less comely young man, no longer a plaything, and he interrupts the free pleasures of the life that she and Minna have designed for themselves. Again she rejects him; he falls into the hands of her husband, who enlists him in the French army. Pascal, the black outsider, it is who comes tumbling over the barricade as part of the troop of soldiers and stabs Minna; Sophia kills him with a shot. This is a very different version of race relations from the poignant idyll of Mr Fortune and his lovely boy Lueli. That enchanting novel explores with delicate compunction the balances between missionary and seeming convert, between sex and love, faith and disenchantment. The rancour of the ending of *Summer Will Show* does not obliterate that earlier work, but it does scrutinise and enlarge its possibilities. *Summer Will Show* is written into the face of Fascism and accepts the full weight of those fickle attachments with which the powerful (which again includes the reader in the economy of the narrative) seek to salve their consciences.

The bleak conclusion of *Summer Will Show* comes at the end of a perhaps over-long narrative indulgence in the private pleasures of a loving relationship. It is not difficult to see personal guilts here in the light of the newly fledged commitment of both Valentine and Sylvia to Communism and activism, a commitment that for Valentine was already uneasy but which carried Sylvia through the period of the Spanish Civil War and some of World War Two.

In *After the Death of Don Juan* she achieves an unflinching comedy about oppression. The work opens in brilliant high pastiche of Mozart's *Don Giovanni*. The sounds of the opera fill out the text. But there is a crucial difference between theatre and narrative. In theatre we see the statue of the Commendatore enter Don Giovanni's dining room, while Don Giovanni is taken down to Hell before our eyes. In narrative, though, there is only Leporello's witness. We have to rely on his account. And so do all the characters, for a while. The staid Goya-like aristocrats rattle through the countryside to tell Don Juan's father of his death, under the inexorable command of Dona Ana's obsession with Don Juan. The book is full of lively character drawings and some sly slapstick. Its narrative eye slowly, intransigently shifts across the arc from aristocrats to the village community. The peasants lack water. Their crops are withering. Don Juan's father, liberal, learned, dilatory, never quite gets the promised irrigation going. Yet after consultation with his village representatives, it seems that at last he may. Suddenly, three-quarters of the way through the tale, Don Juan is back among them. Leporello's story of Juan's death has become in each retelling more threadbare, less probable. Now Juan is all at once there, alive again, crawling out from behind a table.

The comfortable version of these events would be that eroticism must return; it drives desire. Warner makes that reading impossible. The uncomfortable version, worked out in this novel, is that eroticism is economic, mean-spirited, wasting and spending for its own monstrous pleasure, miserly to others. Libertinism feeds on the peasants. It is Fascism and dictatorship. Don Juan says irrigate, and then turn the peasants out, re-let the land. When his father is appalled he imprisons him brutally. The final spare scenes of the book are of absolute disaster. The book keeps its poise. With eerie absurdity the village men find themselves ambushed as part of an uprising that never quite happened and shot down by the soldiery Don Juan has sent for. At the end Juan lurks in a doorway as the forgettable massacre takes place. By then Warner had seen the charred and humdrum horrors of the Spanish Civil War. But yet, in the midst of her bare account, Warner closes with dialogue – a restorative dialogue that acknowledges at the same time anonymity, obliteration, and the significance of the local and the personal. Ramon is dying; Diego kneels beside him and whispers:

> 'You can't fight, they will take you prisoner. I can't leave you to them, Ramon. Shall I kill you? I would do it well.'
> 'I'll see it out.'
> Kneeling beside him he brushed away a fly and smoothed the tumbled lock of hair off the brow.
> 'What are you looking at, Ramon? What do you see?'
> 'So large a country,' said the dying man. 'And there in the middle of it, like a heart, is Madrid. But our Tenorio Viejo is not marked. I have often looked for it. It is not there, though. It is too small, I suppose. We have lived in a very small place, Diego.'
> 'We have lived in Spain,' said the other.
> 'Aye.'
> His gaze left the map and turned to the face bent over him. They looked at each other long and intently, as though they were pledged to meet again and would ensure a recognition.[12]

Later Warner said that this novel was a parable of the Spanish Civil War but later still she refused the idea that the Spanish Civil War was a local war that had ended. Instead she saw a longer compass in the struggle between Fascism and Socialism and faced a struggle continuing past her lifetime. Yet always, alongside that severe conviction, in all her writing whether fiction, verse, letters or diaries, she registered through into extreme old age the tumbling pleasures of the ordinary moment: 'Why does one feel this acknowledging joy?' she wrote one day in 1958 as she looked at a snowfall in the midst of her anger and anxiety about American missile sites in Britain.

Throughout her long career she realised extremity by means of humour and abstention. In Proust and Racine she admired 'the same paucity of language' and knew that she must not 'cool it into eloquence'.[14]

Her own passionate control chimes strangely with the *unforeseeable* quality of her stories. Her narratives cannot be predicted, nor can the droll buzz of the language by whose means she contrives to speak in chords. Her works in the 1930s are imbued with the major historical events and dreads of the time: the persecution of the Jews and of other groups such as gypsies and gays, the sense of betrayal and yet of the necessity for secret organisations, the willingness to be active, the dry despair in the face of overwhelming Fascist forces. But with all that she still writes with a lift, relishes experience that will not fit neatly, improvises pleasure for the reader.

Misfitting, discontinuous, eccentric, imperturbable: as she entered the 1930s she had delighted in the astronomer James Jeans's 1929 book *The Universe Around Us*: 'For one minute I felt quite alert about atoms in orbits being energy, being a going-round, and so filling the entire orbit.' But immediately further questions come to her mind: 'Does it take greater energy to go round in the lesser orbit, or what?' So she writes to Jeans and (admirably) gets a letter two days later: 'He admits that in the end something like a going-round reading may be found to be the right one ... Now I want to know if a centrifugal kick wouldn't supply this for long enough for the electron-life'[15] 'Does it take greater energy to go round in a smaller orbit, or what?' It seems an apt question with which to leave Sylvia Townsend Warner whose wit provides the 'centrifugal kick' and whose 'going-round reading' turns the great issues of the 1930s in the erratic yet concentrated orbit of her insight.

Notes

1. John Updike, 'The Mastery of Miss Warner', *New Republic*, 5 March 1966, quoted in Claire Harman, *Sylvia Townsend Warner: A Biography* (London: Chatto and Windus, 1989), p. 287.
2. 'Reality and its Shadow' in Sean Hand (ed.), *The Levinas Reader* (Oxford: Basil Blackwell, 1989), p. 140.
3. Sylvia Townsend Warner, *Summer Will Show* (London: Virago, 1987), p. 200.
4. Warner, quoted in Harman, *Biography*, p. 79.
5. Claire Harman (ed.), *The Diaries of Sylvia Townsend Warner* (London: Chatto and Windus, 1994), p. 42.
6. Harman, *Diaries*, p. 44.
7. Harman, *Diaries*, p. 17.
8. Sylvia Townsend Warner, *The Espalier* (London: Chatto and Windus, 1935), p. 10.
9. Harman, *Diaries*, p. 44.
10. Harman, *Diaries*, p. 25.
11. Sylvia Townsend Warner, *Summer Will Show* (London: Virago, 1987), p. 31.
12. Sylvia Townsend Warner, *After the Death of Don Juan* (London: Virago, 1989), p. 301.
13. Harman, *Diaries*, p. 243.
14. Harman, *Diaries*, p. 227.
15. Harman, *Diaries*, pp. 45, 48.

7

Rosamond Lehmann's Political Philosophy: From *A Note in Music* (1930) to *No More Music* (1939)

Wendy Pollard

Despite the similarity of the titles of the two works by Rosamond Lehmann published at either end of the 1930s, the novel *A Note in Music* and the play *No More Music*, these works are not merely variations on a theme, but reflect a progression in the writer's political philosophy.

Rosamond Lehmann has rarely been credited with having a political philosophy or with exhibiting any form of social awareness other than in relation to women's issues. Diana LeStourgeon, in the first full-length consideration of Lehmann's work, in 1965, typically declares that it is difficult to place her in relation to other novelists of the inter-war period because, LeStourgeon alleges: 'She has no discernible moral or intellectual, social or political philosophies'.[1] Studies which take a differing view are few but distinguished: Judy Simons has recognised 'Lehmann's sensitivity to her times and her acute political awareness';[2] Ruth Siegel's published American doctoral dissertation engages throughout with the political and economic background of Lehmann's novels;[3] and James Gindin sees Lehmann as representative of a number of 1930s writers 'trying to articulate and assimilate [their] view of the world'.[4]

Born in 1901, Lehmann, in interviews and autobiographical writings, always stressed her awareness that she had had a privileged childhood in 'the pre-1914 sheltered Edwardian world'.[5] That world was of course shattered by the First World War, the memory of which is, as Janet Montefiore has pointed out, 'an unforgotten shadow in much writing of the 1930s'.[6] The political ethos of Lehmann's childhood world has been documented by her younger brother, the left-wing poet and publisher, John Lehmann. Their home, Fieldhead, was, he wrote, constantly visited by 'political personalities who had fought beside my father in Parliament for the Liberal cause we held so sacred'. As a result, he experienced great difficulty in moving away from the received idea that 'men of goodwill' could only be 'Liberals of my father's persuasion',[7] with their overwhelming belief in individualism. The starting point of Rosamond Lehmann's political philosophy too was, as she later made clear, the family Liberalism, but she also held another conviction which, to the best of my knowledge, has not been discussed elsewhere. In the pamphlet *Authors Take Sides on the Spanish War* (1937), Lehmann revealed that she had earlier been 'a pacifist in the fullest sense'.[8] A re-reading of her second novel *A Note in Music* (1930) as a specifically post-First World War work informed by individualistic and pacifist beliefs offers a new perspective on the novel, arguably the most underestimated in Lehmann's oeuvre.

Explicit reference is made throughout the book to many effects of the war. Crucially, it is unlikely that the marriage of either ill-matched couple at the centre of the novel would have taken place but for the war. Norah and Gerald Mackay were, Norah recalls, at the time of their marriage: 'two worn-out relics of war service thrown up by the Armistice'.[9] Norah still constantly pines for her first, charismatic, unfaithful lover, killed in the war; Gerald is corrosively aware that 'the war had put an end to his hopes of a fellowship at Cambridge'. (p. 167) It is clear from Grace Fairfax's rueful reflections that she had fallen in love primarily with Tom's naval uniform. A motherless daughter, she had dutifully left school to look after her ailing father, whose death, also at the time of the armistice, had left the unmotivated Grace with little alternative than marriage to Tom. (pp. 95–6, 245–6) Her husband blames his lowly status as a clerk on the war, which 'had beggared all the old families', from which he, albeit somewhat unconvincingly, claims descent. (p. 3) Without the war, Hugh Miller, the reluctant newcomer to the unnamed northern industrial town in which they live, would not have been called upon to enter the family business. His generation's burden of guilt at having been too young to fight is manifest in Hugh's consciousness of his dilemma, when thinking of 'chucking' it:

> It would be easy to go if the old man were not such a dear old boy: if his two sons had not been killed, so that there was nobody – as the old man so often tremulously said – but himself to

carry on the name and inherit the great arduously-built business. (p. 65)

But the war is a presence in the novel in more than at the levels of plot and characterisation. In his study of the effects of the First World War on the imaginative literature of the post-war years, Samuel Hynes identifies a 'sense of a gap in history', rendered by poets and novelists 'in images of fragmentation and ruin'.[10] Such an image was deliberately chosen by Lehmann for the frontispiece of *A Note in Music*. As the designer, her second husband Wogan Philipps, explained, this illustrates 'a theme in the middle of the book which is put in the mind of the would-be intellectual poet Ralph, and which is really a symbol for the pattern of the book itself'.[11] The woodcut depicts two lovers gazing at their reflections in a pool, but the idyllic scene is to be transformed by hidden menace:

> As their lips met, a shoal of fish came darting through the water and shattered their image into a thousand pieces; and when the surface was still again, it was empty of their faces: they were gone. (p. 152)

He might make something of that, Ralph muses: 'to see one reality and turn it inside out again and again, making of one many, and all conflicting ...' (p. 153)

The multivalence of reality, emphasised by Lehmann's skilful use of a destabilising narrative technique, permeates the entire book. Unlike her first, much-praised, novel *Dusty Answer*, which is narrated entirely from the point of view of its young heroine, *A Note in Music* employs a multiplicity of voices: the narrative is generally mediated through the consciousness of each of the principal characters, as well as by the use of an occasional chorus of neighbours or Norah's relatives. By this means the reader is made aware of the gulf of misunderstanding that divides virtually every character in the book from one another. Ralph, a seemingly minor figure, is nevertheless the agent for making this theme explicit when he considers 'how profoundly each individual life is concealed'. (p. 161)

At times the narrative technique, as in the following passage, deliberately obscures the identity of the speaker initially:

> Misgiving comes, bewilderment, hope, surmise – a host of witnesses, striving to shape the spiritual shape of what has been; till it seems in a moment all will be linked, gathered up into unity and purpose. And the moment does not come, or comes too

briefly, too dubiously to seize; and at length the whirling pace is slackened, the fires grow feebler; they flicker and pause, diminutive in the void: they have vanished. (p. 77)

It is in fact Norah who, in trying to recapture and rationalise the past, is being forced to contemplate 'a comfortless suggestion' that life may be without continuity. (p. 76) This passage cogently illustrates Hynes's contention that inter-war writing constantly expressed 'a fracture in time and space that separated the present from the past',[12] and also a comment made by James Gindin that, for any thoughtful writer of the 1930s, there could be no 'assurances that some permanent perspective could tie past, present and future together.'[13]

Gindin's chapter on Lehmann in his *British Fiction in the 1930s* is entitled 'Rosamond Lehmann's Social and Historical Landscapes'. In the general introduction, he points out that 1930s fiction is 'full of landscapes and provinces as settings, facts and metaphors'. 'Geography', as he succinctly concludes, 'signifies.'[14] Geography in *A Note in Music* is the locus of conflict, and of social and political disquiet. Grace, more than any other character in the novel, associates the North with ugliness, the South with beauty, the town with sterility, the country with fecundity. Brooding about the death of the mongrel puppy she had tried to keep alive, and which she mourns more than her stillborn baby, she reflects that the puppy's 'small person, stamped with the early neglect, disease, and suffering against which her love had been powerless, had become the symbol for the whole colossal ignorance and brutality of the town'. (p. 8) Lying awake at night, frustrated and unhappy, Grace listens to the town trams and yearns for the country. The landscape of her reverie is infused with phallic, heroic imagery: 'Along the hedgerows the tall ash and hazel rods thronged stiffly; they sprang up gleaming in the sun like lances of bronze and silver.' But as a counterpoint, a more pitiful image of war is simultaneously presented in the personification of the last tram of the night, 'the limping tram, the wounded one which screamed and faltered as it went'. (p. 21)

Elsewhere, however, the writing in the novel bears out James Gindin's contention that 'no single set of values, attitudes or even kinds of representation can apply'[15] to the frequent geographical bifurcations in 1930s fiction. When Grace takes her desiderated holiday alone, in the location of which she has dreamt: 'a southern landscape: cottage gardens crammed with flowers; cornfields bordered by great elms; …' (p. 137), she nevertheless recognises that her landlady's six-year-old child is 'slighter and whiter than many a child of northern slums', and the landlady herself shows only a hint of a buried charm, being now 'all given over to the unchanging round of daily tasks and the shadowing doubts and hesitations of her shuttered and dependent spirit'. (p. 196)

In the North, Grace empathises with the isolation of those out of work: working men 'walked in quiet groups from their work, raced their whippets', but the unemployed 'wandered singly, hands thrust in their threadbare pockets, the unmistakable stamp of the degradation of unemployment in their faces, their shoulders, their gaits'. (p. 83) Norah, unlike Grace, is moved to do more than merely observe, but her independent spirit clashes with her rubric as an appointed 'apostle of social welfare'. (p. 265) Investigating housing and health conditions in a new neighbourhood, she transgresses in the first house at which she calls,

> where, besides a woman and some children, several men, in rags, long workless, sat all together by one relic of a fire, stared at her dumbly out of starved eyes in animal faces; and her set speech of a Visitor had died on her lips; and she had given them money to buy food (which was against the rules and precepts of the society) and gone quickly away. (p. 266)

I would suggest that the main reason for the unfavourable reception of *A Note in Music* has been the critics' failure to respond to the characterisation of Grace. If her extreme passivity is seen as consonant with Lehmann's declared pacifism at the time of writing, the focus is radically altered. The complaint of novelist V. S. Pritchett, in one of the most hostile of the contemporary reviews, was that 'nothing happens'. He branded the novel 'a banal, *blasé* and pretentious book about nothing'.[16] In the introduction to the Virago edition, Janet Watts, albeit more sympathetically, comments that: '*A Note in Music* is a study in nothingness: Grace Fairfax is its remarkable example, and the word echoes through the book like a refrain.'[17] But the non-teleological nature of Grace's undoubtedly powerful emotions mirrors the contemporary ethos. The nation, still licking its wounds after the First World War, wanted to avoid further confrontation if at all possible, and the official British policies of non-intervention and later appeasement reflected this. A parallel of inaction might be extrapolated by considering that, deep as her feelings are for Hugh Miller, Grace never contemplates even the possibility of consummation. The most she allows herself to think is that 'if she could but see him for ten minutes every day till she died, she would become the most contented person living'. (p. 169)

Ruth Siegel alleges that Lehmann's *A Note in Music* is 'her *Waste Land* work; that concept', she says, 'permeates the atmosphere, the setting, the intellectual and moral concerns.'[18] Nowhere in the book is this made more explicit than in Grace's final questioning of the role of the 'infinitesimal specks', which are man. This passage crystallises the post-war sense of a crisis of identity, the final line consciously or unconsciously incorporating a phrase from Eliot's iconic work:

> Who am I ... *I?* What is I? What is *knowing?* And what is *dying?*
> ... Christina Grace ... daughter of ... wife of ... born ... died ...
> That is *I.*
> Yes, but that's not it. What happens to *me?* ... Was it going anywhere, this anxious, ignorant, inquiring *I?* ... No, no, how foolish! ... No more than a handful of dust blown away by the wind ... (pp. 310–11)[19]

Lehmann's further two novels published in the 1930s have less overt political resonances. Correspondence in her publisher's files makes it clear that at this time she was under some financial pressure. Her husband's health was poor and she was the family breadwinner. She wrote to her publisher prior to the publication of *A Note in Music* that she had read that: '"The author who is content with reputation for his first book talks of nothing but money when he comes to proffer his second,"' and admitted that 'the cap fitted! ... having now a house to furnish and a family to rear'.[20] Sales of her second novel both in Europe and America, however, fell far below the levels expected after the great success of *Dusty Answer*. This factor may well have influenced Lehmann to take the advice of one English reviewer of *A Note in Music* who urged her to confine her future writing to 'the soul, and not the world'.[21]

Her next novel, *Invitation to the Waltz* (1932), was indeed greeted with almost universal acclaim by the critics, applauding her return to the subject matter of her first novel, to the depiction of what Isabel Paterson, in a review of this later novel, called 'the April moods of adolescence'.[22] The adjectives 'charming' and 'delightful' abounded elsewhere in the reviews, which, for the most part, ignored the novel's subtle analyses of class distinctions within a small rural community. One critique, however, did mention this background but only in order to dismiss the characterisation of Miss Robinson, the downtrodden yet valiant village dressmaker, as a 'rather morbid presentment'.[23] The anonymous writer has, somewhat surprisingly, been identified as a 'Mrs Thirkell',[24] presumably Angela Thirkell, later well-known for her own satirical novels.

In *The Weather in the Streets* (1936), there is still more social criticism although here too, it is generally oblique, with humour acting as the angle of refraction. The literary historian John Atkins has signally failed to recognise this in a lengthy analysis of Lehmann's social attitudes.[25] In his discussion of this novel, he quotes extensively and disapprovingly from the dinner party scene at Meldon Towers, which is explicitly presented through the eyes and ears of Olivia. Already in thrall to the married Rollo, son of the house, next to whom she is sitting, she forces herself, if only by the pudding course, to remember the social conventions and turn away, at which point, 'as if some obstacle to general sight and hearing had suddenly been removed, she became aware again of the room and its other occupants'.[26] Her other dinner partner, the senior diplomat and dilettante connoisseur, Sir Ronald, aware of her neglect, lisps gallantly to her: "'I feared vis uvverwise delightful meal was going to slip by in vain proximity'". (p. 92) Olivia then plays her allotted ingénue role, cooing her responses, 'feeling more and more exquisite, … tossing back and forth … this fragrant nostalgic aesthetical cowslip-ball'. (p. 95) Buoyed up with the illicit excitement of her impending affair, she can smile, as required, 'deprecatingly, sympathetically', at his rabid elitism. (p. 97) The scene is one of high comedy and social satire, shot through with a sexual *frisson*. Atkins' judgment here that Lehmann's 'obvious admiration for a declining way of life is diluted by pricks of social conscience, and the resulting gloom pervades everything' seems very contrary.[27]

Later in the novel, however, when Olivia and Rollo holiday together in Austria, Olivia's willingness to tolerate an 'obstacle to general sight and hearing' seems wilful. John Lehmann, who lived in Vienna between 1932 and 1936 and corresponded from there frequently with his sister, wrote with great sympathy that the post-war generation in Austria 'seemed to have been simply struck out from the roll of human fortune'.[28] Olivia, his sister's fictionalised creation, sees in her cocoon only 'smiling, sociable Austrian faces with their open uncomplicated look of innocence and equability'. (p. 251) Only when, without the blocking influence of Rollo, she visits her friend Jocelyn in Salzburg does any form of political reality obtrude. Jocelyn symbolises the internationalism of his generation of intellectuals: 'Europe not England his country, his point of departure in argument and discussion'. When introduced to his Austrian friends, 'Willi three years without work, Johann's elder brother shot in the Vienna rising', Olivia thinks: 'I should think more about such fates and struggles. If I were free I would, perhaps'. (p. 256) But a more urgent personal worry presents itself: she is 'six, seven days late' (p. 257), and international politics are forgotten, although sexual politics are very much a theme for the remainder of the novel.

International politics were soon to become inescapable. In August 1936, reviewing Graham Greene's *A Gun for Sale* in the *New Statesman*, Rosamond Lehmann wrote that, although the novel was labelled 'An Entertainment' by its author,

> To my mind, it more closely resembles a long elaborate dream-experience: one of those dark disorganising circumstantial dreams ... of intense conspiracies with oneself moving against an Enemy unseen, all-powerful, oneself in the predicament of being obliged to save the world.[29]

Samuel Hynes finds the review interesting because, he says, 'it is not really about Greene's novel, but is rather Miss Lehmann's own parable for ... her generation's nightmare.'[30]

The previous month, the Spanish army had rebelled against the Republican government, and the Spanish Civil War had begun; this seemed for many to be the means by which they might, in Lehmann's phrase, 'save the world'. They did not, however, recognise a single, unifying cause. As sculptor Jason Gurney, a volunteer in the International Brigade, remembers:

> Nobody was concerned with the facts of the situation. The War became a microcosm of all the ideological divisions of the time – freedom and repression, constitutional and arbitrary authority, nationalism and internationalism, the people and the aristocracy, Catholicism and Marxism, and many more. Everyone saw Spain as the epitome of the particular conflict with which they were concerned.[31]

Lehmann's decision to throw herself, as she did, wholeheartedly into efforts for the benefit of the anti-Fascist Spanish Aid movement was perhaps inevitable given that her husband became an ambulance driver in Spain for the Republican cause, and her dearly loved brother and actress sister Beatrix were ideologically engaged as committed Marxists.[32] But at this time there was a further powerful influence in Rosamond Lehmann's life: by the mid-1930s, she was the mother of two children. In a compilation of essays, *On Gender and Writing* (1983), several writers articulate the effect that motherhood has had on their work and lives.[33] Nora Bartlett strikes a common note when she says that: 'nothing in my life has ever surprised me so much as what happens to women when they have children'. She sees her previous life as 'a dim, flat, verbal thing, a spoken monologue' which her son had interrupted, and 'the way that interruption feels, still, is that he gave me the world'.[34] Rosamond Lehmann would have agreed with Bartlett; her children became the declared focus of her life, and two major public anti-Fascist statements made by her expressed her sense of a common bond with parents throughout the world.

The first, already mentioned, was in response to *Authors Take Sides on the Spanish War*, a compilation of the answers to a questionnaire sent out by Nancy Cunard and others under the aegis of the periodical *Left Review*. Valentine Cunningham categorises most of the 149 writers who replied as 'the expected droves of sympathizers', and stresses that it had been important to have 'the rather less expectable names', among whom he counts Rosamond Lehmann.[35] The overwhelming majority of writers declared themselves to be for the Republicans, emphasising the Fascist threat to freedom and culture. Lehmann's was the only reply to introduce a personal, familial note, saying that 'as a mother, I am convinced that upon the outcome of the struggle in Spain depends the future, the very life of my children'.[36]

In May 1938, Virginia Woolf wrote in her diary of 'Rosamond's great meeting for writers to protest against Spain for wh. she has hired the Queens Hall. But hasnt asked us.'[37] Whatever her reasons for not asking the Woolfs (perhaps because, of the two, only Leonard Woolf had contributed to *Authors Take Sides on the Spanish War*), Lehmann was successful in persuading authors with a wide range of political standpoints to speak, or to allow their names to be 'read out', at the meeting, which was advertised as 'Writers Declare Against Fascism'.[38] Lehmann's own speech at the meeting once again stressed the particularity of her beliefs. She addressed parents across national and class boundaries, arguing that: 'The worst grief would be to have to see our children grow up defeated morally, physically, intellectually warped and stunted.' She warned that, under Fascism, this was already happening in Germany and Austria, where Jewish parents were seeing their children 'degraded to the position of something subhuman'. Lehmann then revealed a further development in her political thinking, announcing that she had now come to believe that it was Socialism that afforded 'a sure intention of good, a rational hope of happiness, to the children'. Another platform speaker was the French Marxist Louis Aragon who, according to John Lehmann, 'had an immense admiration for Rosamond and her works', and who therefore had particularly wanted her to become involved at the highest level of anti-Fascist protest to 'give the lie', he said, 'to the legend that has such a hold on continental writers, that English writers are too individualistic to act with their colleagues in defence of all we care about.'[39] It was perhaps to Aragon that Lehmann added: 'It is a popular fallacy that [a belief in Socialism] is not compatible with a belief (which I hold) in the importance of the individual ... Every novelist must be to some extent an individualist.'[40]

There is a problem of chronology involved in a consideration of how far Lehmann's changed beliefs influenced the composition of her play published in 1939. There is evidence in archival correspondence of an unnamed play by her being in the course of preparation late in 1934; however, even if this is *No More Music*, the play performed in 1938 at the artistically prestigious London International Theatre Club, the inclusion of topical references indicate that there must at least have been some rewriting prior to performance. I shall assume that at the time of writing Lehmann's political beliefs were moving towards socialism, and moving away from pacifism towards the view she expressed with regard to the Spanish Civil War in 1937, that 'non-resistance can be – in this case, is – a negative, a sterile, even a destructive thing'.[41]

The action of *No More Music* takes place in a small hotel on a Caribbean island. Lehmann uses the same setting, and even some of the minor characters, in her final novel, *A Sea-Grape Tree* (1976). But the island itself performs very different functions in the play and the novel. In the latter, there are resemblances to Prospero's island; it is a place full of spirits. In the play, the island is a metaphor for the isolationism of contemporary England. As Elizabeth Bowen said in the course of an appreciative review, 'for the duration of these people's visit, the lounge of Miss Leith's private hotel, the tropical light outside, the brilliant coast below have become the world, the sole world.'[42] Jan Loder, a fairly young, once promising painter, and his lover Miriam Ward come to the hotel in an attempt to resolve problems in their volatile relationship; the other guests are an elderly permanent resident, a retired colonel and his wife, and a middle-class widow, with a niece, Hilda, described as having 'a hungry, fanatical-heroic, virginal appearance'.[43] Jan idly plays on Hilda's emotions, and unwittingly incites her to commit suicide. In the final scene, Jan and Miriam come to an uncertain *rapprochement* and agree to leave the island together.

Where *A Note in Music* is a post-First World War text, *No More Music* might be categorised as an end-of-Empire discourse. Although this term is usually applied to British literature of the 1950s, the sense

of impending loss of imperial prestige was also present in 1930s literature. The mountain in Auden and Isherwood's *The Ascent of F6* has to
be conquered by a British team, Mr A., the voice of the public, declares,

> Or England falls. She has had her hour
> And now must decline to a second-class power.[44]

Rosamond Lehmann's internationalist sympathies are a subtext to her
play. Colonel and Mrs Gobbett have openly racist attitudes to the
hotel staff, evidently fossilised during their years exercising colonial
power in Burma. When, on arrival, Jan and Miriam laugh with, rather
than at, Enoch, the West Indian hotel porter, Mrs Gobbett observes
'with a stony eye'. (p. 17) The two waitresses represent changing
attitudes among the colonised: Princess is middle-aged, dignified yet
servile; Caroline is young, pretty and rebellious. Scolded by Princess for
having forgotten flowers for the table, Caroline, in a neat grammatical
inversion, shrugs off responsibility, saying, 'my memory missed.'
Inter-generational conflict, a recurring theme in interbellum literature,
is manifest in Caroline's contempt of the guests prior to the arrival of
Jan and Miriam: 'Dey are all old, and don' laugh plenty, and deir faces
so wrong', and in Princess's shocked reaction: 'So lazy. So cheeky ... in
dese times ... young girls and boys'. (pp. 8–9)

Mr Guthrie, the hotel's permanent resident, represents national
decline more subtly than the Gobbetts. He is described as 'a shrivelled
old man with ... white papery skin' and a 'cultured and pedantic'
voice; the breakfast he orders is emblematic of his effeteness: 'Just
some tea and toast – very weak tea, mind, ... and a little dry toast'. (p.
9) He is half-blind, although it is suggested several times that he sees
more than he admits. Guthrie is complacent about his wasted life:

> In my youth I regarded all professions with equal distaste. I
> desired a life of exquisite sensations. (*Chuckles.*) Oh, I was a figure
> of fun. An aesthete ... Once or twice I have asked myself if a
> more lasting satisfaction is conceivably to be obtained from a life
> of public or even of private duties. (p. 107)

But he is content to see out his days with whisky and music. Lehmann
no longer, however, sympathises with those, like Grace Fairfax, who
are resigned to inertia. The title of the play is taken from Guthrie's
querulous reaction to Hilda's death: 'I don't know what all this distur-
bance is about. All these jarring, wrangling voices. It is most upsetting.
There will be no more music, I suppose? I shall go to bed'. (p. 117)

Purposeless action, however, is also to be condemned; if Hilda's egocentric gesture had been meant to be the crux, the play would have ended with her death, as in *Hedda Gabler* or *The Seagull*. The main theme of the play is a paradigm of Lehmann's attempted reconciliation of her individualistic and socialist beliefs. Early in the play, Miriam, albeit younger, more attractive and superficially more self-assured than Grace Fairfax, reveals that she shares with her a lack of conviction about her own existence. The word 'nothing' again echoes in the dialogue, when Miriam says: 'I'm nothing. Sometimes I say to myself: I hope *he* [Jan] feels sure I'm here – because I don't'. (p. 66) By the end of the play, Miriam, however, has moved to a position of self-affirmation.

In their final meeting in *A Note in Music*, Grace Fairfax and Hugh Miller discuss their Utopia, a place where there would be '"freedom for the individual ... Nobody interfering with anybody else's life"'. (p. 250) But when trying to reconstruct her relationship with Jan after Hilda's death, Miriam realises that it has been Jan's 'false idea about freedom' that has produced the negativity that has blighted them. When Jan insists that he must have personal freedom, Miriam uses the word 'nothing' as a weapon against him, saying, 'then you'll have what doesn't exist. You'll have what's *nothing*. There *is* no freedom for individuals,' other than 'freedom to kick down every construction you make. Freedom to separate yourself from the consequences of your actions.' She appears to persuade him with her argument that 'if we stay together – properly, faithfully together – we'll have a centre; and if we have there's just a chance we can still do something'. (p. 126) The final lines, however, are both interrogative. Miriam, in what she considers to be her triumph, employs a militaristic trope: 'This is the last fight. I couldn't lose, could I?' Jan gently replies: 'Ah, but is it the last fight?' (p. 127)

Music in the titles of *A Note in Music* and *No More Music* clearly represents the civilised values under threat in the 1930s. The individualism inherent in the single note of music has been challenged, but the question as to whether some form of concerted action can negate the threat that there will be no more music remains in the balance.

Notes

1. Diana LeStourgeon, *Rosamond Lehmann* (published doctoral dissertation, University of Pennsylvania; New York: Twayne, 1965), p. 23.
2. Judy Simons, *Rosamond Lehmann* (Basingstoke: Macmillan, 1992), p. 2.
3. Ruth Siegel, *Rosamond Lehmann: A Thirties Writer* (New York: Lang, 1989), *passim*.
4. James Gindin, *British Fiction in the 1930s: The Dispiriting Decade* (Basingstoke: Macmillan, 1992), p. 18.
5. Introduction to *Rosamond Lehmann's Album* (London: Chatto and Windus, 1985), p. 11.
6. Janet Montefiore, *Men and Women Writers of the 1930s: The Dangerous Flood of History* (London: Routledge, 1996), p. 2.

7. John Lehmann, *The Whispering Gallery* (London: Longmans, Green, 1955), p. 88.
8. Rosamond Lehmann, in *Authors Take Sides on the Spanish War* (London: Left Review, 1937), pages unnumbered.
9. Rosamond Lehmann, *A Note in Music* (London: Chatto and Windus, 1930), pp. 143–4. All subsequent page references in the text are to this edition.
10. Samuel Hynes, *A War Imagined* (London: Bodley Head, 1990), p. xi.
11. Wogan Philipps, undated letter to Harold Raymond, Chatto and Windus, received 15 March 1930 (Reading: Chatto and Windus Collection, University of Reading Archives), hereafter called (Reading: C&W).
12. Hynes, *A War Imagined*, p. xi.
13. Gindin, *British Fiction*, p. 1.
14. Gindin, *British Fiction*, p. 15.
15. Gindin, *British Fiction*, p. 15.
16. V. S. Pritchett, review of Rosamond Lehmann, *A Note in Music*, *Spectator*, 27 September 1930, pp. 421–2.
17. Janet Watts, introduction to Rosamond Lehmann, *A Note in Music* (London: Virago, 1982), p. xiii.
18. Siegel, *Rosamond Lehmann: A Thirties Writer*, p. 8.
19. Cf. 'I'll show you fear in a handful of dust', T. S. Eliot, *The Waste Land* (1922), l. 30.
20. Rosamond Lehmann, letter to Harold Raymond, 1 March 1930 (Reading: C&W).
21. K. John, review of Rosamond Lehmann, *A Note in Music*, *Nation & Athenaeum*, 4 October 1930, p. 22.
22. Isabel Paterson, review of Rosamond Lehmann, *A Note in Music*, *Books* (US), 30 October 1932, p. 5.
23. Review of Rosamond Lehmann, *Invitation to the Waltz*, *Times Literary Supplement*, 6 October 1932, p. 712.
24. Letter to author from Eamon Dyas, News International plc, 21 July 1997.
25. John Atkins, *Six Novelists Look at Society* (London: Calder, 1977), pp. 112–34.
26. Rosamond Lehmann, *The Weather in the Streets* (London: Collins, 1936), p. 91. All subsequent page references in the text are to this edition.
27. Atkins, *Six Novelists Look at Society*, p. 116.
28. Lehmann, *The Whispering Gallery*, p. 223.
29. Rosamond Lehmann, review of Graham Greene, *A Gun for Sale*, *New Statesman*, 1 August 1936, p. 164.
30. Samuel Hynes, *The Auden Generation* (London: Bodley Head, 1976), p. 235.
31. Jason Gurney, *Crusade in Spain* (London: Faber and Faber, 1974), p. 18.
32. Wogan Phillips, later Baron Milford, became the only peer to take his seat as a Communist in the House of Lords. John Lehmann, editor of *New Writing*, wrote of believing at that time 'that the solution to the troubles and dangers with which we were faced lay in Marxism, and even in Moscow ...' *The Whispering Gallery*, p. 216. Beatrix Lehmann was co-editor of the Communist literary review *Our Time* and was later on the editorial board of the *Daily Worker*.
33. Michelene Wandor (ed.), *On Gender and Writing* (London: Pandora, 1983).
34. Nora Bartlett, in Wandor, *On Gender and Writing*, p. 11.
35. 'Neutral?: 1930s Writers and Taking Sides', in Frank Gloversmith (ed.), *Class, Culture and Social Change: A New View of the 1930s* (Brighton: Harvester, 1980), pp. 47–8.
36. Lehmann, in *Authors Take Sides on the Spanish War*.
37. Entry for 24 May 1938, *The Diary of Virginia Woolf, V, 1936–41* (Harmondsworth: Penguin, 1985), p. 142 (Woolf's idiosyncratic punctuation).
38. See correspondence (Cambridge: Lehmann Collection, King's Modern Archive).
39. Lehmann, *The Whispering Gallery*, p. 272.
40. Unpublished typescript of speech given at the Queen's Hall, 8 June 1938 (Cambridge: Lehmann Collection, King's Modern Archive).
41. Lehmann, in *Authors Take Sides on the Spanish War*.
42. Elizabeth Bowen, 'Island Life', *New Statesman and Nation*, 5 March 1938, p. 367.
43. Rosamond Lehmann, *No More Music* (London: Collins, 1939), p. 10. All subsequent page references in the text are to this edition.
44. W. H. Auden and Christopher Isherwood, *The Ascent of F6* (London: Faber and Faber, 1936; reprint with *On the Frontier*, 1958), p. 64.

8

In a Class of Her Own:
Elizabeth von Arnim

Alison Hennegan

The writing career of 'Elizabeth von Arnim' spans more than forty years, from the enormously successful publication of her first book, *Elizabeth and Her German Garden* in 1898 to her last, *Mr. Skeffington*, published in 1940, a year before her death, and filmed, after a fashion, in 1944 with Bette Davis and Claude Rains. Usually remembered (and dismissed) as a social satirist with a pleasingly deft touch, Elizabeth is also often assumed by those who know her name but have not read her work to be an irredeemably conservative woman and writer, whose comedies of manners mock the superficial absurdities of aristocratic and upper-class lives whilst implicitly endorsing their norms and values. The truth is rather more interesting.

A hostile critic might claim that Elizabeth had too keen a sense of literary fashion and the marketplace for her own artistic good. Such a one would argue that her first book, *Elizabeth and Her German Garden*, with its first-person musings in diary form, cashed in on a very Nineties vogue for a sophisticated reworking of worldly pastoral, filtered through exquisite and preferably female sensibility, and spiced with gently feminist asides. That *The Benefactress* (1901), her first unambiguously fictional work, in which a young, English-raised, Anglo-German woman inherits an estate in Germany and tries, unsuccessfully, to establish there an all-female philanthropic community, exploits, safely, the turn-of-the-century taste for feminist Utopias – the 'new woman' novel meets *Millenium Hall*, perhaps. That in *The Caravaners* (1909), the tale of a fruitfully disastrous caravanning holiday through Kent and Sussex, Elizabeth transforms herself into The ChesterBelloc to hymn the glories of the rolling English road (and, perhaps, to take an enjoyably reactionary counterswipe at that other new contemporary sub-genre, the motoring novel, of the sort pioneered by the husband-and-wife writing team, Mr and Mrs C. N. Williamson). And that, with her deeply unsympathetic narrator, the Prussian officer, Baron von Ottringel, she moreover makes cheap capital of the anti-German sentiment intensifying in these years immediately preceding the outbreak of war in 1914. That *The Pastor's Wife* (1914), though sympathetic in its depiction of its eponymous heroine, carries that national hostility further. That *The Enchanted April* (1922), with its story of four very different Englishwomen arbitrarily thrown together by their joint holiday tenancy of a 'Small mediaeval Italian castle on the shores of the Mediterranean', trades on the post-war hunger for exotic and newly affordable foreign travel – *A Room with a View*, Mark 2. That *Love* (1925), with its depiction of the havoc wrought when an unhappily married middle-aged woman falls in love with, and is loved by, a man many years her junior, was a thrillingly appealing subject in a world where only two years previously Edith Thompson and her lover, Frederick Bywaters, had hanged for the murder of Thompson's husband (even though most acknowledged that the crime which really sealed her death warrant was that she, a woman of nearly thirty, had taken a teenage lover). Elizabeth remained fascinated by love affairs across the generations, as the adventures of Mrs Skeffington reveal.

Thus our hostile critic. But Elizabeth, in fact, was not just a canny self-promoter with an enviably keen sense of the *Zeitgeist*. If she had an acute sense of the shifts and vagaries of public feeling and literary fashion, it came in part from her own position, in but not of English and European society. Onlookers, notoriously, see most of the game. Even the title-page designation by which generations of readers have known her, 'by the author of *Elizabeth and her German Garden*', misleads, for she was never Elizabeth. Born Mary Annette Beauchamp in 1866, the older cousin of Katherine Mansfield and, like her, an Antipodean, Elizabeth, as she was invariably known after 1898, was, on various counts, an outsider for most of her life: a colonial at the heart of Empire; a British bride in Junker Germany; the widow of a German baron remarried into British aristocracy during the Great War; an aristocrat (but only by marriage) among predominantly petit-bourgeois British intellectuals and bohemians; an anti-Nazi in a casually anti-Semitic world.

A woman who seeks to inhabit so many different worlds must expect to get caught in the cross-fire, and so she did. Katherine Mansfield, who greatly admired the work and loved the woman devotedly (the very last letter she ever wrote was to Elizabeth), could also be maddened by signs of 'Great Ladyness': after one of their rare tiffs, she had her revenge in the story entitled 'A Cup of Tea' (collected in *The Dove's Nest and Other Stories* in 1923). There Elizabeth appears as Rosemary Fell, a wealthy, intelligent but frivolous woman who 'collects' and condescends to impoverished and aspiring artists. Mansfield knew well that there was in fact no contradiction between her cousin's acquired rank and social aspirations and her utter dedication to the perfecting of her writer's craft. Others were more cynical. When, for example, Elizabeth visited Garsington, was she just another of Ottoline Morrell's worthy causes, such as D. H. Lawrence and John Middleton Murry, Mansfield's husband, or one society hostess visiting another? Moreover, in an age when Great Literature was coming all too often to mean dreary realism and grimy maleness, could an author for whom High Comedy was the supreme mode possibly be taken seriously? Some critics certainly thought not. When *Vera* – her devastating portrait of the sour sadism informing one oh-so-respectable marriage, published in 1921, and regarded by many as her masterpiece – received a slating review in *The Times Literary Supplement*, Middleton Murry, who with his wife, much admired the book, consoled her by observing: 'Of course, my dear, when the critics are faced by *Wuthering Heights* by Jane Austen, they don't know what to say.'[1] The bemusement of her contemporaries is matched by the silence of today's academic criticism.

Several major issues preoccupied Elizabeth for much of her life and recur constantly in her work, including the last four novels: *Expiation* (1929); *Father* (1931); *The Jasmine Farm* (1934); and *Mr. Skeffington* (1940). Chief amongst these issues are: male tyranny over women, practised domestically, sanctioned socially and culturally; the links between domestic and national tyranny, links which would become all too horrifically clear as the German people rapidly embraced the Fascism whose antecedents she had so long ago recognized and adumbrated; the morally warping effects of poverty, subordination and spiritual enslavement, particularly for women; the existence of women as a class; and what one might call the 'economy of female beauty'.

Some of these preoccupations emerged from her own experience. Widespread German contempt for women, for example, of the sort her Benefactress experiences at the hands of her loathsome estate Manager, and which the wife of Baron von Ottringel endures in *The Caravaners*, Elizabeth had experienced in Berlin and in Pomerania where she and her German first husband eventually moved to care for his family estate, Nassenheide. (The atmosphere was occasionally lightened by her children's English tutors, aspiring novelists who briefly included E. M. Forster and Hugh Walpole.) As a member of the British Empire in Germany during those extremely tense years waiting for the war that everyone knew was coming, she experienced, too, the arrogant Junker contempt for lesser breeds and nations and its links with misogyny. Later, in *The Caravaners*, her Prussian baron constantly associates the men of other nations with primitive life forms and with effeminacy; the lowest of all are Jews. Elizabeth had already encountered some of the many unlovely varieties of German anti-Semitism during her years in Berlin and Pomerania: hatred posing as Christian religious fervour, for example, terrifying in its mindless 'rabidness' – her own word and one which takes the anti-Semitic metaphor of the Jew as carrier of spiritual and moral disease and turns it against itself.

Male violence, whether verbal, emotional or physical, was also familiar to her; her first husband appears as The Man of Wrath in *Elizabeth and her German Garden* and in *The Solitary Summer* (1899), a supposedly humorous nickname which nevertheless leaves the reader with a sense of unease. Her second husband, Francis, Earl Russell, brother of Bertrand, was the model for Wemyss, the monstrous husband in *Vera*, as he himself was quick to recognize. He threatened a libel action but, on the principle of 'if the cap fits', was persuaded to drop it. The attendant rumours and counter-rumours boosted sales splendidly, to Elizabeth's and Macmillan's delight.

Money – for all women, whether beautiful, young and desirable, or plain, ageing and unwanted – is a constant theme for Elizabeth. The basic question – where is money to come from, on what terms and at what personal and moral cost to the women receiving it? – underpins much of her work throughout her writing life. It is already there in *The Benefactress* and still centrally there in the last, *Mr. Skeffington*. In *Expiation* it is a woman's sudden, unexpected loss of access to money which drives the plot; In *Father*, it is the heroine's decision to opt for a life of independence lived on £100 a year in a rose-covered but insanitary Sussex cottage, rather than material comfort and paternal tyranny in the smoke and smuts of Gower Street. In *The Jasmine Farm* a middle-aged woman of more than slightly dubious morals who has never, in all her life, had enough of any of the things she wants, is prepared to blackmail one of England's wealthiest and seemingly most impregnable women. And *Mr. Skeffington*'s money cocoons his ex-wife in her endless pursuit of expensive pleasures.

Elizabeth saw as clearly as Woolf that certain sorts of freedom – of thought, of choice, of action – are virtually dependent upon economic autonomy. As she writes of Anna Estcourt, the heroine of *The Bene-factress*, a young woman entirely dependent on her wealthy sister-in-law's bounty, 'she had bestowed nothing and was taking everything, and she was of an independent nature; and an independent nature, where there is no money, is a great nuisance to its possessor.'[2] And, it may be said, to those on whom they are dependent. Susie, Anna's sister-in-law, is a reasonably benevolent tyrant, as tyrants go. Other of Elizabeth's heroines are less fortunate: Jennifer Dodge (Jen to her friends and the reader) in *Father*, for instance. Jen is the unmarried thirty-three-year-old daughter of the Distinguished Novelist, Roger Dodge, a writer who for the past few decades has been more admired than read across literary America and Europe. Jen, when eighteen, promised her dying mother never to leave her father. She has kept her promise and over the past twelve years has become his thoroughly efficient and indispensable typist, secretary, proof-reader and chatelaine.

At the book's opening, Father has just broken the news to Jen that he this morning married the nineteen-year-old Miss Netta Baines, a woman hitherto completely unknown to Jen. Unwillingly, and clearly performing a painful duty, he assures his bemused daughter that she is not to assume she no longer has a place in his house. He sets off for his honeymoon in Norway: Jen, at last released from her promise to her mother, joyously takes off for Sussex, armed with a copy of *The Sussex Churchgoer* which is full of useful addresses of very cheaply rentable cottages belonging to clerical landlords. Her cottage found (five shillings a week rent) and furniture moved in, she begins the rural idyll she has long desired. Her landlord, James Ollier, is a young, twenty-six-year old vicar, whose eminently desirable vicarage – magnolia-enfolded Georgian – is impeccably kept for him by Alice, his spinster sister some fifteen years his senior. Alice, like Father, is a tyrant, a bully and adept in all the unworthy skills of psychological management and manipulation: terror and induced guilt are her chief weapons. She employs them not only because the exercise of power affords her pleasure in its own right, but also because her finances are inextricably bound up with those of her brother. His marriage would inevitably threaten and almost certainly destroy her domestic dominion and material security. She may display 'masculine' bullying traits but her reasons are very female.

Father soon finds himself single again: his sexually ignorant and unprepared young orphan bride is so traumatized by her groom's brutal, bungling and incessant sexual rapacity, that she leaves him within days. Determinedly, Father sets about resecuring his once more indispensable daughter. The novel is basically the story of Jen's and James's attempts to break free from their domestic tyrannies. For Jen, as she herself recognises, her father's power over her extends far beyond the straightforwardly economic. 'With father, she had never once, in her whole life, been natural. Probably no obedient creature, she thought, could be so, no creature whose time was spent carrying out orders, and dodging round as the shadow and echo of another human being; no person, that is, who was in any way a slave.'[3]

Yet Jen, who will eventually, by no effort of her own, be most finally freed from Father by his death, risks, as she knows, exchanging one form of slavery for another. As she tells James, on the very first evening she meets him, 'she didn't know which was the more enslaving, – to concentrate on somebody, or be concentrated upon oneself; but she was sure that both were bad. "One has to be free," she finished, as if taking it for granted that he would think so too.'[4]

If union means submergence, or obliteration by fusion, Jen doesn't want it. The book's 'happy ending' is quite ambiguous: yes, Father is dead and, presumably, Jen and James will now marry, but whether they share a common view of the meaning of marriage is far less clear. James's initial response to Jen's cry for freedom would seem to bode ill:

> 'Spiritually [free], certainly,' said James, who, except from Alice, felt he didn't want to be as free as all that, and could picture mutual concentration, under the right conditions, as a very happy thing indeed. What, really, in the whole world could be a happier thing?[5]

Between Jen and James there is a clear imbalance on this point, and Jen is not the only one of Elizabeth's heroines who will almost certainly have to grapple with the problem of male emotional dependency. It is as though once the arbitrary sources of women's dependency are removed – financial, professional, legislative – the full force of male dependency on women is revealed uncamouflaged. Wemyss, the monster husband in *Vera*, is, for instance, hideously dependent on Lucy, his second wife, for his emotional security, and it is his monstrousness which is the index of his need. So, too, Baron von Ottringel would be hopelessly lost without his much-despised Edelgard (who may indeed, although he'll be the last to realise it, be about to leave him).

Marriage is, indeed, the place where many of Elizabeth's enduring preoccupations meet and intersect. Without it, the policing of female virtue can scarcely happen. Marriage is the reward for celibacy maintained before it, and the test of chastity maintained after it. And failing the test can cost you dear, as Milly discovers in *Expiation*.

Expiation deals with the impact upon Milly and her large family of in-laws, the Botts, when her husband's will reveals that the entirety of his estate is being left to a Home for Fallen Women, apart from just £1,000 for Milly, 'for reasons which she will understand'. The reason is adultery (a once-passionate affair, embarked upon some ten years previously when Milly was thirty-five, and now a reassuringly tepid domestic arrangement), which, unbeknownst to Milly, Ernest had discovered. When her plans to run away on the proceeds of the legacy fail (because she makes a gift in its entirety of the money to her also recently widowed younger sister, Agatha), Milly returns to Titford to find that the rest of her life is apparently to consist of being handed round by her in-laws like an unwanted parcel, spending a month in each household, until she's exhausted the roster and has to begin again at the beginning.

Expiation, like much of Elizabeth's fiction, especially her later works, questions conventional ideas of female virtue and, conversely, female vice. Milly, clearly a 'bad' woman, is constantly seen by all around her as good: she looks good, she feels good, she makes other people feel good; the creature she is most often compared to is a dove, with both its peaceful and sacred associations. Milly's dove-like goodness in fact enrages her nearest (though never dearest), who feel cheated of their moral certainties. Just as Hardy raised disturbing questions by subtitling his more sombre work, *Tess of the d'Urbervilles*, 'a pure woman', so too Elizabeth implicitly asks constantly whether the commonly accepted definition of virtue in a woman is actually big enough to do the job.

The virtues of other of Milly's sisters-in-law prove equally, though less spectacularly, delusory. (Mabel, for instance, is merely stupid, Ruth besotted, Edith tolerating a loveless marriage for only as long as it seems a better bet than a divorce with a generous settlement.) And sometimes 'virtue' can be positively vicious, as it is in Agatha, once as unvirtuous as her sister Milly but rapidly subsumed within a life of marital virtue and grinding poverty. Physically worn and spiritually hardened, she is reduced to the unyielding practice of the chilliest virtues.

Vicious virtue receives Elizabeth's most uncompromising dissection in *The Jasmine Farm*, the first of her novels published in the 1930s. This magnificently accomplished novel, one of Elizabeth's most exuberantly written and plotted, uses High Comedy, with occasional descents to pure farce, as the vehicle for some of her most serious work.

Daisy, Lady Midhurst, now fifty-three, is one of the undisputed social leaders of London society. Born into one of England's oldest families and married into the other, she has been for sixteen years a widow. Her daughter, Lady Terence Chilgrove, is beautiful and good, as befits one whose mother is the moral arbiter of England's nobility. Daisy, also beautiful – with a great deal of painstaking and expensive help from coiffeuses, manicurists, cosmeticians, *corsetières* and dressmakers – is the scourge of the sexually immoral: to have the entrée to her house is to have one's morals vouched for; to lose it is to join the ranks of the fallen and excluded. Unbeknownst to Daisy, unbeknownst, indeed, to anyone, her daughter has for the past seven years been the lover – at her own most pressing instigation – of Andrew Leigh, a man now fifty-nine, once a fellow officer of Daisy's husband, and the man who brought her news of Midhurst's death in action in 1918 and stayed to become her indispensable secretary. Leigh is married, has been since the war when he entered impetuously into a disastrous match with the seventeen-year-old Rosie, an aspiring revue actress, beautiful, empty-headed and utterly cold. To make matters worse, Rosie has a mother, herself once an actress, now the formidable Mrs de Lacy (title by courtesy of her third husband who, with a degree of cowardice still bitterly resented by his relict, yelled one evening that he'd had a bellyful, disappeared into his study, locked the door and blew his brains out. Life, for Mrs de Lacy, more usually known as Mumsie, has not been easy.) When, in a moment's carelessness, Lady Terence unwittingly reveals the fact of her affair to an old friend who loves her dearly but is nevertheless the leakiest man in London, the Midhurst family, Andrew Leigh, Rosie, Mumsie, a German Count and an English Cabinet Minister are precipitated into a series of unseemly melodramas which reach their culmination at the Jasmine Farm, which Daisy's hopeful young husband bought for her, in the early years of the century, during their French honeymoon, and where Daisy, for the first and only time in her life, permitted herself, during five weeks or so, to give and receive sexual pleasures.

At the Jasmine Farm, to which Daisy has withdrawn (in something more closely resembling a rout than a retreat), Daisy is forced to face a number of long delayed and very unwelcome truths about herself, about her purity, about her cowardice and her own betrayals of love. Her purity has, it becomes hideously clear to her, been little more than pique, self-regard – and self-punishment for the passion she did briefly feel and could not bring herself to honour. Fear – of her own emotions and the vulnerability they bring – and a determination to punish the man who has aroused them make up a great deal of her much vaunted 'purity'.

Moreover, she must recognize a host of unexpected affinities with other, supposedly 'impure' women – the déclassée Mumsie, for example. Throughout the novel Daisy will sometimes, unwillingly, hear a small, tiresome voice which whispers 'So do you' or 'So are you' when she's indulging in some hostile formulation about Mumsie. Learning to acknowledge that the voice is right is almost the most important part of the moral self-education which Daisy undergoes during the course of the book.

Both women have been beautiful ('a fine woman' or 'a handsome piece' may have been the terms more usually applied to Mumsie, whilst Daisy has been described with more veneration), but each has had beauty and is now losing it. Both women battle to preserve their beauty as long as possible. Daisy can do a better job because she has more money and less worry, but she is as desperate as Mumsie to hold Age at bay. Each uses beauty as a form of power. By concentrating on physical beauty, Daisy can indefinitely delay troubling questions about her own moral beauty and whether it may already have decayed far more dramatically than her face and body. Beauty also enables her to postpone the painful discovery that most of her power and influence over the influential and powerful are directly linked to her physical appearance. Mumsie needs her physical attractiveness for reasons of simple livelihood: since all three of her husbands did the dirty on her by dying (although only one was rat enough to die at his own hands), and left little enough behind them, she must secure a succession of Friends, willing to 'lend' money when conventional bankers prove unwilling. And, with each passing year, Friends are harder to find.

Rosie and Daisy also share unexpected attributes. Rosie is as sexually cold as Daisy; she, too, though still blessed with comparative youthfulness, husbands her looks as thriftily as any merchant. Completely unstirred by sexual passions, she accepts compliments and gifts as the debt due to beauty but has nothing but impatience or distaste for sexual emotions. She isn't even narcissistic: it's her clothes – expensive, fashionable, eye-catching and tasteless – which excite her, not her own body.

Unlike Rosie and Daisy, Lady Terence has an easy pleasure in the body, inherited perhaps from her father. And yet, in some rather unexpected ways, Terence is undoubtedly her mother's daughter. Although, on the face of it, Terence has flouted Daisy's moral code, she resembles Daisy in the mercilessness with which she allows no possibility that Andrew – many years her senior, not physically very strong after the privations of a hard war, and morally always utterly miserable about the affair upon which they are embarked which involves not only adultery but also betrayal of Daisy's trust – may be better served by ending the affair.

In *The Jasmine Farm* (and even more so in *Mr. Skeffington*), women, and beautiful women in particular, are seen to form a class, however divergent their own individual class positions may be. For Daisy, Mumsie and Rosie their faces are amongst their most important assets; but their faces also provide one of the most important elements in their own sense of identity: from them they take their sense of who and what they are, what their place in the world is and what is owed to them by the world.

But faces are also fertile of metaphor and proverb. Faces fall metaphorically, in disappointment, and literally, with the sagging of muscle and tissue. (Sometimes, even more horrifically in this period, faces pumped full of 'rejuvenating' wax literally fell, slipped and rotted.) Faces may freeze or solidify, so intransigent is the carapace of cosmetics they carry. Daisy, whose eyebrows sit in a face as 'enamelled' as Queen Alexandra's and Queen Mary's were in real life, can scarcely raise them, even for purposes of admonishment. Mumsie, whose more limited budget will stretch only to 'corking', has greater freedom. Daisy's constraints and Mumsie's liberties are not confined to their eyebrows and cheek muscles: each woman's cosmetic status accurately reflects her differing psychological states, states caused by a combination of individual temperament, social and class factors, and the interrelation of the two. A face which permits virtually no physical indication of emotion is a face that functions as a mask, and, as such, most useful and appropriate in a society as formally layered and choreographed as Daisy's.

You may, also of course, 'lose' your face (to the ravages of Time or illness), or 'lose face' (in the eyes of your peers or dependents), by unseemly, foolish or disreputable conduct, or by the simple loss of power and influence. One of the questions which Elizabeth has constantly before her in *The Jasmine Farm*, and to which she returns in *Mr. Skeffington*, is whether for a woman to 'lose her face' may inevitably entail 'losing face'.

And virtually every significant character in this novel is in some respect 'two-faced'. For Daisy, the biggest challenge presented to her by the disaster which nearly engulfs her is to discover and acknowledge her real faces, both literal and metaphorical, and to consent to wear and inhabit them from now on.

The same dilemma faces Lady Frances Skeffington (Fanny) in *Mr. Skeffington*, Elizabeth's last novel, published in the year before she died, in America, a refugee from Hitler's Europe. Fanny is about to be fifty. One of her age's greatest beauties, a serious illness has wrecked her looks which, she gradually realizes, are almost certainly never going to be regained. Some twenty-two years previously before the Great War, she married Job, Mr. Skeffington, the adoring and enormmomously wealthy Jewish financier whose millions saved her father's heavily mortgaged ducal acres (three lots of death duties in five years, as heir after heir fell in the Great War, had all but obliterated the family estates). Fanny's younger brother Trippington (Trippy) loathes her marriage to a beastly Jew, even though (unbeknownst to him) she marries in part to secure Trippy's inheritance; he is himself killed within days of enlisting. He was, she often believes, the only man she ever really loved.

Fanny soon divorces Job, although he continues to adore her, because of his weakness for typists; after the seventh, Fanny decides enough is enough and secures a divorce settlement of fabulous value, many times greater than her legal entitlement. Since then, she has lost sight of Job, though the casual gossip of male business friends suggests he is abroad somewhere. She has embarked upon a series of – what? – flirtations? *amitiés amoureuses*?; fully fledged affaires?; – no-one's quite sure, though many a slighted wife is sure she has cause for grievance. With the departure of her beauty – temporary, she hopes; permanent, she fears – Fanny, like Daisy, is forced to confront questions and fears which her beauty has kept at bay. A succession of encounters, some farcical, all disastrous, with some of the men in her past, pushes her remorselessly, though resistingly, to recognize that her 'love days', as Stilton Byles, the ultra-fashionable, very expensive and extremely insulting women's nerve specialist, calls them, are well and truly over. Not that she'd asked for his opinion about that; she'd actually consulted him about Job's recent and unnerving appearances in her house – behind the fish-dish at breakfast, for example, or tucked away behind the back of the writing desk. All very inexplicable because he clearly isn't actually there. Ghosts, suggests Byles rudely, need to be laid, and Fanny had better find a way of doing so.

As Fanny proceeds in the spiritual and moral journey that she must undertake if she is eventually to accept the loss of her beauty, she also, unwittingly, journeys closer to Job. Her cousin George, a friend from childhood, is a man tormented by cruelty and injustice, fired by the need to combat it at home and abroad. He has found Job – no longer the financial wizard who dominated the London markets, but an old and broken man of seventy-two, bankrupted, tortured and blinded by Austrian Nazis. Traumatized and terrified, brought somehow back from Vienna to England, he has been discovered by George who, impulsively, brings him and his guide dog unannounced to Fanny's house, desperate to prove to himself that Fanny's essential kindliness will triumph and that she will take back the husband who always loved her and to whom she owes so much. Driven by the vanity which has not entirely died, Fanny at first refuses to see him; she has been told little of his plight, other than that he is now poor, and she cannot bear that he should see her so dreadfully changed. Seeing her, of course, is what he will never do again – the far more dreadful changes inflicted upon him guarantee that. Her horrified realization, first of his blindness, and then of the manner of his blinding and the meaning of all that has been done to him, effects a reconciliation of passionately protective forgiveness.

Again, as in *The Jasmine Farm*, physical facts about the senses work both literally and to provide a constant metaphorical and symbolic framework for a consideration of other forms of perception, grasping, seeing, being blind. Hearts see as well as eyes. Physical beauty has a meaning and value beyond those who possess it – it has a social/ spiritual function, too, it genuinely warms and lightens the lives of those it touches. Part of what's going on in this novel (and which makes it different from *The Jasmine Farm*) is that a battle rages within it – voiced explicitly by some characters, implicitly in the interactions of others – a battle between a pagan, hedonistic joy in Beauty, and a particularly sour sort of Christian suspicion and hatred of the human body. This is a book which questions an either/or opposition of Spiritual Beauty versus Bodily Beauty, and keeps insisting that there is, or should be, some genuine movement between the two. The men amongst Fanny's previous attachments who have most 'died' are those who have let themselves become oblivious to that knowledge: Lanks, now a money-obsessed and desiccated barrister making far too much a year to deign to be Home Secretary; and Father Hyslup, his religion now a thing of joyless negation and harsh dominion in reaction to his despair at being dropped by Fanny.

Threaded through the text of *Mr. Skeffington* are countless scraps and echoes of great poems and Biblical passages extolling human beauty, sexual passion and Divine Grace. Technically the occasion of them is provided by the fact that Fanny, who has numbered many well-read men and poets amongst her conquests, has the sort of rag-bag memory which is crammed to overflowing with half-remembered phrases culled from works once read to her. But in fact their function and cumulative effect is to keep constantly before us the proof and embodiment of the way in which carnal love has constantly provided a gateway to the soul.

From the earliest pages of *Mr. Skeffington* male characters have discussed gravely 'the European situation', although Fanny always wished they wouldn't:

> Certainly the European situation was enough to make anybody talk out loud, but ever since she could remember there had always been something the matter with it, and it hadn't in the slightest way interfered with amusing, silly things being whispered in one's ear.[6]

By the novel's end, its invasion of her life – and Job's – has altered both irrevocably:

> 'This then', she realizes, 'was life, beneath the smiles. While she, in the sun of its surface, was wasting months in shamefully selfish, childish misery over the loss of her beauty, Job was being broken up into a sort of frightened animal. How could one live, while such things were going on? How could one endure consciousness, except by giving oneself up wholly and for ever to helping, and comforting, and at last, at last, perhaps healing?'[7]

Mr. Skeffington, engaging directly with 'the European situation', is the most obviously political of Elizabeth's novels in the sometimes rather narrow sense in which many of those who work on the literature of the 1930s recognize politics. In this essay I have tried to suggest and show that Elizabeth von Arnim's sense of the political encompasses a perhaps unexpectedly wide range of concerns in which economics, class, gender, sexuality, nationalism and power are inextricably inter-related – a startlingly PC list for such a very un-PC author. Elizabeth would almost certainly be wryly amused.

Notes

1. Karen Usborne, *'Elizabeth', The Author of* Elizabeth and her German Garden (London: The Bodley Head, 1986), p. 231.
2. Elizabeth von Arnim, *The Benefactress*, pocket edn. (London: Macmillan, 1929), p. 2.
3. Elizabeth von Arnim, *Father* (London: Macmillan, 1931), p. 103.
4. von Arnim, *Father*, p. 106.
5. von Arnim, *Father*, p. 106.
6. Elizabeth von Arnim, *Mr. Skeffington* (London: Macmillan, 1940), p. 10.
7. von Arnim, *Mr. Skeffington*, p. 231.

9

The Reception of Nancy Cunard's *Negro* Anthology

Tory Young

U ntil recently the works of Nancy Cunard, poet, publisher, political activist, journalist and biographer, were omitted from almost
every study of the 1930s. Cunard's achievements have also been disre-
garded in wider studies of the Spanish Civil War and campaigns for
racial equality. During the last few years, however, revisers of the
literary history of the 1930s have found a place for Cunard, her *Negro*
anthology and her poems.[1] Jane Marcus has begun to dissect the
reasons for her marginalisation by intellectuals and historians; detailing
the objections to the activism of a promiscuous white, upper-class
woman by both black and white.[2]

It is not hard to see why feminists have been slow to champion the
works of a woman who expressed doubts that rape could ever occur, in
her support for the wrongly accused in the Scottsboro trial, one of the
most famous rape cases in the 1930s to which I shall return (although
in the silence surrounding Cunard such objections have not even been
heard). However, studies of *Negro* have been most recently inspired
not by feminist re-readings of the 1930s, but by those engaged in
another project of revision. Cunard's anthology has been widely discussed at every recent conference on the Harlem Renaissance. In these
forums, whilst hostility to Cunard as primitivist, negrophiliac and
misguided liberal is widely voiced and debated, the process of contextualisation has also begun, for example relating the influence of French
surrealism upon *Negro*.[3] It is my aim in this essay to also provide a
context in which to discuss Cunard's anthology, its reception and
reasons for its neglect which have not been fully identified so far. In so
doing I intend to focus upon the text and authorial politics rather than
the figure of Cunard herself. It is my belief that earlier attempts by

113

Hugh Ford to draw attention to *Negro* failed where current critics succeed, because of his imposition of the figure of Cunard upon her anthology. The biographical details which form a fascinating introduction to his abridged reprint, and pictorial emphasis on her representation, perversely have the effect of marginalising the text and diminishing her project.

Hugh Ford abridged and republished *Negro* in 1970 as a celebration of both the anthology and its editor. He begins his foreword by stating 'One of the most astonishing facts about *Negro* is its existence; another is its author'.[4] In order to simultaneously celebrate the book and the woman, Ford removed some of Cunard's more controversial statements – for instance her comments on rape and her opinions of W. E. B. DuBois, the black activist and founder of the National Association for the Advancement of Colored People – and in so doing has removed clues not only to the text's marginalisation, but also to Cunard's own agenda. It is important to consider Ford's revisions as his reprint continues to be widely read and considered as representative of the whole.

Apparently unable to perceive *Negro* as the first of Cunard's many protests against Fascism and social inequity, Ford strains to find reasons for the compilation of a black anthology. His comments are framed in the racist discourse of the primitive, proposing a layperson's psychoanalysis; 'this kinship with blacks, always so spontaneous and honest, so natural that it seemed inevitable, can perhaps be traced to a muted desire expressed in' a childhood dream;[5] and offering the purely patronising: 'one of the elements that help to explain Nancy's defense of the black man is her appreciation and understanding of his musical accomplishments'.[6] His celebration of Cunard goes so far as to introduce her image into the text in which she originally chose not to appear. Ford negates her significant decision to include only the photographs of black contributors and inserts paintings and photographs of the editor herself. He praises and includes almost all her articles, increasing their prominence by vastly reducing the number of other contributions. Ford's abridgments and insertions distort the face of the book, destroying its significant black representation, and its emotional impact. Her defence of the Scottsboro boys, seven youths from Alabama wrongly accused of raping a white woman, was intended not just to rally support for their case but to inspire horror at the countless injustices it typified. By removing the details of hundreds of lynchings which had taken place in the first half of 1933, Ford also unintentionally weakened Cunard's argument.

It is clear that Ford was deeply impressed with Cunard's achieve-ment: 'one of the most astonishing facts about *Negro* is its existence'.[7] However remarkable it may have been, Ford's celebration of Cunard within the reprint and his removal of contentious statements, give the impression of him being content to merely marvel at the fact a white woman compiled a black anthology. In lauding the existence of *Negro*, Ford also disregards the series of black anthologies compiled in America since the beginning of the century, for example *A New Negro for a New Century* and *The New Negro*. In this essay I hope to suggest that Cunard's anthology can be seen as a response to this tradition, and that considering it in relation to other black anthologies, rather than only in isolation as the product of a white woman, will provide further enlightenment as to its lack of contemporary popular appeal.

Cunard does not seem to have intended to locate black experience at one geographical site. She visited North America twice and collected material which forms the largest section of the anthology, but also collated articles under the headings: West Indies, South America, Europe and Africa. Not content to document the brutalities of the American lynch mob, and the injustice of white rule in the colonies, she sought also to provide a record of discrimination in Europe. In 1931 she instigated her plans for an anthology to be titled *Color* by leaving her French home for London. There she intended to perform conventional research in libraries and galleries, but also in the company of her black lover, Henry Crowder, to witness the racial prejudice of the English at first hand. From the moment of inception, therefore, Cunard proposed to span a range of genres: historical thesis was to stand next to contemporary testimony. The couple's visit provoked as much sensation as Cunard had anticipated. Indeed, it was the money she gained from later suing the Allied Newspapers group which was eventually to fund the anthology's publication. Forced to retreat to France, she devised a plan of contents to be circulated with letters requesting contributions.

This circular reveals that Cunard's approach was unscholarly: 'It will be published ... as soon as enough material has been collected'.[8] However, those who criticise *Negro* for failing to fulfil academic criteria disregard the telling urgency of Cunard's appeal. Her anthology was intended more as a call to arms than an encyclopedia. This can be testified in its lack of index and biographical data and also in her decision not to pay for contributions (a policy which was to cause trouble and accusations of racism, most notoriously from Claude McKay). The contents of the final collection are distributed among eight and not four sections, but their subject matter and range is surprisingly close to Cunard's plan, suggesting that her methods were not as chaotic as has been supposed. Her communist sympathies, occasionally revealed in angry editorial comments, give the volume more coherence than has usually been credited.

Nevertheless, in compiling an expansive and generically disparate anthology, Cunard was especially vulnerable to the criticisms which are generally levelled at the anthology as a form. The collation of materials suggests a process of discrimination, claims of representativeness and meritocratic selection, which challenge any reader to discern questionable inclusions and surprising omissions. Whilst she felt the strength of her text to lie in the variety and number of its contributions and contributors, contemporary reviewers were more conventional in their estimation of the anthology. Lord Olivier, in the *New Statesman and Nation*, assumed that absence in the text equalled absence in the world, musing that 'the literary exhibit ... invites speculations as to why the Abantu never produced an Iliad'.[9] Spike Hughes in the *Daily Herald* found the 'section of the book devoted to Negro music and the theatre ... absurdly inadequate'; he railed: 'this sort of thing does nobody any good and is out of all proportion'.[10]

The anthology, published on 15 February 1934, was most widely reviewed in British newspapers; the paper's political slant dictating the position of the notice (those to the left classified its publication as news, those to the centre-left placed it in the books pages, those to the right did not mention it at all). *Negro* does not appear to have been reviewed in any literary journals. The most common response of those who did review it is one which is still voiced by critics today. After perhaps expressing admiration for the volume's size (more than 800 pages), reviewers proceeded to focus upon one area of personal interest or knowledge, find flaws and regard these as reason enough to disregard the rest of the anthology. In her focus upon America and Africa, and exclusion of extracts from writings of contemporary black French writers, Cunard may be regarded as a proponent of exoticism and primitivism. The absence of any literature other than poetry is significant. Although she is careful to include dissenting voices, both black and white, the editor's political sympathies are strongly apparent in the anthology at times. Nonetheless, the book collated a myriad of voices and, whether it is deemed to have succeeded or not, was intended to illustrate the conclusion to Cunard's pamphlet 'Black Man and White Ladyship' that 'there are many truths'.[11]

Anne Chisholm, Cunard's biographer, notes of her subject that 'objectivity never interested her at all'.[12] This lack of neutrality troubled some contemporary readers. Presenting her own views explicitly, led Lord Olivier to voice the opinion that so many others (later including Hugh Ford) shared, that Cunard had somehow adopted a black psychology herself: 'she must ... discipline her sometimes rather characteristically negroid methods of controversy'.[13] Believing her to be thus, not merely partial but 'other', Olivier concludes that Cunard is an unreliable spokesperson, declaring: 'I should discount by at least 33 per cent. any statement she made on her own uncorroborated observation, by 33 per cent. more when it reflected on the virtues of black men – and by 33 per cent. more when it reflected on the vices of white men'.[14] Again, the multiplicity of voices and the diversity of opinions are negated by this focus upon Cunard. Critics in the 1930s were disgusted by the thought of a white woman taking a black lover; critics now accuse her of negrophilia, an emotional and irrational love of black people which would brook no criticism. Whilst some objections may stand, all have served to obliterate *Negro*'s status as an anthology, reducing it to the one voice of its editor, and in so doing, precisely denying its purpose.

Cunard opens her foreword: 'it was necessary to make this book – and I think in this manner, an Anthology of some 150 voices of both races'.[15] She presented the book as a multiracial collaboration which celebrated difference and offered diversity of opinion. She wanted to give a voice and a face to the Negro, whom, as symbolised by the Scottsboro case, she regarded as forced into silence by those within the law and the violence of those apparently outside it. 'The Scottsboro frame-up is more than an attempt to electrocute 9 innocent black Alabamians – it is part of the effort to force into the dumbest and most terrorised form of subjection all Negro workers who dare aspire to live otherwise than as virtual slaves'.[16] Cunard's campaigns to free the Scottsboro boys, incarcerated, repeatedly tried and put on trial again over the three years of the anthology's production, seem to have caused her to sharpen her response to the New Negro movement, which is discussed more fully later, and inspired her decisions about the readership of her anthology. In introducing *Negro*'s contents she stated that 'the chord of oppression, struggle and protest rings, trumpet-like or muffled, but always insistent throughout'.[17] This emphasis on protest rather than the celebration of black achievement as the way to win equality, not only underlines Cunard's sympathy for the communist stance but also indicates a shift in thinking about *Negro*'s audience.

Cunard's circular reveals that the anthology was originally to be titled *Color*. The spelling and dedication 'primarily for the Colored people' seem to indicate that it was largely intended for a black American audience. Primarily, and somewhat patronisingly, she hoped to disseminate black histories and global black experience to black Americans. It seems, however, that as her outrage grew, so did her horizons, with more of the material aimed directly at white Europeans. The title *Negro* not only removes the specificity of an American audience but also signals a more explicit engagement with the trope of the New Negro. As Henry Louis Gates has shown, this term originated during the process of black re-presentation 'in the court of racist public opinion'.[18] Gates considers the trope's development in the early twentieth century by reference to the black anthologies produced during that period. In 1900 Booker T. Washington, Fannie Barrier Williams and N. B. Wood edited *A New Negro for a New Century*. This bulky volume of 428 pages collected black histories, journalism and biographical sketches with the aim of refuting racial stereotypes and presenting black achievement (particularly of black soldiers) as just cause for equal citizenship.

The phrase 'New Negro' was transferred from the political to the artistic arena. Alain Locke's anthology of 1925 took the trope as its title. *The New Negro* originated as a special edition of the *Survey Graphic* journal entitled 'Harlem: Mecca of the New Negro' and is generally regarded as spearheading the movement which became known as the Harlem Renaissance or Negro Renaissance. Locke and the *Survey Graphic* editor Paul Kellogg felt that the thriving cultural activity centred around Harlem offered a 'new approach' to the struggle for equality: 'different from the political approach of Negro rights, lynching, discrimination, and so forth'.[19] Instead of social complaint, therefore, *The New Negro* was largely a celebration of literary talent anthologising the poetry, drama and narrative fiction of authors such as Sterling Brown, Countee Cullen, Langston Hughes, Zora Neale Hurston, James Weldon Johnson and Jean Toomer. Locke has been described as attempting to make the Negro, and not the Negro Problem, known. However, by the 1930s the Harlem Renaissance was widely deemed a failure (although it has been revalued in recent years). Criticisms of the movement were many and varied but can be broadly summarised as relating to the absence of political commitment and the issue of white patronage. Although Locke was no doubt aiming to draw attention away from old stereotypes to previously uncelebrated talents, his literary focus has been criticised, as here by Henry Louis Gates: 'It was *not* the literature of this period that realized a profound contribution to art; rather, it was the black creators of the classic blues and jazz whose creative works ... defined a new era in the history of western music'.[20]

Cunard praised the literary achievements of the 'Negro Renaissance'; she admired Locke's anthology and the subsequent 1929 collection by V. F. Calverton, *Anthology of American Negro Literature*. However, she found the trope 'New Negro' a bourgeois construct far from 'representative of the Negro masses'.[21] For an emotional observer of the tortuously protracted case of the Scottsboro boys, and a communist sympathiser, loudly voiced protest was the only way to induce necessary change. Cunard's anthology, therefore, more closely followed the model of Booker T. Washington's but its blunt title *Negro* aimed to embrace all black social groups. Cunard, admirably and idealistically, desired not reconstitution of the Negro, but reconstitution of society. Perhaps in response to this rejection of the trope of the New Negro, her anthology contains no narrative or dramatic fiction. Instead *Negro* has a sociological bent, with articles in the American section on the experience of racially motivated violence and oppression; the Negro vote; 'The Negro and the Supreme Court'; 'Education and the Negro'; 'The Negro in the Present Appalling Trade Depression'; 'Negro Folklore and Expression', to name a few. Cunard's anthology, like so many subsequent individual testimonies, privileged experience above art; thus for instance including not Zora Neale Hurston's fiction, but her anthropological essays on 'Spirituals and Neo-Spirituals' and 'Characteristics of Negro Expression'. Cunard hoped to explore black culture in its widest sense. The large section on music frames international debate on varieties of black music, printing scores and lyrics to American, Creole, West Indian and African songs as well as celebrating jazz. Although the anthology has a poetry section containing one of Cunard's poems, her narrow definition of poetry in the foreword accords with this material, rather than artistic purpose, of the book:

> There is no laughter in any of the *Poetry* here, for facts have made it, and the reflector of life a poet is supposed to be is, in the case of the coloured poet, doubly sensitive. Perforce he carries the burden of his race, it is mostly his theme. Sterling Brown is the most racial of the poets, his subject and his tone are as fine as a saga. Langston Hughes is the revolutionary voice of liberation.[22]

It was this desire to portray the horrific truths of racial prejudice in America which led to Cunard's argument with W. E. B. DuBois and the National Association for the Advancement of Colored People (NAACP). Cunard violently disagreed with the NAACP's policy of counting as lynchings only those which had been investigated rather than reported, and vigorously attacked this policy in an article which preceded one by DuBois in the anthology. Cunard's vitriol was removed by Hugh Ford from his reprint. In emphasising the widespread nature of the crime of lynching, Cunard was voicing the shock of a white European and hoping to reproduce this horror amongst other Europeans to whom it was less widely known. She was trying to canvas support amongst widely differing readerships: black Americans and white Europeans. In highlighting injustice, however, many have found, and do find, her motives regressive, again leaving her open to charges of being overly reliant on discredited ideas. Her argument with DuBois, meanwhile, provides a stark reason for *Negro*'s failure to find approbation amongst the NAACP even though articles by its members and extracts from its journal *Crisis* were included. The strength of support for the NAACP and DuBois was clearly underestimated by Cunard and was such that the lack of a review in *Crisis* carried more weight than any favour it found with those who did share her views.

Although *Negro* found some support in America, this was rarely expressed in the public arena. In the *Amsterdam News* Henry Lee Moon agreed with Cunard's view of the Scottsboro case as not an 'isolated instance of race terrorization' but a 'link in a whole system of oppression', but greatest praise came from Alain Locke in a letter shortly after publication:

> I congratulate you, – almost enviously, on the finest anthology in every sense of the word ever compiled on the Negro. When I saw the announcements, I feared a scrapbook, but by a miracle of arrangement, you have built up a unity of effect and a subtle accumulative force of enlightenment that is beyond all contradiction and evasion ... The serious analyses of Jazz by Antheil and Goffin are path breaking. You will have endless vindications in the years to come.[23]

Locke was less than prescient in his anticipation of wide praise and a favourable reception for *Negro*. Reading the anthology persuaded him that its scale was not injudicious as he had feared; however, *The New Negro*, his own generically specific collection, reached a far wider audience and achieved a place in the canon of black literature. Despite Locke's private approbation, what Cunard had always perceived as a strength, the scale of the project and diversity of subjects, was to prove a weakness. Moreover, in attempting to appeal to so many audiences – black, white, American, European and communist – Cunard's anthology failed to meet the expectations of any of them and found no group to champion it. I would suggest, however, that by disregarding national boundaries in this way Cunard's anthology shows intimations of a black Atlantic sensibility. Cunard always aspired to the global when fighting for justice and equality. Embarking on a vaguely autobiographical project in later life, she wrote the following note:

> When of SELF writing: Re the 3 main things.
> 1. Equality of races.
> 2. Of sexes.
> 3. Of classes.
> I am in accord with all countries and all individuals who feel, and act as I do on this score.[24]

This note, like her impassioned crusades, underlines the aspiration, if not always the achievement, of Cunard's intent and also the occasional lack of self-awareness which sometimes aroused the disbelief of both collaborators and detractors. As a European and an Internationalist, she tried to respond to the inequity of both black experience and representation by anthologising *Negro*. Her book is not 'the finest anthology ... ever compiled on the Negro' as Locke claimed, but as a response to earlier collections, such as those I have discussed, it deserves careful consideration.

Notes

1. I am extremely grateful to Mary Joannou for introducing me to the works of Nancy Cunard and drawing my attention to the research of those who have already begun to acknowledge her achievements; Jane Marcus is currently writing a book on Cunard, and Janet Montefiore's article about her will appear in *New Left Review*.
2. Jane Marcus, 'Bonding and Bondage: Nancy Cunard and the Making of the *Negro* Anthology', in Mae Henderson (ed.), *Borders, Boundaries and Frames: Cultural Criticism and Cultural Studies* (New York: Routledge, 1994) pp. 33–63.
3. As discussed by Jacqueline Chénieux-Gendron at 'The Harlem Renaissance: Tensions et Stéréotypes', Université François Rabelais, Tours, February 1998.
4. Hugh Ford (ed.), *Negro: An Anthology Collected and Edited by Nancy Cunard* (New York: Frederick Ungar Publishing Co., 1970), p. xi.
5. Ford, *Negro*, p. xii.
6. Ford, *Negro*, p. 252.
7. It is perhaps unfortunate that Ford's version seems to have become more widely available and read than the 1969 facsimile published by the Negro Universities Press.
8. Ford, *Negro*, p. xvii.
9. Lord Olivier, 'Miss Cunard and the Negro', *New Statesman and Nation*, 10 March 1934, pp. 351–2.
10. Spike Hughes, 'Book Shows Up Empire's Masked Slavery', *Daily Herald*, 14 February 1934.
11. Nancy Cunard, 'Black Man and White Ladyship', in Hugh Ford (ed.), *Nancy Cunard: Brave Poet, Indomitable Rebel, 1896–1965* (Philadelphia: Chiltern Book Co., 1968) pp. 103–9.
12. Anne Chisholm, *Nancy Cunard* (London: Sidgwick & Jackson, 1979), p. xii.
13. Olivier, *New Statesman and Nation*, p. 351.
14. Olivier, *New Statesman and Nation*, p. 351.
15. Nancy Cunard, *Negro Anthology Made by Nancy Cunard, 1931–33* (London: Wishart & Co., 1934), p. iii.

16. Cunard, *Negro*, p. iii.
17. Cunard, *Negro*, p. iv.
18. Henry Louis Gates, 'The Trope of a New Negro and the Reconstruction of the Image of the Black', *Representations*, 24, 1988, pp. 129–55.
19. George Hutchinson, *The Harlem Renaissance in Black and White* (Cambridge, MA: The Belknap Press of Harvard University Press, 1995), p. 393.
20. Gates, 'The Trope of a New Negro', p. 148.
21. Cunard, *Negro*, p. 146.
22. Cunard, *Negro*, p. iv.
23. Marcus, 'Bonding and Bondage', p. 56.
24. Chisholm, *Nancy Cunard*, pp. 402–3.

10

Lorca's Mantle: The Rise of Fascism and the Work of Storm Jameson

Sylvia Vance

The impulse that turned so many of us into pamphleteers and amateur politicians was neither mean nor trivial. The evil we were told off [sic] to fight was really evil, the threat to human decency a real threat. I doubt whether any of us believed that books would be burned in England, or eminent English scholars, scientists, writers, forced to beg for hospitality in some other country. Or that, like Lorca, we might be murdered. Or tortured and then killed in concentration camps. But all these things were happening abroad, and intellectuals who refused to protest were in effect blacklegs. In this latest quarrel between Galileo and the Inquisition they were on the side of the Inquisition.[1]

This passage, from Jameson's heralded autobiography *Journey from the North*, is one that could be quoted by those critics interested in exploring the impulse of writers in the 1930s who turned their energies toward the politics of the day or, especially, the decade. The rise of Fascism turned the tide of many writers' political interests and much of the work driven by political impulses has had a profound impact on the development of Modernism. Modernism is still a particularly male domain, formed, among other things, by ideas about war, politics, the fracturing of language and the nature of the individual in his society. The pronoun used here is intentional, as it has become more and more apparent that what women writers were doing, what they were concerned with, was quite different from the men. Virginia Woolf, the allowed great Modernist woman writer, becomes more intriguing as critics avail themselves of the political impulses in her work. We have moved from an aesthetic in Woolf to a denser reading that includes politics and her intense involvement in the commonplaces of her own day.[2] By comparison, critics have tended to focus on Jameson's politics rather than her literary outpourings (she was prolific), for if Woolf is the allowed great woman Modernist of the 1930s, Jameson is the allowed political woman of the same period.[3]

She is that because of her political acuity – she recognised early the threat of Fascism and Nazism and wrote vehemently against them, both in her journalism and her fiction. Although later she disparaged her 1933 novel *No Time Like the Present*, at the time it was published she wrote to Evelyn Sharp asking for a review:

> I am sending you a book written first against war. I thought that I should more or less have to trick people into reading anti-war propaganda, so started the book with autobiographical sections. ... I feel a little ashamed to be asking help for anything I have written, but I feel so desperate about the war danger I would do anything to get myself heard.[4]

This early understanding of the threat of war had become consolidated by the time she became president of PEN in 1938. At the same time, she had solidified her position as a political and critical commentator, particularly confirmed by articles she wrote for *Left Review* and *Fact*.[5] From 1938 to 1944 her activities as president were unceasing and valiant as she attempted to rescue and bring to English shores those intellectuals and writers who were being threatened and persecuted on continental Europe. It was that period she was commenting upon in the quotation at the beginning of this chapter, a quotation from her autobiography, *Journey from the North*.

Her autobiography can contribute greatly to our understanding of the 1930s and is a neglected classic. The impulse to this very large work, which was published in 1969 and 1970, is the 1930s, and Jameson gives an inordinate amount of detail about her political life in that decade. The text, however, was written with hindsight, a hindsight that had to encompass an already formed and accepted construction of the 1930s and the driving political forces of the time. The construction of self in autobiographies written decades after the events in and of themselves deserve study, and Doris Lessing's recently published two volumes could bear that kind of scrutiny. The same way we now understand historical revisionism – that the politics of the present, for example, shape how and which historical events are privileged – could inform the way we understand autobiography. At the same time, attention should be drawn to Jameson's reliability. She was a writer who put her life in her fiction – her Mary Hervey Russell novels are clearly and admittedly autobiographical – but who also fictionalised her life according to her own limitations.[6] Like any one of us writing our own life would be, she was self-serving and duplicitous, and those impulses were complicated by an insecurity about her fiction writing and passionate hatred of confrontation. In a portrait of herself upbraiding a politician in the 1930s, for example, she describes her actions as coming out of a compulsion (she could not *not* confront him) at the same time as feeling utterly defeated and shattered by the notion of having exposed herself and having failed to be persuasive because of that very exposure.

She avoided confrontation to such a degree that she could not tell Vera Brittain that she was no longer a pacifist by 1938, even though they were the closest of friends (close enough after Winifred Holtby died for Brittain to name Jameson custodian of her children if she and Brittain's husband were to die).[7] Brittain writes briefly and bitterly of Jameson in her autobiography; Jameson writes of Brittain not at all. Yet Jameson's anti-war and then pacifist position greatly affected her politics and her fiction. She says she was a pacifist between the wars and was ever after ashamed at what she called her own cowardice for leaving pacifism. Certainly, she had joined the Peace Pledge Union as a sponsor before Brittain and figured on the PPU's letterhead long after she had left. Her anti-war position is clear through the novels of the 1920s and 1930s – *The Happy Highways* of 1920 and *No Victory for the Soldier* of 1938 are clear examples.[8] She also wrote anti-war articles (her series for *Peace News* probably articulated her position best, even in its ambivalence)[9] and her shame at having left pacifism, which caused the final rift with Brittain, was mollified by her clear anti-Fascism and anti-Nazism, the Nazis, as Rose Macaulay so astutely phrased it, making pacifism impossible. Jameson was anti-war in the 1920s and 1930s and that position is clear in her novels, leading to a clear and precise connection of politics to art and a more complex understanding of Jameson's politics and fiction in the 1930s.

Valentine Cunningham has titled his work *British Writers of the Thirties* in spite of the fact that he fends off any question of including women as serious subjects in his study by his statement:

> The neglected sister – why didn't we know more about Shakespeare's sister, Virginia Woolf asked, famously and influentially in *A Room of One's Own* (1928), inspiring numerous recent feminist inquiries – was finding her modern voice in the '20s and '30s,

and her critical and editorial brother was still trying to stifle it …
What mattered was the sisters' new-found audibility. What was
striking was their brothers' deaf ears. We, for our part, now,
cannot rest happy at remaining among those who still do not have
ears to hear. This particular book lacks the space to do full justice
to anything like all of these customarily absented authors.

He continues, 'But at least the gap that commonly denotes their absence
can be defined, they can be granted the mentions and some of the
respect they deserve, and their place can be marked on the '30s map
for future reference.'[10] In eight mentions of her name, no Jameson
novel is cited by title and only once is she mentioned as a novelist,
among many other 'competent' novelists of the period.[11] Storm
Jameson's place in Cunningham's book is as political commentator,
one he considers especially potent in her important 1937 essay 'Documents'. In that essay, she challenges Orwell's notions of living dirty,
and the resulting *Wigan Pier*, as of no significant value, since, 'If he
[the socialist writer] happens to have been born and brought up in
Kensington the chances are that he has never lifted the blind of his
own kitchen at six in the morning, with thoughts in his mind of
tumbled bed-clothes, dirty grates, and the ring of rust on the stove.'
Jameson continues, 'The first thing a socialist writer has to realise is
that there is no value in the emotions, the spiritual writhings, started
in him by the sight, smell, and touch of poverty. The emotions are no
doubt unavoidable. There is no need to record them. Let him go and
pour them down the sink.'[12] What she was emphasising here was the
nature of the socialist writer focusing on his own responses, his own
observations contextualised within an emotionality that lent little
awareness except of the emotional state of the writer. But she was a
socialist writer also concerned with poverty.

The narrative in *A Day Off* (1933) is a lyricism harsh and uncompromising. Nothing in the situation of the main character (only named
'her') is pleasant nor does the narrator give the reader any relief from
the desperateness of 'her' life. In the end, the reader lives through the
grime, dust and constant humiliation that 'her' faces and is complicit
in 'her' moments of despair. The exploration of emotional layers and
the shifts of awareness are extraordinary:

> Men haven't the gumption to marry a woman with my experi-
> ence and go. I daresay they know enough to know that a woman
> like me sees through them – to their mean dirty bones I see.
>   She felt an inexplicable joy and satisfaction – as though for a

moment she had been folded in a familiar clasp. There was a knowledge she had forgotten, a body of which she was a member, a connection not yet broken between her and the grass she pressed, the clouds, big and tumbling, the moist earth. She felt this, but only in her blood, and when the momentary thrill faded she was more than ever aware of her thickened body and the pain of now.

'Oh God,' she said quietly.[13]

Jameson's prose experiment here is accomplished. The reader is inextricably bound to the experience of 'her', forced through the layers of consciousness and recognition while sustaining evaluative moments brought about through shifts in the narrative. This reading can be a considerable demand on the reader, for 'her' is not accomplished nor is she a woman whom Woolf may have explored, that is, any man's educated daughter. She does not even have a language: 'she had no words at hand to describe her state. So far as she was concerned no words for it had ever existed' (p. 156). She is among those women to whom, in principle, we may have politically sympathy, and she is also among those we have all tried to avoid, as Jameson forces the reader to recognise in a scene where 'her' has been sitting in the park, then moves toward a group of young people who are on a picnic,

lurching from the stiffness of her knees and ankles, her hat fallen back, her face red. Just as she reached them she fell. Her toe caught in some unevenness of the ground and down she came, on both knees, with a groan.

One of the girls jumped up to give her a hand. The young man holding the thermos called out: 'I say, bad luck. Have some tea, won't you?'

She was about to thank him and take it when she saw that they were all struggling not to laugh. At once her manner altered.

'Here,' she said aggressively, 'what d'you mean by planting yourselves where people can fall over you? Who d'y'think you are. The Prince of Wales?'

'You didn't fall over us,' one of the young men began.

A girl interrupted. 'Don't take any notice of her.'

She set her arms. 'So – that's *it*, is it?' she said with bitter slowness. 'I'm to be knocked down – a nice business – and then you'll take no notice. You – dressed-up young – monkeys!'

The boy tried quelling her. 'Clear off now,' he said in a loud authoritative voice. She had begun to enjoy the scene, and rocking from side to side she told them what she thought of them. For this she had words enough.

They had turned very red but they ignored her. One of them, altering a knob, increased the volume of organ music until it all but drowned her voice. She raised her voice against it but she was defeated: she had to go. She made a twitching movement with her hands. The sun fell across the back of her neck like a whip and a quiver ran through her. Dropping her head suddenly, she went. (pp. 157–9)

In the same way that Orwell's arguable affinity with the working-class man has remained the assumption on which his work is examined, Jameson's similar assimilation into the consciousness of a working woman should be recognised. This is a poignant scene, played out through a narrative quite different from anything else Jameson attempted. She thought *A Day Off* 'perhaps the only genuinely imaginative book I have written.'[14] More important, though, is Jameson's attempt to explore the questions of gender and what women's dependence on men, both financial and emotional, signals. By presenting an unheroic woman, caught in the machinations of a patriarchal system that she neither recognises, understands nor can articulate, Jameson explores the gulf between the sexes with radical acuity. As 'her' mother cryptically explains it:

> 'If you want to know what I think – I think it's much the same life for a woman whatever she does, she has to eat humble pie. Either to her husband or her children, it's all the same. They do as they like, and she waits on them – mending their clothes, on her knees cleaning after them. Nobody asks her if she wants to go to bed or to get up or to have children … There's bad days and good, and what else? Nothing – if you ask me.' (p. 140)

This portrait of woman as victim is unrelieved in the novel, which is particularly explicit about the fate of women in war. Here, unlike in other novels, Jameson's character has neither an interest in politics nor even in day-to-day political events, war or elections. But they have an impact nevertheless. At twenty-eight, Jameson's 'her' has become Mrs Ernst Groener, working hard in a restaurant owned by her husband. He has a wife in Germany, however, which does not allow him to marry, so the relationship is a tenuous one (whatever Jameson's progressive attitudes, she remains constant about the necessity of marriage providing security for women). When war is imminent, and even when she realises he is 'still a German', 'she quite hoped for war. The consequences, to Ernst and herself, were still outside her grasp'. (p. 111) After he is forced to leave the restaurant, she tries to carry on under the name Green but business cannot recover. She packs everything she can carry and leaves in the middle of a dark night. Later, she reflects:

> To have finished with Mrs Groener like that. It was horrible; it made out that you were nothing – she struck her breast – you, you here, nothing. She felt a deep – not grief exactly – confusion, a dull misery, as though all she did had been useless. You worked, cried, made plans, got up morning after morning in the dark, scrubbed the shelves – but it was nothing, it tailed off. (p. 119)

As 'she' is called Mrs Groener, with an impudent smile by someone she has hired, even when she is clearly English, so is an old woman distrusted during the war, although she has become English through marriage. The difficulties for any woman who does not live most conventionally are delineated in this novel in the most remorseless fashion, until finally 'she' recognises the absolute horror of her situation. She has stolen a handbag from the old woman she befriends in a tea shop and takes it to be pawned. Offered ten shillings, next to nothing, she responds:

> She wanted to tell him what a mean lousy bastard he was but kept it back. The very quietness of his manner frightened her. Something was in, yes in the quietness, some rag of her fears flew out in it; she felt terror. It was nothing actual that she feared; she did not think that he would get her into trouble – or do anything to her. In a way, her fears had nothing to do with Mr Gapalous. She felt that she was flat down, with her face in the dirt, and these safe people were treading on her. It was an animal terror – the fear without mitigation of thought that shows in the eyes of animals, no wordy veil comes between them and the menace of *things* – but the spasm tore her inwardly. It lasted in her only the fraction of a second and then the ordinary sense of resentment and annoyance flowed back. He had done her, mean wretch. She had expected it, and yet hoped for miracles. It's because I'm a woman and I haven't a man behind me protecting me, she thought bitterly. They're all alike, I'll say that for him, they all take advantage of us

– how would they like it, I wonder, if we robbed them right and
left – (pp. 192–3)

Always, the they, the enemy – men – permeate the text, accompanied
by a responsive memory snatch recalled, then lost again, seemingly
Jameson's response to Joyce's Penelope section and Molly Bloom in
Ulysses and to Eliot's *The Waste Land*:

> Oh God it's over and this time last year we were where, in
> Ramsgate, I shan't ever forget it, if I live to be a hundred, the heat
> and the dust and the sea smooth like milk, and then afterwards,
> no I shan't forget. All he said then to me and his look. It was like
> the canal at Staveley when we lay out there, that other, that boy
> he was: I was young too then I didn't know, but I remember the
> water shining and sucking in the darkness and that one lovely
> light, yes lovely. (p. 217)

Finally, at the end of the day, the narrator paints 'her':

> She lies there in the darkness, her mind a meeting-place for every
> kind of event. A multitude of the quick and the dead exist in it.
> It is exquisitely poised to make her laugh, cry, speak, exult, suffer,
> and dream. Exactly as the separate parts of her body are held fast
> in equilibrium until an instant in a not unguessable future.
> Turning on her back, she makes a loud strangled noise as she
> breathes. The pulse in her arm lying on the dirty sheet is one of
> the stages of a mystery. Look once more and you can see how
> beautiful she is.
>   Poor woman, let her sleep. (p. 219)

This poignant ending, which leaves the character's position
unresolved, finishes the lyrical nature of the text so exquisitely sustained by Jameson throughout. It is not only a novel hugely imaginative, as Jameson claimed, but beautifully written. More, the writing
sustains a persistent and consistent discussion about the place of women
and maintains a constant exploration of the issues of gender. In *A Day
Off* Jameson explores the role of woman as victim, her unrecognised
and powerless position in society, and it is a considerable change from
Jameson's earlier novels where, in the novels that are not strictly
autobiographical (which we might call historical), her *Triumph of Time*
trilogy, for example, she has strong women as protagonists. After the
last novel in the *Time* trilogy, published in 1932, these women do not
appear again.

Some of the novels of the 1930s are precursors to Jameson's more well-known *The Black Laurel* (1947) and other novels written after the Second World War. They explore the relationship of victim, and the nature of victimisation, to the rise of Fascism and the increase in the possibility of war. They also explore the nature of Fascism, what it is in men that allows for a belief in Fascism to be constructed, and it is in these works that Jameson extends the necessity of entering as a writer the male-centred text of war.[15] This exploration is particularly prevalent in *In the Second Year*, Jameson's significant speculative novel of 1936. It is a dystopia, narrated by a man, and is singularly outside the rest of Jameson's oeuvre, however much we recognise how wide ranging the works in it are. The first-person male narrative is the first in Jameson's work, after seventeen novels. The narrator is Andrew Hillier, cousin to the prime minister (also a Hillier) and brother to Lotte, who is married to the commandant of the Volunteers – a home force which fought any armed opposition to the present government. The novel is set in the not-so-distant future and accounts for 1930s' political movements, details the reasons for their destruction and relates the futures of familiar writers, politicians and public figures who were alive at the time Jameson was writing the novel. She takes, for example, the fate of a particular novelist, who is arrested then executed. Alternatively, she reports on the dictatorship's appropriation of one of the union movement's strongest leaders and his pathetic diminishment and ineffectiveness as a government spokesman. One of her more poignant reports is about the novelist Sophie Burtt.

Andrew, who was abroad at the time of the revolution, has returned from Norway to England a sceptic. He has heard much negative news about the new regime but does not believe most of what he hears. Jameson uses him as a narrative foil; his continuing education reveals, to his and the reader's increasing horror, the cost of the regime in human terms. Determined to learn more about the regime, he gains entrance, on a visitor's pass, to one of the training camps for those opponents of the government who have not been killed, or those who have only used a careless word. Until Andrew enters the Winchell Training Camp, he has not formed an opinion about the new regime. He trades on that openness when first entering the camp, telling the Commandant, '"I am a professor, and I am eager to have a sight of your methods of dealing with anti-social elements."'[16] He is then shown the camp by a man he presumes to be sixty years of age, 'becoming numbed by the discomfort and naked misery of the huts, each alike with its rows of sleeping bunks and the bench and table between'. (p. 59)

Realising that he has met the man before, a well-known journalist, who is not much more than forty, Andrew persuades him to reveal more about the camp, especially the rumoured floggings:

> [Holman] 'You mean, is it true that we are flogged regularly? It is true.'
>
> He spoke in a quiet soothing voice. I felt the wooden frame of the door under my hand. 'Why are you flogged? When?'
>
> 'When we break a rule,' Holman said. 'There are a great many rules, more, many more than there were in the army. I was in the army as a boy, did you know? I enlisted in the last year of the last war, when I was sixteen. I gave my age as eighteen, of course.'
>
> 'What rules? Don't be so correct,' I mumbled. I felt unfitted to play his game with him.
>
> 'Disobedience. That is, not running quickly enough when called, forgetting to salute, slackness in drill, persistent untidiness, that is folding blankets the wrong way. And of course any serious offence, answering back, trying to send unauthorised letters out of the camp, deliberate refusal of duty ...' (p. 61)

Stunned by this information, Andrew is then staggered to find that Sophie Burtt, a writer who has been reported by *The Times* to have gone abroad, is in the camp. Worse, she is the only woman to have been flogged (for insolence to the camp commandant), after which she lost her reason and now only sings. Andrew hears 'a thin voice, I thought it was a child's and my heart turned only to think of a child in there' but it is Sophie Burtt singing her only song:

> *Me farver was the skin of a Spanish onion*
> *And so was Ma*
> *So there you are.* (pp. 62–3)

There are more revelations, each in its way a condemnation of Andrew's willing ignorance, until he says to himself 'I was sunk'. (p. 64) 'I thought I should remember all that was said,' he remarks. 'But I don't. There was a middle-aged writer, another novelist, and he was the only man without any hope. I should have been like that man'. (p. 65) In a sense he is like that man already, as when he leaves the camp, 'I felt anger and despair. All the fears of my childhood rushed through me in a dark flood. I fell on the moor and passed the night there, with my face on the ground'. (p. 71) And when he leaves the camp, he remains unchanged.

In part, the Andrew unchanged suits the novelist's technique; the more unchanged the character, the more suitable he is as a foil. But on another, more significant level, an unchanged Andrew presents the powerlessness of the liberal in the face of Fascism. Andrew acknowledges that he is 'a liberal, a mule, as Pollock would say, an animal without hope of posterity'. (p. 68) With that liberal disengagement with the future, he feels dismay at the men in the camp still arguing about the past, about whose fault it is for the state of the country (the most damned is the Labour Party, who could not drive 'their socialist cart and plough in an emergency' p. 661), and he can listen openly to the story of one of the men's heroes, Tom Lloyd, a Labour leader of the Welsh miners, who at the beginning of the government takeover moved from village to village in Wales, calling out the men to fight (they came out 'to one man' p. 691). Then, Holman tells the story of how Tom Lloyd

> And five hundred men were forced back into one of those valleys of dead bones over the mines, and how the Government offered all except Tom a free pardon if they came in before noon the next day, and how five only went down and were received in silence by the Volunteers and one of the five drowned himself afterwards when even his wife would have nothing to do with him. And how the others were bombed out of their place, ... (p. 69)

As a liberal without hope of a future, he can only be caught up in events, cannot have an impact on them. Events are controlled by those with an eye to and the goal of achieving posterity, the Fascists.

What Jameson is so successful at portraying is the psychic condition necessary to produce the Fascist mind-set. It is a condition possible in every man, as she demonstrates by giving us the childhoods of the two main characters, Richard Sacker and Frank Hillier. At the same time, the visionary notion elaborated on in *In the Second Year* attempts to elucidate the progressive nature of the Fascist psyche, giving us an almost sympathetic Hillier at the beginning of the novel who exists to do the best for his country to a Hillier near the end of the novel who believes himself to *be* his country. In a sense, Jameson portrays the notions of service and sacrifice as inherently corrupt and those notions themselves as the seeds of Fascism:

> 'One thing is greater than I am,' he said, 'that is the State. My individual life is nothing – if the only way to save the State were for me to lay down my life I would lay it down gladly. It may come to that yet, to one dying that others may live. But while I

live all men must be loyal to me, and to the historic task we have undertaken, to restore England to its greatness, and how can England be great and sound at heart until its heart is sound? And how is that heart sound when the blood shaking it is not sound, and what is that blood if it is not credit, the country's credit? We must cleanse the blood, we must wash the bones and the veins, we must rebuild the credit. The heart of the State is an economic heart.' (pp. 256–8)

Finally, Andrew watches 'the saviour of his country emerge from him [Hillier] and take full possession':

'I tell you that death means nothing to me. I shall go on living, I shall escape all sorts of deaths, because my work is not yet done. I can't die and I can't fail. My work is not finished until every man in the country has work, bread, and security. Work, bread, and security for the labourer, security and opportunities for the educated, security and profits for the employer of labour. So I shall not die. Whoever dies, England must not die!'

He held his arms out and said 'England!' very softly, and then with a yell – 'England!' (p. 259)

In the Second Year marks a change in Jameson's work. Alec Brown, in his 1936 review, claims that her portrait of Sacker is crafted, first, with Jameson's usual

Succinctness and ordinary realism; this is the former Storm Jameson, and the craftsman's tool is, if any different, keener than before. But the third paragraph goes into the man's mind and produces another succinct picture which not only concretizes his mood and his life, but also concretizes, symbolizes, the essential detachment of the fascist leader from the mass of people whom he has pretended, to them and perhaps even to himself, to lead.[17]

Brown focuses appropriately on the delineation of the nature of the Fascist leader that Jameson explores but attempts to counter complaints about the negative nature of the novel falling short of convincing, as he says the novel is not a 'prophecy, *but a warning to liberals*'. Continuing his evaluation, he responds to the 'snarls, shrieks, judicious shakings of the head, and a good deal of stammering' from the Right and the 'profound whispers' about the novel from the Left'.[18] *The Times*, for example, had condemned it for its anti-German position (there is no mention of the novel's anti-*Times* sentiment). To contradict him from the text is unnecessary, as Jameson had earlier published an excerpt of the novel under the title 'Circa 1942, Scenes from a New Novel.'[19] Clearly, she did mean the novel to be a prophecy. Brown's occasionally insightful comments become limited by his final analysis of Jameson as having discovered 'socialist realism', for what Jameson has discovered is a way of writing about Fascism that has nothing to do with the Soviet School.

Until *In the Second Year*, she had written semi-autobiographical texts or those almost exclusively engaged with women. Her protagonists were women and were, generally, women in positions of power. Her three major trilogies centred on women of status and concentrated on a form of historic-domestic novel with women as decision-makers and managers of their own, and others', lives. Even one of her most romantic novels, *The Single Heart* (1932), which has a central character literally dying of love (or of the effort required to sustain that love), has that character organising, supporting and being the major power in the lives of the men in her life. It has its anti-war moments, even in the midst of a love story, as the narrator comments on the trip of a couple to America to

> Persuade Americans to enlist their ideals more directly in the cause of civilisation – as expressed in the tears of the women, the sighs of the children condemned by the Allied blockade, and the growing piles of torn male flesh, severed limbs, and entrails hanging down like bunches of unwashed tripe in a butcher's shop.[20]

When she wrote *A Day Off*, however, it was with the recognition that women had lost, maybe had never had power, even on the domestic front. From that publication, Jameson published novel after novel that was concerned with men in positions of power, the nature of Fascism and the resulting chaos for women's lives. Her Spanish Civil War novel *No Victory for the Soldier* not only had a male protagonist, but was written under a male pseudonym, James Hill.

The issues surrounding the ways we receive Jameson's texts that lend a reading to them guided by the influence of the rise of Fascism demonstrate that she is more than a commentator on the 1930s and more than a competent novelist. She is trenchant and perceptive, writing both in the 1930s and about the 1930s at a later date in an extraordinary range of novels from the Modernist to the sweeping historical to the dystopic. Her work can be studied because of its interesting structure, lyricism and experimentation. It also needs to be studied because it was produced by one of the most involved and intriguing activists of the day. That activism informs her work with an unmatched political acuity and can reflect on our understanding of both historical and literary events of the period. At this time, of the fifty-four books she wrote in her lifetime, there is only one of her books in print (in hardback at £35): *The Writer's Situation and Other Essays*. At the end of her autobiography, Jameson wrote: 'The absence of my name from critical summaries is not wholly deserved'.[21]

Notes

1. Storm Jameson, *Autobiography of Storm Jameson: Journey from the North*, 2 vols (London: Collins and Harvill Press, 1969–70), pp. 293–4.
2. See, for example, Gillian Beer's *Virginia Woolf: The Common Ground* (Edinburgh: Edinburgh University Press, 1996), earlier work by Jane Marcus, especially *Virginia Woolf and the Languages of the Patriarchy* (Bloomington: Indiana University Press, 1987) and Mark Hussey (ed.), *Virginia Woolf and War: Fiction, Reality and Myth* (New York: Syracuse University Press, 1991).
3. See Joanna Labon, 'Tracing Storm Jameson', for a tracking of some of Jameson's political involvement (*Women: A Cultural Review*, vol. 8, no. 1, Spring 1977, pp. 33–47). A recovery of the extent of Jameson's political activities is a necessary antidote to Virago's introductory notes to its reprints of some of Jameson's novels in the 1980s, where, for example, Elaine Feinstein mistakenly claims that Jameson 'joined no [political] party' ('Introduction' to Storm Jameson, *Company Parade* (London: Virago, 1982), p. xii).
4. Storm Jameson to Evelyn Sharp, 8 April 1933, Letter 52 (Letters to Evelyn Sharp 1933– 1945, Bodleian Library, Oxford, in Ms. Eng. Lett. D. 278).
5. She was a regular contributor to both periodicals on social, political and economic issues. A sophisticated understanding of economics and her commitment to socialism informs, for example, her review of *This Final Crisis* by Allen Hunt (see 'Crisis', *Left Review*, vol. 2, no. 4, January 1936, pp. 156–9). See also 'To a Labour Party Official', *Left Review*, vol. 1, no. 2, November 1934, pp. 29–34, where she catalogues her long relationship with the party, and 'Socialists Born and Made', *Fact*, May 1937, pp. 87–90.
6. The trilogy consists of *Company Parade* (1934), *Love in Winter* (1935), and *None Turn Back* (1936).
7. For one version of Brittain and Jameson's falling out, see Paul Berry and Mark Bostridge, *Vera Brittain: A Life* (London: Chatto and Windus, 1995). I must thank Mark Bostridge for meeting with me to discuss Brittain and Jameson's relationship and for sending me information about Jameson that was not included in the Brittain biography.
8. In *No Victory for the Soldier*, written under the pseudonym of James Hill, Jameson portrays the impulses of John Knox, a concert pianist and composer, that force him to volunteer as an ambulance driver in the Spanish Civil War. When a friend asks why he is doing it he says he is not volunteering 'for the Spanish Government's sake' but for 'a new experience', continuing, 'I want to act in a different kind of way' (London: Collins, 1938), p. 292. For a similar perspective by a woman writer on why men volunteered for the Spanish Civil War (that is, one uninformed by a political understanding), see Rose Macaulay, *And No Man's Wit* (1940). *No Victory for the Soldier* is important not only as a male-centred text but because it is Jameson's 'effort at a portrait of the Thirties' written during the 1930s (*Journey from the North*, vol. 1, p. 408).
9. See, for example, 'Storm Jameson's Message to the World's Writers', *Peace News*, 13 October 1939. She was a pacifist of greater conviction earlier in the decade, in 'Women's Work for Peace', *Modern Woman*, January 1935, pp. 7–8.
10. Valentine Cunningham, *British Writers of the Thirties* (Oxford and New York: Oxford University Press, 1988), pp. 26–7.
11. There has been very little critical work done on Jameson and what there is does not always address the complexity and variety of her work. Douglas Robillard, in his very slight article that focuses only on the later works of Jameson, states, 'In a time that has included much

literary experimentation, she has not been an experimenter. Her novels are conservative in their structure, shapely, well-expressed, careful to stay within their limits' ('Storm Jameson as Novelist and Critic', *Essays in Arts and Science*, vol. 17, May 1981, pp. 63–4). This statement is not true of her work in the 1920s, 1930s and 1940s. *A Day Off* is clearly experimental, as is the structure of *The Single Heart*, which has a first chapter of sixty-one pages and a last of nine. She also experimented with form in the 'Unreal City' chapter in *None Turn Back* (1936).

12. Cunningham, *British Writers of the Thirties*, p. 244.

13. Storm Jameson, *A Day Off* (London: Ivor Nicholson, 1933), pp. 150–51. All further references are to this edition and page numbers are given in the body of the text.

14. Jameson, *Journey from the North*, vol. 1, p. 285.

15. Only in the 1930s, for example, does Jameson publish under male pseudonyms: James Hill for *Loving Memory* (1937) and *No Victory for the Soldier* (1938) and William Lamb for *The World Ends* (1937). Similarly, Katharine Burdekin published five novels in the years 1922 to 1930 and three under the male pseudonym Murray Constantine in the 1930s, the most famous being her dystopia *Swastika Night*. Other women writers were also writing dystopian novels that engaged the possibility of a future England ruled by Fascists. See, for example, Naomi Mitchison's *We Have Been Warned* (1935) and Aelfida Tillyard's *The Approaching Storm* (1932). In contrast is the woman dictator in Elise Kay Gresswell's utopia *When Yvonne Was Dictator*, who rules successfully through a Charter that 'merely gave to women that which men had and would not relinquish – their human selves apart from being male' (London: John Heritage, 1935), p. 304.

16. Storm Jameson, *In the Second Year* (London: Cassell, 1936), p. 58. All further references are to this edition and page numbers are given in the body of the text.

17. Alec Brown, 'It needn't happen here,' *Left Review*, vol. 2, no. 6, March 1936, p. 281.

18. Brown, *Left Review*, p. 280. Actually, the reviews were not nearly so negative as he implies.

19. Storm Jameson, 'Circa 1942, Scenes from a New Novel', *Left Review*, vol. 2, no. 4, January 1936, pp. 148–54.

20. Storm Jameson, *The Single Heart* (London: Ernest Benn, 1932), pp. 76–7.

21. Jameson, *Journey from the North*, vol. 2, p. 373.

11

Naomi Mitchison's Historical Fiction

Elizabeth Maslen

The Thirties is a fascinating period in which to explore the decisions of many women writers about how they should write their fiction, given that they wish their novels to express various kinds of political commitment. Many take decisions which support critical claims for the mutual dependency of realism and modernism both in the visual arts and in literature: Virginia Woolf in *The Years*, for instance, or Sylvia Townsend Warner in *After the Death of Don Juan*. Valentine Cunningham, in a recent article, attacks the idea that, during the Thirties, modernism lost out to a realism favoured by writers of the left, and argues persuasively for the value of 'changing the model' when one mode of writing no longer answers the requirements of contemporary writers. He also pours scorn on those critics whose judgment is based

> On a very usual set of judgements about literary value, prejudgements or prejudices no less, heavily reliant on the very traditional assumption that overt political propaganda, in fact instrumentality of any kind, let alone sentimental disposition of materials, and simplicity of address to readers, will axiomatically mark a poet or poem down. According to these views, temporal or worldly interests and commitments automatically make a work of less importance than more formalist, or more language-centred, or (save the mark) more 'eternal-verity' writings – even if the 'eternal-verities' in question are, in the end, just as ideologically skewed as the propagandistic dispositions which are being disallowed.[1]

And women writers of the Thirties who were intent on exploring the various political issues of their day certainly do not adopt a mode of writing which is already in existence, either realist or modernist, without 'changing the model', if what they wish to say requires such changes. Realism in the hands of women in the Thirties, who wished to use their fiction as something more than a vehicle for entertainment, is by no means a vehicle for cultural conservatism or a surrender to patriarchal modes of writing. It is reshaped and adapted, sometimes borrowing techniques from modernism, always probing for satisfactory ways of conveying commitment to ideas.

For these writers also have another problem: how to get their readers to engage with the issues of the age. Both Alison Light and Gill Plain have shown how important it is to acknowledge that conservatism and radicalism exist side by side in any age, and that both will be reflected in the works of writers.[2] What is more, both will be reflected in works by the same writer, since each writer has to contend with what is frequently a fascinating blend of conservatism and radicalism within each reader. Fiction, with its ostensible priority of 'entertainment', deploying realism with its emphasis on a strong story line and character placed in a well-drawn, recognisable setting, makes up an ideal vehicle for persuading a reader to engage with radical ideas, while sustained by a cushion of conservatism. If the writer is going to deal with contentious issues, there is a need to get past censorship, not only the official censorship of Thirties' society, but also personal and consensus censorship which a reader may have absorbed from the political, cultural and moral climate of the times.

As a response to these problems, many of the women writers of the Thirties resorted to a kind of writing which supplied entertainment on one level, the story level, for those who merely sought entertainment, but also offered signals (by epigraphs, for instance) that the story cover could be penetrated by readers who shared the writer's political concerns, and could then be read at another, subversive or polemic level. This method of communicating ideas was termed Aesopian language by writers under the Russian Empire and Soviet Union to get past the strict censorship of the State, so that:

> By innocent-seeming tales of other lands or times, by complicated parables, animal fables, double meanings, overtones, by investing apparently trivial events with the pent-up energies of the writer ... the reader [is] compelled to dwell on them until their hidden meanings bec[o]me manifest.[3]

Of course, it is easy to understand why the politically committed may see the use of Aesopian language as less than honest; it was certainly condemned by many such in Russia up to the time of Lenin. But writing openly about sensitive issues of the present moment could be a risky business, not only under the Tsars and Communist regime in Russia, but in Thirties Britain, as Naomi Mitchison was to find out. Fiction arguably reaches a much wider audience than non-fiction and so is a useful vehicle in which to test ideas. But when a large percentage of the readership which is in the habit of patronising fiction has no wish to engage with controversial or disturbing issues, the writer faces severe problems. This was as true for novelists as for writers offering stories to magazines; so it is instructive to read the advice given by the Anglo-American Manuscript Service to those writing for periodicals, which Q. D. Leavis quotes tellingly, and which, she maintains, was as relevant for the British market as for the American:

> Avoid *morbidity*. The Americans don't want *gloom*, but something that will brighten life. The sun must always be shining. Treat *sex* reverently, and avoid its unsavoury aspects. Don't be *vulgar*. Remember that serious thought is not looked for in the majority of American magazines. Don't discuss *religious* questions in a manner that would offend national sentiment ... *Religion* that brings out its boons and its blessings to long-suffering humanity is deemed praiseworthy. Leave *social* and *political* problems to take care of themselves.[4]

A discouraging list for the politically committed writer to confront, if she wishes to reach out to a wider audience. But if she takes advantage of Aesopian language, and places her work in the past or the future, it seems that more can be made acceptable to the conservative reader. Thus we find many of the women novelists of the decade, when they want to address some aspect of the contemporary crises, turning to the historical or futurist novel. Sylvia Townsend Warner, Katharine Burdekin, Susan Ertz and Edith Pargeter are striking examples of writers who turned in these directions in some or all of their work.[5]

Naomi Mitchison also figures among these writers, and she is interesting for a number of reasons. A consideration of her work in the Thirties highlights dilemmas facing the writer who wants to engage with issues of her time: the style in which she writes, as well as her priorities in relation to content are well worth examining in some detail – not to mention what happens when she abandons writing novels based in the far past for those in a contemporary setting. I am going to concentrate on three works: *Corn King and Spring Queen*, published in 1931; *We Have Been Warned*, published in 1935; and *The Blood of the Martyrs*, published in 1939.[6]

As for style, it is easy to underestimate Mitchison when one reads her work for the first time, as she opts for a very accessible idiom. This is not in line with the 'highbrow' novelist of the day, nor even the 'middlebrow' (to pick up on Queenie Leavis's undefined categorisation, which none-the-less throws light on the intellectual's approach at the time she wrote her *Fiction and the Reading Public*). Mitchison's style meets many of the criteria for 'lowbrow' writing – it sets us little challenge for the most part, though this is clearly a matter of choice; she is perfectly capable of fine writing, as she demonstrates in many descriptive passages. But in the bulk of her fiction, it is as if she aims to reinvent for adults the storytelling mode found more commonly in children's literature, offering the illusion of an oral tradition. This in itself should give us pause, as Mitchison is from the intellectual Haldane family and is highly cultured. Yet since, by the inter-war years, she has become increasingly 'left' in sympathy (though very idiosyncratically so), should we be surprised that she adopts the accessible language of the 'lowbrow', when she wants to reach a wide audience? The magazines that were sensitive to their potential markets, as Q. D. Leavis shows, know what to ask from their writers both in content and style, and the literary style of the 'highbrow' and 'middlebrow' writings ring true only to a limited audience for, as Deborah Cameron points out,

> Whenever some aspect of a language is codified and standardised, the standard is invariably based on the usage of an élite class. Their norms are universalised, while others are stigmatised. What we now know as 'standard English' is the historical reflex of the variety spoken by the London-based court and mercantile class in early modern England.[7]

What we find in Mitchison is a keen awareness of an audience beyond her own class, a keen ear for idiom, and a refusal to 'write down' to any section of that audience. When writing a historical novel, she does not indulge in false archaising of the language, either in dialogue or in the body of the narrative. In the opening lines of *Corn King and Spring Queen*, for instance, the young girl, Erif Der, is presented as our contemporary by Mitchison's use of language. And only gradually do a casual reference to magic and a description of clothes which would appear to be foreign rather than those worn at the time of writing lure us into a setting which is 250 years BC. But the first few paragraphs reassure the reader that this girl is familiar, reacts like the reader's contemporary and is not inaccessible.

However, *Corn King and Spring Queen* is not a simple narrative; in it we find a number of different societies interacting. A democratic movement replaces conservative capitalist tyranny in Sparta for a time; a decadent autocracy rules a population which keeps its links with the world of nature in Egypt; and then there is Erif Der's tribal society in Marob, where fertility rituals rule and magic is practised. This last kind of society, painted with all the fervour of primitivism, is very dear to Mitchison, tending quite often to override her commitment to conventional socialist issues, even while she is honest enough to show her vision of such a society as very far from perfect. Indeed, she shows it as both conservative in its commitment to the cycle of the seasons, and adopting what it sees as the best from the Stoicism and Epicureanism of Hellas: a kind of protosocialism with green roots, one might say. The novel as a whole is full of explorations of sex and sexuality (rape and homosexuality are frankly discussed), as well as very astute probing of the practice and repercussions of the various political stances in the different countries Erif Der and her kinsmen visit. Mitchison's knowledge and understanding of both Stoicism and Epicureanism, the former looking beyond the surface of things in its pursuit of the good, the latter stressing the importance of personal happiness, undoubtedly are impressive. Yet while she can offer characters who reach eagerly and unashamedly for their ideals, she shows the drawbacks of such a pursuit as well as the beauty. Her 'barbarians' from Marob in the end are more astute about the survival of their society than the more sophisticated societies they encounter, more committed to evolution than to revolution, not losing their faith in their traditional links with the cycles of nature, even in the face of apparently more successful political and social systems.

It is interesting to speculate that Mitchison's post-World War Two bonding with Africa is foreshadowed here in her distrust of purely rationalistic world views. There is much in Mitchison's depiction of Marob which links to the passage in Ngugi wa Thiong'o's *Petals of Blood*, where a teacher educated in European methods rebukes a pupil for seeing the colour of petals as 'blood', telling him he must call them 'red', thus destroying for the child his uninhibited assertion of his bond with the plant and, through it, with the world which he inhabits.[8] It would seem that Mitchison's argument in *Corn King and Spring Queen* very clearly reveals a danger within her own society of losing touch with roots, and what happens in her story also warns against the aridity of self-interest which is rationalised in the capitalist ethic; but the reader who has no wish to confront such issues as part of their own world can relax in a reading which remains firmly rooted in 250 BC.

With the success of *Corn King and Spring Queen*, Mitchison made a fateful decision: to tackle contemporary history in a contemporary setting in her next novel, *We Have Been Warned*. This work fails to satisfy for a number of reasons, but its failure is in itself illuminating and repays analysis, as it highlights the politically committed novelist's dilemma. For instance, it is intriguing to see Mitchison grappling with the problem of how to lead us in to her novel. There are the epigraphs she chooses for each section of her book, drawn from a telling range of poets (for example, W. H. Auden, Charles Madge, G. D. H. Cole and Stephen Spender). Then, the first two chapters show her far from unaware of alternatives to conventional realism: she moves easily from the self-reflexive reading of just such a historical tale as she is writing herself to a fluent handling of stream-of-consciousness, echoing but not overstating shifts in idiom as English and Scottish partners dance at a Highland party. The book opens with the protagonist, Dione, looking at her own thumb on the margin of the book she is reading, and then dipping into the narrative of the witch Green Jean, while never abandoning the reader bent over the book. But the characters of Jean's story degenerate into whimsy as they keep invading the realist world of the rest of the novel, always at critical moments. And while their intrusions are apparently meant to signal the many centuries of unchanging hostility to those, like Dione, who explore the boundaries of what society will tolerate, unfortunately Dione's world, the early Thirties' world, cannot accommodate the slippage between actuality and intrusions from imaginary, fabular layers of consciousness which worked so well in *Corn King and Spring Queen*.

Whereas the Marob Spring Queen in the earlier novel lived in a world readers accepted, and whereas her magic (a kind of manipulation of the psyche) is acknowledged as not so effective within the political climate of Sparta, in this next novel Mitchison seems to have lost her sense of an artistic decorum which limits what modes of expression can sit comfortably with each other. Whimsy in the form of elephants and illusory tractors is merely embarrassing when it intrudes on earnest debate about what socialism stands for – it does not make the debate more acceptable to the reader. And when Mitchison introduces other elements from her historical novels, such as a political murder which is condoned, a rape which is forgiven, free love within an 'open' marriage, and vivid descriptions and debate about abortion, what worked in historical fiction proves too much for her publishers. All such issues were part of the dynamic of *Corn King and Spring Queen*, but

Mitchison's publishers, Jonathan Cape, took fright at their intrusion into a very realistic portrayal of a Labour campaign and its aftermath, and refused to publish. It was true that such issues as free love and abortion were indeed debated by the fringe intelligentsia of the Labour movement. But to introduce them into the conversation (and actions) of a Labour party candidate and his wife, as they wrestle with the problems of their constituency, and with their reactions as visitors to the Soviet Union, was to introduce too many conflicts of interest, too many things which would not get past consensus and personal censorship, too many things which Mitchison's usual readership would find hard to swallow, quite apart from the aesthetic problems which the novel posed for the reader.

Eventually another publisher, Constable, took the book on. It is interesting that, during the previous year, this firm published Jean Rhys's novel, *Voyage in the Dark*. This work also engages with love outside marriage and with abortion – and indeed with two clashing worlds, one the society in which Rhys's protagonist, Anna, lives, one the Caribbean world she keeps within her head. But the comparison of these two novels shows only too clearly why one satisfies and the other does not. Certainly, the publication of these two books shows Constable willing to run the gauntlet of consensus and personal censorship, but the worlds of these works are poles apart, in both style and content. Rhys's protagonist, Anna, is a young girl without roots in this country, driven by poverty towards sex and abortion. Mitchison's protagonist has the luxury of options: she decides free love is acceptable and can choose whether to have an abortion or not. Social status makes all the difference. But as Mitchison's novel also deals centrally with party politics and was, moreover, dedicated to a large number of left-wing friends, some very well known, Constable insisted on a disclaimer to be printed at the front of the novel, which, for all its defiant tone, reveals a great deal about what a readership of the day could be expected to accept:

> In deference to the intensive criticism which this historical novel about my own times has already received, I wish to state most earnestly that the views on socialism and in general on social morality expressed by the main characters in the story do not represent either the official Labour Party attitude nor the views of any Left-wing or 'intelligentsia' group. Nor do they, to the best of my knowledge, represent the views of any person in the dedication of this book ... May I add that the final chapters of

the book were written before the events of summer 1933 in Germany, and before the counter-revolution of 1934 in Austria and Spain.

But the novel, despite some very pertinent debates and memorable moments, was in many ways disastrous for Mitchison, as she never quite regained the popularity she had formerly enjoyed through her sure touch for a historical fiction which could both be true to its own time and illuminate issues of the reader's own time. What I find interesting are the reasons why a writer with so sure a sense of how to present issues in her earlier works loses her judgment so drastically when writing fiction about her own society. All sorts of gremlins emerge once she moves into the Thirties, one of them being class. Dione's upper-class ambivalence about her husband's working-class constituency is even more disturbing than Orwell's ambivalence in *The Road to Wigan Pier*, precisely because it appears to reveal what an upper-class candidate's wife might be feeling even while she worked beside him. And the confusion generated by the condonement of a political murder – Dione helps the communist perpetrator to escape to Russia – shows where Dione's priorities are: he is a member of her own Scottish clan, the MacLeans. Tribalism wins over democracy, and while this may reflect the way many react in an emergency, the incident cannot but jar in a novel supposedly showing the importance of democratic socialism. As one emerges from the novel, one can only reflect on how much better Sylvia Townsend Warner succeeds when dealing with politics through history or legend; and Winifred Holtby in *South Riding* is more successful, using conventional realism to trace her schoolmistress protagonist's path through a local Yorkshire community, letting the politics form part of a rich backdrop which the author knows well and has been part of. Storm Jameson, too, deals with the contemporary scene more effectively, using as she does many of the literary journalist's strategies which Orwell adopts. Mitchison, in her urge to engage her reader's interest by strategies of entertainment, fails to produce a work which gives the bulk of her contemporary audience a sense of a true reflection of their own day – she introduces too many fringe issues and sticks them centre stage. Sex and politics, then as now, produced too volatile a combination to be served to a wide readership without the reassurance of historical distance.

Mitchison does not make the same mistake again. The book she publishes a year after *We Have Been Warned* is a collection of stories, poems and drama, in which she successfully demonstrates an impressive ability to alter her style according to the effect she is aiming for. In this collection, *The Fourth Pig*, this versatility is used with tact, matching the wide range of subject matter.[9] Many of the stories in this collection rewrite fairy stories, turning them into vehicles for political, sexual or broadly psychological themes. Some follow the general rules of standard English; but others experiment with idioms which Q. D. Leavis would call lowbrow, anticipating the sorts of experimentation that Alan Sillitoe and Sam Selvon would develop in their very different ways so successfully after World War Two so as to give a voice to sections of society not represented by standard English. In 'The Snow Maiden', for instance, Mitchison adapts the traditional legend, bringing the maiden literally down to earth (where she can be hidden from the jealous sun god) and telling her story in a chatty, 'over-the-garden-wall' style which gradually reveals the stultifying effect of marriage on a bright young girl, full of potential ('Clever she was, too, and most of all with what's not common in a girl, and that's mathematics' (p. 65); but after the marriage 'she just seemed to melt away, to fade right out somehow. Like an ice-cream sundae on a hot afternoon'. (p. 79)) So, neatly, Mitchison makes a comment on a certain kind of sun god who operates well beyond the controlling force of class privilege.

Her next novel, published at the end of the decade, *Blood of the Martyrs* (1939), returns to the past, to the persecution of the Christians under Nero, and uses this subject matter to explore a world increasingly threatened by Fascism and Nazism. This is a serious book with a serious subtext. As Mitchison says in her dedication:

> Books are never written only and entirely by their authors. There are always others who have helped to shape them. It will be obvious that this book could not have been written, or, with the same plot, would have been written very differently, a few years ago.

She goes on to name a number of dedicatees and then continues:

> And beyond and behind these known and certain and consciously collaborating individuals, there are other men and women whose names I may not even know; but my thoughts and imagination fashions and chooses and eliminates because of our mutual participation in events. There are Austrian socialists in the counter-revolution of 1934, share-croppers in Arkansas in 1935, ... and the named and unnamed host of witnesses against tyranny and superstition and the worship of the State, witnesses for humanity and reason and kindliness, whose blood is crying to us now and

whose martyrdom will help to build the Kingdom which we all want in our hearts ...

As before, Mitchison uses religion to show the common roots of spiritual and ideological ideals: the land of Marob knows no distinction between the material and the spiritual, while the sections in *We Have Been Warned* carry titles drawn from Bunyan's *The Pilgrim's Progress*. *The Blood of the Martyrs* explores the seeds of a socialism which bind together the dispossessed in Nero's Rome: slaves and poor freemen form the grass roots of the movement through their Christian meeting groups. Their Christianity has no concern with an afterlife, but is more of an ideology; its ideal state is envisaged as here on earth, and indeed Paul of Tarsus is brought into the story to be reprimanded for complicating the picture by his references to an afterlife. The novel is also very conscious of the ever-growing threat of war – Nero is clearly a Hitler figure, his persecutions of the Christians and the reasons given echoing Nazi rationalisations of their persecution of Jews. And it also engages through Flavia, the spoilt daughter of a senator, with the debate of where to assign the main blame for Fascism, a debate which had been powerfully developing throughout the decade. The blame was most commonly assigned to men – but Katharine Burdekin[10] and Stevie Smith,[11] for instance, show women as quite capable of Fascist behaviour. Then, on the brink of World War Two, Amabel Williams-Ellis's novel *Learn to Love First* portrays a woman, blinkered by self-interest, condoning Fascism;[12] while the book written by 'Cato' (Michael Foot and friends), *Guilty Men*, published in 1940,[13] was quickly followed by Richard Baxter's *Guilty Women* in 1941.[14] Mitchison does not go so far as this, but she does show the greed and decadence of over-indulgent women as very ready to espouse the Fascist side for purely selfish motives.

Mitchison's novel may be compared with Edith Pargeter's *Hortensius Friend of Nero*, published three years earlier. Mitchison's is a far bleaker tale, her Christian slaves and freedmen constantly discussing the value of brotherhood and non-violence as they live under the ever-present threat of persecution: they stand very clearly for the Jews and other victims of the Nazi regime, while Nero, the second-rate artist and volatile tyrant, mirrors Hitler. As two of the senators, Stoics who disapprove of Nero and his ruthless henchman Tegellinus, agree:

> If the authorities round up a few hundred Christians, put them through a solemn trial and find them guilty, then they'll get all the curses, and Nero will only have to appear on his balcony in

uniform to have all Rome lining up below and shouting Hail!
(p. 232)

Pargeter's Christians do not discuss their beliefs very often or in great
depth; clearly they are against violence, but they obey the English
convention of not discussing religion. They are also people of rank,
unlike Mitchison's Christians who are for the most part slaves and
freedmen. And there are no signals in Pargeter's novel that we are
reading Aesopian language: only the choice of subject matter suggests
a link with the increasing tyrannies of the Thirties. However, while
Pargeter's Nero is a less depraved figure than Mitchison's emperor, the
weight of the guilt for persecution and mass destruction is placed more
firmly on the Roman people, as Nero points out when Hortensius
protests at the massacres of Christians:

> Do you realise, my Marcus, that you are born out of time? Rome
> wants blood, loves blood, has no use for mercy ... If I wished to
> open the prison gates now, I dare not. (p. 106)

Pargeter's novel is intelligently written, and pleasingly structured, but
in the end it is the personal fates of Hortensius and his Persian lover
which dominate the book; the persecutions are their backdrop. For
Mitchison, personal stories are all subsumed within the vast social
tragedy which is taking place in the Third Reich, just as it did in one
of that Reich's models, imperial Rome. And her characters are well
drawn, not relying on easy stereotyping. While Nero is a gruesomely
decadent tyrant, he is also seen as a product of his time. While many
of the wealthy are power-hungry and impelled by self-interest, there
are those who still maintain high standards in public life. While many
of the slaves and freedmen value brotherhood and compassion, there
are those who betray everything under pressure and there are others
who are simply uninterested in the movement their fellows value so
highly.

Mitchison writes this historical fiction with confidence and flashes
of real flair. She changes idiom to suit the personality of her characters,
using stream of consciousness to blend thought and speech in ways
that reflect both the temperament of the individual and the occasion.
She draws us well into the novel before she signals that she is using
Aesopian language, in the epigraph from William Morris heading the
second section of the book. (p. 169) It is not until the third section,
with its epigraph from Bartolomeo Vanzetti, that the parallels with
socialism are clearly signalled; from then on, such chapter headings as

'The Bosses', 'Ends and Means' and 'The Individual and the State' urge us to interpret.

In the end, what Mitchison attempts to do throughout the Thirties bears witness to Virginia Woolf's argument in 'The Leaning Tower'.[15] Here Woolf stresses the inevitability, for writers with any sense of responsibility to their readership, of writing with political awareness throughout the Thirties. She also points out that there was practically no precedent for the kind of writing the inter-war years made necessary for such writers: up to 1914, writers had been for the most part creatures of privilege, inheritors of a great tradition, unthreatened by war. But from about 1925, says Woolf,

> When they looked at human life what did they see? Everywhere change; everywhere revolution ... There was communism in one country, in another fascism. The whole of civilization, of society, was changing ... The books were written under the influence of change, under the threat of war. (p. 167)

And Woolf uses the image of the leaning tower to show how hard it was for a writer in the Thirties to achieve a well-balanced view, since the great tradition which had created a strong secure tower up to the outbreak of World War One was no longer set on firm foundations. Later she says:

> The poet in the thirties was forced to be a politician ... If politics were 'real', the ivory tower was an escape from 'reality'. That explains the curious bastard language in which so much of this leaning over prose and poetry is written. It is not the rich speech of the aristocrat: it is not the racy speech of the peasant. It is betwixt and between. The poet is a dweller in two worlds, one dying, the other struggling to be born ... 'All that I would like to be is human' – that cry rings through their books – the longing to be closer to their kind, to write the common speech of their kind, to share the emotions of their kind, no longer to be isolated and exalted in solitary state upon their tower, but to be down on the ground with the mass of human kind. (p. 173)

Woolf pinpoints a crucial aspect of writing for the politically committed in the Thirties: the need to communicate widely and persuasively, and the inevitable problems encountered when trying to find the right mode of expression. Communication is clearly what Mitchison aims for in her fiction and, while she does not always succeed, at her best she achieves a great deal more than what Woolf calls 'bastard language'.

For at her best, she revives the art of a storytelling that takes old tales and makes them new for the troubled decade she was aiming to delight and instruct.

Notes

1. Valentine Cunningham, 'The Age of Anxiety and Influence; or, Tradition and the Thirties Talents' in Keith Williams and Steven Matthews (eds), *Rewriting the Thirties: Modernism and After* (London and New York: Longman, 1997), pp. 5–22, 6. See also James Malpas, *Realism* (Movements in Modern Art series, London: Tate Gallery Publishing, 1997) and Charles Harrison, *Modernism* (Movements in Modern Art series, London: Tate Gallery Publishing, 1997).
2. Alison Light, *Forever England: Femininity, Literature and Conservatism Between the Wars* (London: Routledge, 1991); Gill Plain, *Women's Fiction of the Second World War: Gender, Power and Resistance* (Edinburgh: Edinburgh University Press, 1996).
3. Bertram D. Wolfe, *Three Who Made a Revolution* (1948; Harmondsworth: Penguin Books, 1966), p. 36. See also Lev Loseff, *On the Beneficence of Censorship*, tr, J. Bobko (Munich: Verlag Otto Sagnerin Kommission, 1984).
4. Q. D. Leavis, *Fiction and the Reading Public* (1932; London: Bellew Publishing, 1990), p. 29.
5. See, for example, Sylvia Towsend Warner, *Summer Will Show* (1936; London: Virago, 1987) and *After the Death of Don Juan* (1938; London: Virago, 1989); Katharine Burdekin (as Murray Constantine), *Proud Man* (1934; New York: The Feminist Press, 1993) and *Swastika Night* (1937; London: Victor Gollancz, 1940); Susan Ertz, *Woman Alive* (London: Hodder and Stoughton, 1935); Edith Pargeter, *Hortensius Friend of Nero* (London: Lovat Dickson, 1936). All further references are to this edition and page numbers are given in the main body of the text.
6. Naomi Mitchison, *Corn King and Spring Queen* (London: Jonathan Cape, 1931); *We Have Been Warned* (London: Constable, 1935); *The Blood of the Martyrs* (London: Constable, 1939). All further references are to this edition and page numbers are given in the main body of the text. See also Janet Montefiore, *Men and Women Writers of the 1930s: The Dangerous Flood of History* (London: Routledge, 1996) for thought-provoking analyses of these novels; and Jenni Calder's biography, *The Nine Lives of Naomi Mitchison* (London: Virago, 1997) for further contextualisation and analyses.
7. Deborah Cameron, 'Language: Are You Being Served?' in Colin McCabe (ed.), *Critical Quarterly*, vol. 39, no. 2, Summer 1997, pp. 99–100.
8. Ngugi wa Thiong'o, *Petals of Blood* (Oxford: Heinemann, 1977), p. 19.
9. Naomi Mitchison, *The Fourth Pig* (London: Constable, 1936). All further references are to this edition and page numbers are given in the main body of the text.
10. Katharine Burdekin, *The End of This Day's Business* (written but unpublished, 1935; New York: The Feminist Press, 1989).
11. Stevie Smith, *Over the Frontier* (1938; London: Virago, 1980).
12. Amabel Williams-Ellis, *Learn to Love First* (London: Victor Gollancz, 1939). I am grateful to Dr Maroula Joannou for reminding me about this novel.
13. Cato (M. M. Foot, P. Howard and Frank Owen), *Guilty Men* (London: Victor Gollancz, 1940).
14. Richard Baxter, *Guilty Women* (London: Quality Press, 1941).
15. Virginia Woolf, 'The Leaning Tower' (1940) in Rachel Bowlby (ed.), *Virginia Woolf, A Woman's Essays* (London: Penguin Books, 1992). All further references are to this editon and page numbers are given in the main body of the text.

12

Back from the Future:
Katharine Burdekin and Science Fiction
in the 1930s

Keith Williams

In the 1930s, women were establishing permanent bridgeheads within the traditionally male-dominated genres of futuristic and utopian fiction. Many of their texts were prophetic cautions against the rise of totalitarianism, set in imagined near futures, such as Naomi Mitchison's *We Have Been Warned* (1935) or Storm Jameson's *In the Second Year* (1936). Others, such as Susan Ertz's *Woman Alive* (1936), dealt specifically with the destructive impact of sexual politics on modern history, but perhaps Katharine Burdekin's *Swastika Night* (1937) (thanks to the single-handed rescue of her oeuvre from canonical oblivion by Daphne Patai) has now become known as *the* Thirties dystopia which confronted the implications of the Fascist 'cult of masculinity' directly and, perhaps, with greatest foresight, taking Nazi ideology to its logical conclusions in a state set some 600 years from the present. However, the crucial formal and intellectual foundations for *Swastika Night* had already been laid by Burdekin in *Proud Man* (published in 1934, using, for the first time, her masculine pseudonym 'Murray Constantine').[1] This represents a significant intellectual and discursive nexus between Modernism, sexual politics and dys/utopian science fiction. It enabled Burdekin's gender critique, as it developed, to fully identify Fascist ideology not as a historical aberration but as an extreme reaction against the idea of progress in human equality, rooted in an ancient tradition of misogyny. Indeed, in the novel Burdekin wrote the year after *Proud Man*, *The End of this Day's Business*, her futuristic heroine Grania relates how, in the twentieth-century struggle between modernity and reaction, the Fascist gender backlash posed the greatest threat to human progress.[2]

Born Katharine Penelope Cade (1896–1963) ('Burdekin' was the surname of her husband, from whom she separated in 1922), she was at the cutting edge of the progressive thought of the inter-war period. Burdekin knew and/or corresponded with H. D., Radclyffe Hall, the Woolfs and the Russells, among others. Her work also contained one of the earliest, feminist critiques of D. H. Lawrence as the literary emissary of patriarchal reaction. *The End of this Day's Business*, identifies him as the prophet of the irrationalist cult of blood, soil and death hysteria (see especially pp. 64–5). (Earlier he featured as 'Carapace' in *Quiet Ways* (1930).) Crucially, *Proud Man*'s investigation of the psychological link between anxieties inherent in masculine socialisation and militarism shows that Burdekin was also in step with advanced thinking about neurasthenia's connection with theories of the 'hysterical male'. 'Shell shock' was the vernacular expression for neurasthenia in the Great War. W. H. R. Rivers's noted victims of it exhibited hysterical symptoms hitherto associated with the 'passive', domestic situation of women. Rivers concluded in his *Conflict and Dream* (1923) that the stalemate of the Western Front had a 'feminising' effect on soldiers because of the inactivity and helplessness it induced.[3] *Proud Man* extends such thinking to post-Great War male unemployment and Fascist belligerence. Because masculine identity demands compensatory self-esteem from the shame of 'feminising' inactivity, 'the next war will probably be started by that nation which has the most neurasthenic unemployed males'.[4]

Proud Man uses the same back-from-the-future strategy as H. G. Wells's *The Dream* (1924), in which a highly evolved human dreams of a time trip back to the present. In effect, it is a feminist reworking of Wells's text, which questions contemporary notions of social development and superhumanity. This essay will show how Burdekin built on the contemporary critique of masculinity epitomised by the 1932 feminist symposium *Man, Proud Man* (Rebecca West's contribution in particular); also how she drew on early insights into the centrality of gender ideology in Fascist politics, by writers such as Winifred Holtby, and speculations about literary 'androgyny', proposed in the work of Modernists such as Virginia Woolf.

Wells often used displacement in time or space as an imaginative principle for reconsidering civilisation and *The Dream* was a particular precedent for Burdekin.[5] Sarnac, a Utopian neurobiologist, dreams a 'past-life regression' in the late nineteenth and early twentieth century as Harry Mortimer Smith. What he effectively recollects is the genteel poverty of Wells's own upbringing, as fictionalised in his social-realist novels. *The Dream* gives it a futuristic perspective to defamiliarise and criticise (almost) every institution of the age. Creating what Sarnac calls a 'standard outside ourselves' allows Wells to metaphorically sidestep the 'normal' subjectivity such institutions produce.[6]

The Dream has much in common with *Proud Man* in its diagnosis of the problems of past civilisation, especially in presenting the cult of militarism as the primary cause of the apocalyptic social collapse in which it perished. Wells's text is largely about repression and the deathliness of socially conditioned roles, and Sarnac denounces the mystification of sexuality in particular. He sees all the physical and psychological traits of the dysfunctional past as fatally interconnected, but his author does not *systematically* raise the question of gender. Wells's utopian alternative is arguably a version of the flawed classical-masculine ideal of hygiene and pure reason, rather than, as in *Proud Man*, an attempt to imagine an inclusive, *ungendered* humanity. In contrast, Burdekin highlights the role of gender in the gathering patri-archal reaction against equality in the Thirties.

What is inchoate or marginal in *The Dream*, becomes central to *Proud Man* and to how Burdekin adapts the key Wellsian argument – that the unconscious contradiction between anachronistic mentality and advanced technology prevents the full realisation of modern hu-manity's potentials. In effect, she develops Sarnac's point that the future's consciousness is its fundamental difference from the past: 'Our motives took us unawares ... We were only beginning to learn the art of being human'. (p. 433) Consequently, the 'relation between the self and the not-self', as *Proud Man* phrases it, is made central to becoming fully human, but involves first and foremost 'transcending gender'.[7] The situations of Sarnac's female peers are not subjectivised on their own terms. Burdekin's first-person narrator has empathy with both male and female experience from inside. By making her dreamer a hermaphrodite telepath, she provided a more radical strategy for re-imagining 'normal' subjectivity than Wells's text.

The proposition that *Proud Man* reworks *The Dream* is corroborated by Rebecca West's 1928 fantasy *Harriet Hume*, which probably sug-gested both the form and direction that reworking took. This features a woman gifted with telepathy who enters the mind of a 'man of power', Arnold Condorex, so that he cannot conceal his unconscious motiv-ations from himself:

> She had burgled his mind and seen that he had meant to do that very thing. Damnable witch, she had enchanted him into feeling

a sense of loss and shame for what is no crime but the world's constant practice ... For she had come between him and every human being's right not to know quite what he is doing.[8]

There are close parallels between Burdekin's critique of gender and Karen Horney's essays of the 1920s,[9] but perhaps the decisive evidence that West was instrumental in mediating Wellsian ideas and strategies is a pioneering collection of commentaries, *Man, Proud Man*, published two years before Burdekin's novel. Though far from consistently feminist,[10] their underlying implication is that masculinity might be as much of a cultural product – or 'performance', in Mark Simpson's terms[11] – as femininity. West's own essay purported to be revelations picked up by a medium from a distant future of female intellectual superiority, rather like that in Burdekin's *The End of This Day's Business* (written in 1935).[12] Similarly, West's utopian future was not so much a social blueprint as a polemical device for defamiliarising the present. Her future woman is a crusty old matriarch, insisting on men's 'natural' incapacities and fulminating against fashionable doctrines suggesting otherwise. (M,PM, pp. 278–9)

Like *Proud Man*'s narrator, West's stresses that psychology tears down 'the façade of consciousness' and lays claim to the ability to render the mind transparent. (M,PM, pp. 267, 278) Her premise, that men's disguising of the psychological motives for their behaviour, even from themselves, is the root of masculine self-destructiveness, is especially relevant to Burdekin's novel. Its key terms are '*competitiveness and confusion*', which made men's monopoly of power in past history a cumulative catastrophe. The perennial cause of war was not external danger but a hysterical death wish produced by the unconscious, conflicting pressures of masculinity. Militarism submerged responsibility for individual self-knowledge, exchanging 'the burdensome freedom of the will for the psychologically easy servitude' and heroic delusions of 'premature and communally sanctioned death'. (M,PM, pp. 252–3)

West followed Wells's diagnosis that society is sick, but argued that misogynistic religion perverted the soul's medicine into an aggravator of its condition, an assumption also shared with Burdekin's novel (especially Part II, 'The Priest'). Christianity was hijacked by self-aggrandising ascetics (M,PM, pp. 254–5), so that masculine competitiveness and psychological confusion led to the inverted priorities of mind–body dualism, while celibacy and denigration of family relationships denied men's origins in, and continued dependence on, the 'sinful' female body. (M,PM, pp. 268–74) Similarly, in Burdekin's fiction, misogyny is driven by the memory of infantile dependence.[13] West's narrator concludes that both ancient self-martyrers and 1930s Fascists pursued 'honours due to supermen', topically spotlighting the present gender backlash. (M,PM, p. 267) Through her narrator's final admonition to male liberationists to remember their 'shame' (M,PM, pp. 284–5), West also implicitly acknowledges the symbolic basis of the social order her text inverts, prompting Burdekin's own explicit critique of phallocentrism.

Although West's contribution is most obviously relevant, Burdekin may have picked up prompts about the nature of difference from others. Mary Borden's 'Man, The Master, An Illusion' shows how myths of feminine weakness magnify men's achievements and conceal their anxiety about emasculating incapacity. (M,PM, pp. 11–38, especially 11–13) Moreover, like Burdekin she argues that fear of women is 'one of the most powerful forces in history', comparing the Biblical heroes' contempt for women (Samson is the classic male anxiety narrative) with that of modern dictators. (M,PM, pp. 16, 23) The erosion of men's traditional supremacy under the conditions of modernity, which tend to render mere physical strength redundant, has increased men's angst and accounts for the backlash against women as 'rivals'. However, Fascist attempts to reinstate the traditionally complicit feminine love of the 'strong man' are, ironically, their own undoing, 'For he does not and cannot survive intimacy', dominating whole nations without being able to confirm the submissiveness of his mate. (M,PM, pp. 24–5) Similarly, E. M. Delafield's 'Man and Personal Relations' could have highlighted for Burdekin that construction of feminine personae in male-authored discourse might be a literary impersonation or drag act, based on cultural stereotypes rather than the facts of sex and experience. (M,PM, pp. 41–74)

The imaginative method of *Proud Man* furnishes, in effect, a kind of ethnographic report on the gender practices of modern society from a detached or alien viewpoint, as Patai points out (PM, p. xv), and the principle of 'Anthropology at home'[14] is also marked in the essays. Susan Ertz in 'Man As Pleasure-Seeker' anthropologises the 'homosocial' (to use Eve Kosofsky Sedgewick's term)[15] cults of sport, work, ritual display, crowd behaviour, sexuality, etc., as if she were reporting on a 'primitive' society. (M,PM, pp. 77–101) Also a possible influence on both Burdekin's 1934 novel and Woolf's 1938 *Three Guineas* is G. B. Stern's 'Man – Without Prejudice (Rough Notes)', a kind of encyclopedic documentary montage which fractures the abstract homogeneity of Man into the identities of individual men in specific contexts. Like Borden, Stern also emphasises the social indulgence of masculine infantilism, or the 'Peter Pan' tendency. She connects it with fear of mature female sexuality and, therefore, 'life itself', an idea Burdekin embodies in the child-murderer of Part IV of her novel. (M,PM, pp. 177–217, especially 178, 212–17)

But perhaps Sylvia Townsend Warner's 'Man's Moral Law' is both the most satirical and explicitly 'anthropological' contribution in the way it demystifies taboos. An important parallel with Burdekin's defamiliarisation of common concepts in *Proud Man* is her focus on the gendered nature of ordinary language, ideologically riddled with, for example, game-playing terms. Such 'metaphors we live by'[16] infiltrate cultic values which exclude women from activities such as politics. (M,PM, pp. 221–245, especially 227ff) She also shows how masculine values are literally fetishised, by pinpointing the investment of gender characteristics in commodities, especially clothing and cars, by the semiotics of advertising. This process continuously reflects and reinforces Man's mystique, as the absolute and universal human subject, suggesting that Warner's unconscious cultural mechanisms adapt primitive beliefs to contemporary conditions. (M,PM, pp. 237–9, 241–5)

Such ideas and tactics enabled Burdekin to adapt *The Dream* for imagining a more radical kind of 'escape from subjectivity' (Patai's phrase in PM, p. xvi). The person does not experience the past with no 'memory' of the future, but with full consciousness. Moreover, the definition of 'human' they bring back has drastically changed: the future species has evolved to the point where sexual characteristics are no longer split and cultural elaboration of biological differences is unknown. Consequently, the person regards twentieth-century people as 'sub-human' because they are still biologically male and female and subject to fictions of polarised gender roles. Of course, the term 'sub-human' is politically laden, especially in the 1930s context. Nazi ideology was predicated on pseudo-scientific distinction between races as more or less evolved: Jews and Slavs were 'subhuman', or *Untermenschen*, and Germanic races the embodiment of Nietzsche's 'supermen' or *Übermenschen*. However, *Mensch* can mean 'person' as well as 'human'. Thus, not only does Burdekin subvert Nazi use of 'subhuman' by turning it against their ideological distinctions (racial and/or sexual), she also implicitly deconstructs the hierarchical pairing sub/superhuman by problematising the concept that it significantly elides: i.e., 'human' itself. *Proud Man* is concerned, therefore, with how different categories of inferiorised 'otherness' are interrelated, but can also be seen as initiating her specific critique of the Fascist 'cult of masculinity', as elaborated in *Swastika Night* (1937). This was the most militant form of the contemporary patriarchal backlash against equality. Nazi doctrine posed the most urgent of threats to any progressive notion of being human. Moreover, its misconceived bid for superhumanity eventually plunged the world into unprecedented depths of barbarism against 'otherness' in all its manifestations.

Though investigating how socialisation overall prevents human beings from achieving individual potentials, *Proud Man* also contains one of the earliest and most astute responses to Fascist gender politics. Ingram and Patai argue that Burdekin preceded Woolf in locating 'the germ of Fascism in the patriarchal family'.[17] But contemporary thinking by some other feminists accorded with Burdekin's fictional vision. For example, in 'Black Words for Women Only', published in the same year, Winifred Holtby made the same points: that gender is central to Fascist ideology and that it was different in degree, but not kind, to patriarchal substructures in 'democratic' states. She observed that Oswald Mosley's *The Greater Britain* typified 'that Fascist inclination to dream of an eclectic Olympus of virile he-men (Romans, Britons or Teutonic Aryans) separated sharply from all lower forms of being'. Holtby also compared Mosley's promises with Hitler's performance as evidence of what reassertion of 'natural' roles meant in practice. The Nazis quickly reversed provisions for women's rights enshrined in the Weimar Constitution. But throughout history, 'Exalting woman's sex until it dominated her whole life' had been the State's 'excuse for political or economic disability', sacrificing to it 'the citizen, the worker and the human being'.[18]

Burdekin's attempt at a comprehensive gender critique shapes both the structure of her novel and its diagnosis of crisis at every level. *Proud Man* falls into four parts. Part I, 'The Person', begins with a comprehensive 'report' on subhuman psychology and social order from his/her defamiliarising perspective to his/her peers. Part II, 'The Priest', opens the narrative proper by dramatising the reactions of a 'typical' subhuman family when their remote, sexually-ambiguous descendant materialises near their farmhouse. S/he is finally taken in by an untypical clergyman, whose own disaffection from organised religion as the ultimate horizon of patriarchal ideology is crystallised in the course of their intellectual exchanges. In Part III, 'The Woman', the person, still passing as a woman, moves to London and surveys its cultural life with an aspiring but divided woman novelist, held back by gender disability, as his/her guide. Finally, in Part IV, 'The Man', the person assumes a masculine guise and builds up a psychotherapeutic intimacy with a serial killer, whose dysfunctional sexuality is made representative of the fundamental problems of his/her ancestral race. Wells's text concluded that the world economy was distorted by the inverted production priorities of war and unrationalised advances in technology, creating both international friction and mass unemployment. However, Burdekin's text understands economics in patriarchal terms: capitalist competition for money had superseded feudal land ownership by a symbol of virile success. (See for example PM, p. 59)

Because of its 'alien and critical'[19] method, *Proud Man* defamiliarises ideological keywords (most obviously 'human') to reveal their contradictions. For example, the concept of 'privilege' assumes 'some subhumans are, by reason of the colour of their skins, or their rearing, or their sex, *better* and more worthy' than others. However, although their society cannot exist without hierarchy, the latent antagonism which it engenders, prevents 'the stability necessary to its permanent existence'. The person sees that privilege is, paradoxically, both the grounds of social order and its undoing, since it is bound up with a 'subhuman necessity, the exercise of power'. (PM, pp. 17–18) Anticipating Foucault, s/he detects power and coercion arrogated around their whole system, but regulated by laws creating conscience and preventing reversion to instinctual predatoriness. This leads to another major contradiction: individuals are forbidden to murder, but collectively sanction 'large organised killings called wars'. Designating soldiers 'killing males', s/he notes the insidious connection with anxieties inherent in the cult of masculinity that makes future wars inevitable. In this way, conscription is also a psychological dynamic, a necessary test of both individual and national virility. In the Great War, fear of appearing unmanly, not courage or desire for 'glory', drove the conflict. (PM, pp. 19–22)

Burdekin uses hermaphroditism as a metaphor for the imaginative androgyny of fully human individuality. Alternatively, 'the root cause of all subhuman wretchedness' is sexual dimorphism, distorted through cultural fictions of gender difference. (PM, pp. 22–3) Aggravated by male jealousy of greater biological importance (i.e., 'womb envy'), this 'poisons the natural relation of the females to the males'. (PM, pp. 42–3) The exclusion of women from warmaking is powerful compensation for the masculine sense of inferiority, in giving death not birth. Patriarchy created masculine 'self-esteem', but only through its complement – feminine self-hatred and interiorised complicity in subordination. The person, therefore, anticipating Lacan, recognises that sacralisation of the penis is the origin of what we now call 'phallocentrism'. (Cf. Patai, afterword to PM, pp. 325–6) Conversely, as West also argued, religious misogyny inculcates female 'uncleanness'. The only idealised femininity is virginity, negating the reproductive function. Conceiving of femininity as 'lack' makes subhuman females grow up devitalised and inauthentic, with 'intense secret envy of the phallus, the sign of power'. (PM, pp. 28–30) The person notes that the cultural period in which s/he has materialised is one in which the backlash against limited emancipation has seen 'the complete emergence of sex antagonism' (PM, p. 32), especially in the writings and cult of D. H. Lawrence.

Because patriarchy operates through hegemony rather than crude domination, its system denies women an equal level of mental development, since 'The higher consciousness can always enslave the lower'. (PM, p. 33) But Burdekin also builds on Ertz and Warner's essays on gender rituals and taboos to anticipate contemporary feminist thought on the effects of 'homosocial' groups, in the sense of the damage done by segregating activities irrelevant to sex. Men can escape 'to some large or small homosexual pack which clings together and excludes all females, such as a *regiment*, a *club*, or a *bar*', but women are encouraged to be indifferent or even hostile to their sex, to prevent them objectifying its situation in any organised way. (PM, pp. 33–5)

According to the person, the advanced consciousness necessary to be human depends on 'a true idea of the relation of the self to the not-self', i.e., to 'otherness', encountered in various forms, climaxing in the child-killing 'monster' of Part IV. (PM, p. 47) Since what West calls 'competitiveness and confusion' are endemic to the unconscious of patriarchy, subhumans cannot conceive of difference as anything but opposition and conflict. This mystification leads to fear of women, masked as contempt or loathing, and the latent threat of emasculation, of losing 'the power which dwells in the symbol of power'. Demonisation of 'effeminacy' explains the apparent contradiction whereby masculine education requires constant intervention in, and reinforcement of, what is 'natural' in order for boys to become men, such 'a delicate and exotic thing' is virility. Middle-class boys are removed to the homosocial environment of public schools, making 'inevitable sex antagonism … sharper and more bitter by abysmal ignorance'. But Burdekin does not subscribe to the fashionable Thirties Proletkult, which worshipped the greater 'naturalness' of working-class identity. Proletarian boys still band together in homosocial gangs, instilling similar cultic values. (PM, pp. 51–4)

Advanced feminist thought and Modernist experiment fuse together in the narrator of *Proud Man*. As a telepath, the person can read the thoughts of both sexes and his/her own ambiguity has formal as well as psychological implications. Patai notes how this forces readers to question any 'objectivity' claimed by conventional narrative viewpoints, because s/he neither divulges their 'real' name, nor fits the categories of subhuman pronouns, occupying an ungendered textual space. (See Patai's afterword to PM, pp. 342–3) Through her persona, Burdekin imagines a state in which, paradoxically, imagination is redundant because ideological barriers, including language, which prevent one subject empathising with an 'other', appear deconstructed in a common identity between 'self and not-self'.

As the priest realises, s/he impersonates or passes for both sexes by assuming the material gender symbols and roles of either as demanded by the situation (PM, p. 146), revealing that even for biological women and men gender is a mutual performance, albeit unconsciously scripted. Similarly, clothing is shown to both conceal and exaggerate sexual difference (see for example pp. 66–7, 74–6, 80–81), but language and writing are also entangled in this fetishism. Significantly, the priest dubs him/her 'Verona', an Italinate-Shakespearean name echoing Woolf's own sexual metamorph.[20] Through the figure of Orlando, Woolf *diachronically* cross-sections changes in gender roles and literary discourse over four centuries. Similarly, Burdekin uses the person to *synchronically* cross-section contemporary sexual politics. The person's shifts between male and female consciousnesses are also a kind of 'impersonation of style', deriving from the way Modernist texts move between the interiority of multiple personae or 'voices'. In this s/he resembles T. S. Eliot's Tiresias in *The Waste Land* (1922), Bloom's 'womanly man' in the 'Circe' chapter of Joyce's *Ulysses* (1922) and, most particularly, the mentally androgynous writer of the future Woolf imagines at the end of *A Room of One's Own* (1929).[21] His/her mind-reading is often presented as sequences of free indirect discourse or interior monologues, quintessentially Modernist innovations for depicting subjectivity. For example, the thoughts of aspiring novelist Leonora Simon, of Part III, 'The Woman', are described as 'very jerky, for everything she saw and heard had a front place in them. Had she expressed them in words they would have been something like this'. There follows an extended first-person sequence composed of apparently random impressions, musings and memories, but poetically concentrating and interweaving the novel's main themes. (PM, pp. 164–6) The person concludes Leonora is 'drowning in a river' (p. 230), because her stream of consciousness is troubled and confused, though s/he is able to discern its underlying pattern, like a psychoanalyst with the professional advantage of knowing how patients' words genuinely correspond with their thoughts.[22] However, overtly experimental techniques are used sparingly in the novel, probably because, like so many other radical writers by the mid-Thirties, Burdekin became convinced the political crisis was too urgent to risk obfuscating her message, especially since it was already so far in advance of its time.

While adapting the intellectual and literary legacy of Modernist feminism, Burdekin was concerned to broaden its appeal. She did this not by returning to naturalistic realism, nor by simply feminising more popular literary discourses, such as science fiction, but also through making intertextual connections with feature film. There is, for example, a crucial parallel between Part IV, 'The Man', and M, directed by Fritz Lang (1931).[23]

Thea von Harbou's 1931 screenplay was based on the case of the 'Monster of Düsseldorf', Peter Kürten, internationally notorious at the time. However, the Nazis regarded the questions it raised about difference as dangerously subversive. Because the final scene allows the killer to presents himself in his own subjective terms, they banned it as the cinematic epitome of 'degenerate art'.[24] Similarly, the final subject of Proud Man, though 'set apart from all his kind' by apparent monstrosity (pp. 251–2), actually epitomises the emotional crippling of men. Gilbert Hassall, unable to have a relationship with sexually mature women, suffers from the misogyny inherent in 'normal' masculine socialisation, aggravated by circumstance. The major difference from the screenplay is that Burdekin attempts to answer the question of the social motivations of his compulsion as well as raising it.

Not only does Burdekin reveal the typicality of the psychological background to his crime, she also examines the ambivalence behind the public hysteria it engenders, just as Lang's film investigates mob frenzy on the eve of the Nazi takeover (significantly, its title was to have been Die Mörder sind unter uns, 'The murderers are among us'). In Proud Man, patriarchy scapegoats 'monstrous' individuals, while sanctioning the genocidal slaughter of war. As in M, Hassall's periodic compulsion is based on some repressed trauma from which murder affords temporary 'lightening and peace'. (PM, pp. 256–7) The person senses it is a displacing symptom: 'You don't really want to murder the little girls. You want to kill the thing behind the dreams'. (PM, p. 260) However, his psychopathic tendencies are exacerbated by the response from a community that considers him 'a fiend in human form'. (PM, p. 263)[25] He even gets a kind of thrill from this 'monstering', imagining himself a kind of superman – a perversity mirroring the appeal of Nazism's atrocities without their ironic bonus of social sanction. Consequently, Burdekin demystifies the psycho-social duplicities and taboos which make such a 'monstering' possible. (PM, pp. 269–70)

The person finally watches Hassall's nightmare like a symbolic film, climaxing in the equivocal splitting of his subjectivity between tenderness and brutality as in M's speech: 'It was because he loved the child and something terrible was waiting for it behind the next boulder. It was himself, and he knew it was himself, so he wept and wept, and always they had to walk towards the stone'. (p. 271)[26] Burdekin makes explicit what is arguably implicit in the final speech of Lang's psychopath: he 'preserves' his prepubescent victims from consciousness of the world of adult sexuality by which he was prematurely traumatised himself. The person helps him recognise he kills 'to stop them growing up'. (PM, pp. 280–85)

Hassall, thus, typifies the psychological confusion of all subhumans – 'He had to know his own mind' (PM, p. 297) – which, as West suggested, is particularly prevalent in the construction of masculinity. The father's emotional autism makes the 'recovered' childhood trauma about his mother's epilepsy the more devastating because it transformed the maternal source of love and security into something terrifying and demonic. (PM, pp. 304–5) As the root of Hassall's antisocial behaviour, it focuses Burdekin's critique of hysteria onto conversion of fear of otherness into hate, an emotion which does not undermine the masculine ego in the same way. The person concludes that Hassall's condition, in which sexuality distorted by gender finds outlet in a vicious cycle of 'blood sacrifices and blood atonements', is neither monstrous nor unique, because the same catastrophic pattern is writ ever larger in the course of subhuman history. (PM, p. 305) However, set against that is Hassall's psychotherapeutic 'abreaction' to the source of his personal angst which places him 'beyond doubt and fear'. (PM, pp. 311–13)

Consequently, Proud Man confirms the individual's potential to learn 'the art of being human', but also warns against totalitarianism's whipping up of hysteria against the 'not-self', sexual, racial, political, etc., which jeopardises the moral evolution of the species. (PM, pp. 317–18) Although subsequently overshadowed by Swastika Night (reprinted by the influential Left Book Club in July 1940, as one of the only two topical novels it promoted as 'book of the month'), Proud Man was instrumental in Burdekin's reshaping of a traditionally 'boys' own' genre in the 1930s. Her critique of gender ideology expanded both the scope and form of dys/utopian writing, but *Proud Man* strove to convey her radical view of the crisis of modernity in reader-friendly discourse, neither mandarin High-Modernist, nor stylistically conservative social realism, but a pragmatic synthesis, in which the two traditions mingled freely with futuristic science fiction and progressive aspects of the new popular culture of film.

Notes

1. Assumed to protect her family from potential Fascist harassment. For detailed biographical information, see Daphne Patai's afterword to Katharine Burdekin, *The End of this Day's Business* (New York: Feminist Press, 1989), especially pp. 161–7.
2. Burdekin, *The End of this Day's Business*, pp. 55–85.
3. For a recent account of the impact of his theories, see 'Male Hysteria: W. H. R. Rivers and the Lessons of Shell Shock', in Elaine Showalter's *The Female Malady: Women, Madness and English Culture 1830–1980* (New York: Pantheon, 1985; reprint London: Virago, 1987), pp. 167–94. Also her *Hystories: Hysterical Epidemics and the Modern Media* (New York: Columbia University Press, 1997), pp. 72–4, 96.
4. Katharine Burdekin, *Proud Man* (London: Boriswood, 1934; reprint New York: Feminist Press, 1993), pp. 39–40. All further references to PM are to this edition and page numbers are given in the main body of the text.
5. Daphne Patai in her edition highlights other contemporary sources using spatial or temporal displacement, such as Charlotte Perkins Gilman, *With Her in Ourland* (1916) and, especially, Olaf Stapledon, *Last and First Men* (1930), a Neptunian's history of 'post-human' civilisation. Though she omits Wells, her own distinction makes the 'fit' with *The Dream* even closer: 'Whereas Stapledon writes *of* the future *for* the present, Burdekin pretends to be writing *for* the future *of* the present, while, of course, actually writing for the present about its own peculiarities and its desperate need to take stock of itself.' (See Patai's foreword to *Proud Man*, p. xv.) There are other telling parallels: Sarnac speaks to an audience of future peers; the 'Person's' narrative is addressed to his/hers. Both 'dreamers' are killed in the present as a way 'back to the future'.
6. *The Dream* (London: Cape, 1924; reprint as a volume of the Odhams uniform edition, 1930–), p. 294.
7. Patai, foreword to Burdekin, *Proud Man*, p. x.
8. See Rebecca West, *Harriet Hume: A London Fantasy* (1928; reprint London: Virago, 1980), pp. 109–10.
9. Collected as *Feminine Psychology* and building on the work of Georg Simmel. (See Patai's afterword to *Proud Man*, pp. 324–5.)
10. Both titles derive from a speech in Shakespeare's *Measure for Measure* (II, ii, 117–23) contrasting the judgment of men and gods. For an extended commentary on the collection, see Elizabeth Maslen, 'Man, Proud Man? Women's Views of Men Between the Wars', in Maya Slater (ed.), *Women Voice Men: Gender in European Culture* (Exeter: Intellect, 1997), pp. 58–60. Maslen argues that 'in these essays "man" is a term used in both essentialist and constructivist contexts: as yet there is no readily available vocabulary for separating traits associated with sex from those relating to gender' (p. 58), which accounts in some measure for their inconsistent blend of conservatism and radicalism. Nonetheless, Burdekin's response to the collection highlighted and developed whatever sporadic and incipiently feminist distinctions it contains between biology and cultural fictions *avant la lettre*, as I show below.
11. See introduction to Mark Simpson, *Male Impersonators: Men Performing Masculinity* (London: Cassell, 1994), pp. 1–20.
12. Rebecca West, 'Man and Religion', in Mabel Ulrich (ed.), *Man, Proud Man: A Commentary* (London: Hamish Hamilton, 1932), pp. 249–85, 249. All further references to M,PM are to this edition and page numbers are given in the main body of the text. West's 'superwomen' parody the Wellsian socio-technocratic ideal. They evolved through 'hormone enhancement

therapy', boosting women's working capability and lifespan, as well as *in vitro* gestation, shortening pregnancy and producing better children. (See *Man, Proud Man*, p. 280.) Daphne Patai notes, both the form and subject matter of West's contribution are particularly relevant to Part II of *Proud Man*, 'The Priest', which also explores religion as the ultimate horizon of patriachal ideology.

13. In *Swastika Night*, the whole Nazi programme of organised forgetting is founded on that 'perpetual affront to male vanity' as Patai puts it. See Patai's afterword to *Proud Man*, pp. 324–5 and Katharine Burdekin, *Swastika Night* (London: Victor Gollancz, 1937; reprint Lawrence and Wishart, 1985), p. 81.

14. The principle became integral to the 1930s documentary impulse, exemplified by Mass-Observation, to which Malinowski applied the phrase, and which was jointly founded by professional anthropologist Tom Harrisson. See Bronislaw Malinowski's essay 'A Nation-wide Intelligence Service', in Charles Madge and Tom Harrisson (eds), *First Year's Work 1937–38, by Mass-Observation* (London: Lindsay Drummond, 1938), p. 120.

15. Eve Kosofsky Sedgewick, *Between Man: English Literature and Male Homosexual Desire* (New York: Columbia University Press, 1985).

16. See George Lakoff and Mark Johnson's eponymous classic of socio-linguistics *Metaphors We Live By* (Chicago and London: Chicago University Press, 1980), p. 3.

17. Introduction to Angela Ingram and Daphne Patai (eds), *Rediscovering Forgotten Radicals: British Women Writers 1889–1939* (Chapel Hill and London: University of North Carolina Press, 1993), p. 18.

18. *The Clarion* (24 March 1934), reprinted in Paul Berry and Alan Bishop (eds), *Testament of a Generation: The Journalism of Vera Brittain and Winifred Holtby* (London: Virago, 1985; pbk. 1986), pp. 84–6. Holtby stressed the significance of the connections by extending her review into a chapter of *Women and a Changing Civilisation* (London: Longman, 1934; reprint Chicago: Academy Press, 1978). Burdekin was evidently monitoring the struggle between progress and reaction in Weimar Germany closely: her pacifist novel *Quiet Ways* (1930) has a Germanically named heroine, Helga. Similarly, in *The End of this Day's Business* the women's world council is in Munich, as a tribute to German feminism's pioneering role. For a discussion of Woolf and Burdekin in relation to the Nazi backlash against Weimar feminism, see Maroula Joannou, *'Ladies, Please Don't Smash These Windows': Women's Writing, Feminist Consciousness and Social Change* (Oxford: Berg, 1995), pp. 166–70.

19. Significantly, the person is called 'an alien without passport'. (p. 140) Both Burdekin and Woolf turned the split consciousness induced by feminism into imaginative strategies: '"in walking down Whitehall … from being the natural inheritor of that civilisation, [a woman] becomes, on the contrary, outside of it, alien and critical."' See *A Room of One's Own*, p. 93, and cf. Patai's foreword to *Proud Man*, p. xvi.

20. Joannou rightly compares *Proud Man* with *Orlando* in *'Ladies, Please Don't Smash These Windows'*, p. 182.

21. Woolf uses similar metaphors to Burdekin (e.g., 'self-fertilising') in a psychological sense. See Virginia Woolf, *A Room of One's Own* (London: Hogarth, 1929; reprint Frogmore: Granada, 1977), especially p. 99. Grania's theory of art in *The End of This Day's Business* is also based on androgyny. (See pp. 56–7.)

22. Burdekin's serial killer assumes the person is 'a peculiarly brilliant psychiatrist', but himself bears witness to the failure of conventional analysis. (See pp. 263–4.)

23. There is a wealth of parallel details, including the same murder weapon – a cut-throat knife. Burdekin's killer is mild-mannered, sensitive, anonymous, just like the figure Peter Lorre plays. His surname 'Hassall' may be a pun on *haß alle*, 'hate everyone'? A potential victim is called Else, like M's 'Else Beckmann'. Both killers are, paradoxically, attractive for, and tender to, children. (See, for example p. 284.)

24. For the scripting and political impact of the film, see Patrick McGilligan, *Fritz Lang: The Nature of the Beast* (London: Faber, 1997), especially pp. 148–58.

25. The etymology of fiend remains more obvious in German (as in key Nazi concepts such as *Rassenfeind*, 'racial enemy').

26. Graham Greene reviewed Peter Lorre's performance in similar terms, noting 'the expression of despairing tenderness he turned on his small victim, the hapless struggle in his face of a habit he could not break' (*World Film News*, July 1936; reprinted in David Parkinson (ed.), *Mornings in the Dark: The Graham Greene Film Reader* (London: Carcanet, 1993), pp. 403–4).

13

Three Guineas and the Photograph: The Art of Propaganda

Elena Gualtieri

As the most explicitly political of Virginia Woolf's works, *Three Guineas* has been the object of innumerable commentaries from all sides of the political spectrum since the time of its first publication. Written from an openly declared anti-Fascist position, and yet critical of anti-Fascist support for the idea of military intervention, Woolf's book-length essay[1] sets out to demonstrate the existence of a causal link between war, Fascist ideology and the psychological and institutional make-up of patriarchal society. It does so through the deployment of the type of argumentative skills that earned for Woolf the title of 'the most brilliant pamphleteer in England'[2] when the essay was first published, and have in more recent years led to its recognition as a major feminist text. Yet, although *Three Guineas* remains one of the most famous and most widely read of Woolf's essays, very little has been written on its extraordinary use of photographs both as illustrations of its arguments and as rhetorical figures.[3]

When first published in 1938, *Three Guineas* was accompanied by five photographs of representatives of the professions: (i) a general, (ii) a group of heralds, (iii) a procession of university dons, (iv) a judge and (v) a bishop, all of whom are depicted in their official robes of office.[4] The position of these photographs within the text and their relation to its arguments clearly signalled them as satirical illustrations of the pomposity, arrogance and self-importance that Woolf associated with patriarchal institutions. Each of the plates was placed opposite to particular lines of writing which functioned as a kind of indirect commentary guiding its interpretation. The first three plates were grouped together quite closely in the first section of the essay, while the last two were spaced out in the second and third sections respectively. In the post-war years the reproduction of the five plates became somewhat erratic. They were dropped from the Hogarth Press edition after the fourth imprint, which appeared in 1952, as well as from the American paperback edition brought out by Harcourt Brace in 1963. More recently, the plates have once again been reintegrated within the essay both in the Penguin 1993 edition, where they appear in their original location, and in the World's Classics one of 1992, where they have been reprinted at the centre of the text.

There are to date no records to indicate where the originals of these photographs came from, but their contents, style and composition resemble very closely those of similar illustrations that can be found in the scrapbooks Woolf compiled between 1931 and 1937 in preparation for the writing of *Three Guineas*. Now preserved in the Monks House Papers collection at the University of Sussex Library, these scrapbooks offer the possibility of witnessing the process that led from the gathering of the evidence on which Woolf's arguments came to rest to the published version of *Three Guineas*. Most of the material collected in the scrapbooks forms, in fact, the backbone of the footnotes that accompany the essay, and it is often possible to trace back the origin of an argument developed in *Three Guineas* to a particular quotation, article or image in the scrapbooks.

The story of Frau Pommer is an instance in kind. It appears in one of the notes of *Three Guineas* as a modern-day version of Antigone's struggle against tyranny and it was first reported in an article in *The Times*, 12 August 1935, which is pasted in to the second volume of the scrapbooks.[5] With a technique that anticipates the juxtaposition of texts and images that Woolf is to deploy later in *Three Guineas*, the cutting detailing Frau Pommer's act of resistance is flanked in the scrapbook by two pieces of counteracting evidence. At the bottom left-hand corner Woolf pasted a glamorised picture of Count Ciano (Mussolini's son-in-law and Italian foreign minister) 'in flying kit', while at the opposite end of the page an article reports a speech by the Führer which proudly announced the birth of a 'Nation of Men'.[6]

Other material from the scrapbooks did not find its way directly into *Three Guineas* but nevertheless shows a strong resemblance to the five photographs printed there, as well as having a clear link to many of the arguments for which the plates function as illustrations. Woolf's comments in *Three Guineas* on the double standard which classifies women's fashion as frivolous but men's ceremonial dresses as 'venerable' (TG, p. 374, n. 6) are graphically conveyed in the scrapbooks through the striking juxtaposition of two sets of photographs, both taken from the 30 May 1936 issue of the *Daily Telegraph*. In the first one, four heralds are shown 'proclaiming the coronation of King Edward [VIII] in London',[7] while in the second four women in hats at the races offer mirror mages of the heralds in terms of extravagance of dress and composition of the photographs.[8] Both these cuttings are preceded by a third picture of the Pope 'on his throne in St Peter's Rome',[9] which in its combination of opulence and hieratic character strongly recalls the image of the bishop featured in the fifth plate of *Three Guineas*. Another photograph of the Lord Mayor's show 'passing through Moorgate' taken from *The Times*, 10 November 1937,[10] clearly illustrates the strong visual sense which informs Woolf's use of the march of the professions in *Three Guineas* as a metaphor for the staid and unswerving course of patriarchal history.

The importance of images to the structure of *Three Guineas*, both as illustrations of a point and as records of events, is also borne out by the presence of a second set of photographs, which the narrator of the essay claims to have received from the Spanish Republican Government during the winter of 1936–7. (TG, p. 164) Unlike the photographs of the representatives of the professions, this second set, which is said to portray civilian casualties of the Civil War, is not reproduced as an image but simply given a verbal description. Although these photographs do not appear to have survived in Woolfs archives, they are usually linked to those mentioned by Woolf on 16 November 1936 in a letter to Julian Bell, who at the time was working at a Chinese university but would be returning later to Europe to join the Republican side in Spain. They represent Woolf's first mention of the Spanish War in her correspondence and are described as 'a packet of photographs from Spain all of dead children, killed by bombs', which Woolf received with the morning post.[11]

The date of the letter to her nephew, Woolf's description of the photographs and the circumstances under which she received them, all suggest that she might have been referring to photographs of the children of Getafe, an airport town near Madrid which was the target of a German air raid on 30 October 1936. The photographs from Getafe were used as explicit evidence of Fascist brutality in a propaganda campaign run by the Spanish Communist Party in the attempt to raise international support for the Republican cause during the first weeks of the siege of Madrid. According to Arturo Barea, who worked in the Foreign Press Censorship Department of the Republic during the Civil War, they reached Madrid a few days before the beginning of the siege on 7 November 1936.[12] In the chaos that ensued after the removal of the Republican Government to Valencia, Barea rescued the photographs from destruction and, sometime after the arrival of the International Brigade in Madrid on 8 November, took them to the office of the Communist Party 'to be used for propaganda posters'.[13]

Copies on paper of the photographs from Getafe, of which plates 1 and 2 are a selection, can be found in the International Brigade Memorial Archive in London. Each of these copies carries a caption in Spanish which identifies the child as one of the victims of the Getafe air raid and gives the child's name and address when known. Some of these pictures were published in Britain by the *Daily Worker* on 12 November 1936, a few days before Woolf wrote to Bell. According to Caroline Brothers, the photographs of the children from Getafe were the first ones to 'contravene in every respect the conventions regulating the representation of death in the British Press', where images of the casualties from Spain had until then always been 'symbolic, incidental, euphemistic or aesthetic' in character.[14] They were therefore accompanied by a lengthy editorial that attempted to justify the decision to publish them by appealing to their value as documents of Fascist brutality, but which in fact had the effect of sidelining the account of the events to which they referred and foregrounding instead their use as propaganda.

Although there is no certain proof that Woolf saw the photographs from Getafe, the weight of circumstantial and textual evidence appears to support this hypothesis. At around this time, in mid-November 1936, Woolf was engaged in writing an article on the relationship between art and politics in the 1930s which was published by the *Daily Worker* a month later.[15] Her diary uncharacteristically offers no mention of the photographs of 'dead children' described in her letter, but it nevertheless records Woolf's feelings of 'strain' and tiredness on 10 November in connection with 'The Daily Worker article. Madrid not fallen. Chaos. Slaughter. War surrounding our island'.[16] On 24 November, a week after receiving the Spanish photographs, she announced that she had 'beg[u]n 3 Gs.' the day before '& liked it'.[17]

This chronological connection between the photographs 'of dead children' and the inception of *Three Guineas* is confirmed textually by a manuscript page of notes which Woolf jotted down in preparation for the essay. It is part of a collection of 'random ideas and sketches' which Brenda Silver dates between October 1935 and January 1937,[18] and it provides what is effectively a compendium of the first part of the argument in *Three Guineas*. As she will do in the essay, Woolf reflects here on the connection that might exist between her sense of 'horror' at the sight of 'maimed' and 'mauled' bodies in the 'Spanish photographs' and the need for practical action against war. Clearly addressing an unknown interlocutor, who in the essay will become her male correspondent, she remarks that it is 'only too easy to be moved' when confronted with those images, 'but' she interjects 'you don't want tears; you want a suggestion how to prevent war'.[19]

The dialogic character of these notes echoes Woolf's 1936 letter to Julian Bell and highlights the intersection of personal concerns and wider historical events that the Spanish photographs represented for her. Bell's decision to go to Spain, and his subsequent death in the battle of Brunete in July 1937, left a lasting impression in Woolf's mind, forming some of the background against which the arguments of *Three Guineas* were developed.[20] Both his death and the photographs 'of dead children' had a determining influence on the final shape of the essay, whose form as a letter underscores the sense of a continuing dialogue with Woolf's deceased nephew, while its deployment of photographs grapples with the artistic and moral problems raised by the use of such disturbing images for propaganda purposes. Although the argument of *Three Guineas* appeals to the same emotions of 'horror and disgust' (TG, p. 65) that the *Daily Worker* of 12 November 1936 aimed to elicit from its readers, it radically distances itself from the sensationalising of death carried out by that paper by refusing to publish the images that prompted Woolf's reactions. The Spanish photographs are consequently replaced in her text by the plates of the representatives of the professions in a way that prevents *Three Guineas* itself from participating in the exploitation of those harrowing images, while at the same time suggesting the existence of a connection between British patriarchal institutions and the victims of Fascist aggression.

This omission of any reproduction of photographs of the Civil War from the published essay allows Woolf to turn the record of a specific historical event into a generalised scene of death and destruction. Stripped of their original context, the Spanish pictures become in *Three Guineas* a universally applicable illustration of the evils of war which transcends any distinction between just or unjust causes:

> Here then on the table before us are photographs. The Spanish Government sends them out with patient pertinacity about twice a week. They are not pleasant photographs to look upon. They are photographs of dead bodies for the most part. This morning's collection contains the photograph of what might be a man's body, or a woman's; it is so mutilated that it might, on the other hand, be the body of a pig. But those certainly are dead children,

and that undoubtedly is the section of a house. A bomb has torn open the side; there is still a birdcage hanging in what was presumably the sitting-room, but the rest of the house looks like nothing so much as a bunch of spillikins suspended in mid-air. (TG, p. 164)

In its subdued tone this description differs radically from the detailed and explicit quality of the photographs from Getafe and their exploitation by the pro-Republican press. Here wounds and mutilations are not graphically rendered but rather transformed into a metaphor for the devaluation of human life produced by the blast, which has deprived the human body of any distinguishing features. Absence and death are signified indirectly, through the survival of familiar objects in utterly defamiliarised surroundings. On the whole, this is a stylised, iconic representation of the horrors of war whose conventional character is confirmed by Woolf's use of the image of the birdcage, by that time an established cliché of war reportage in Spain which even journalists were discouraged from deploying.[21]

This recourse to worn-out phrases and the attendant refusal to animate these images is not typical of Woolf's writing and may be understood as the result of a stylistic choice that is consistent with the arguments laid out in the essay, rather than as a failure of the imagination. The photographs from Spain are introduced within *Three Guineas* to override the language of 'biography, autobiography' and 'the daily paper' (TG, p. 159), which all offer a bewildering multiplicity of opinions on 'the rightness or wrongness of war' but no 'absolute point of view', no 'moral judgement that we must all, whatever our differences, accept'. (TG, p. 163) The Spanish photographs are seen to counteract this proliferation of diverging points of view by bringing about a univocal condemnation of war that admits of no distinctions or differentiations between their viewers:

When we look at those photographs some fusion takes place within us; however different the education, the traditions behind us, our sensations are the same; and they are violent. You, Sir, call them 'horror and disgust'. We also call them horror and disgust. And the same words rise to our lips. War, you say, is an abomination, a barbarity; war must be stopped at whatever cost. And we echo your words. War is an abomination, a barbarity; war must be stopped. For now at last we are looking at the same picture: we are seeing with you the same dead bodies, the same ruined houses. (TG, p. 165)

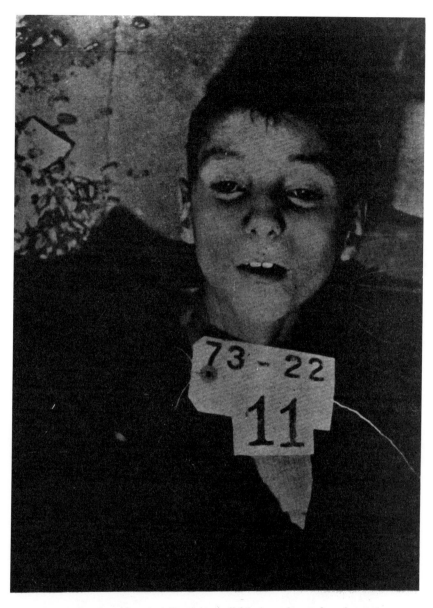

Fotografía obtenida en el Depósito Judicial el 31 de octubre de 1936.
Corresponde a **PEDRO CARRASCAL PUERTOBARRERO**, domiciliado en la
calle del Amparo, núm. 12, que falleció a consecuencia del bombardeo aéreo
efectuado el 30 de octubre de 1936.

Plate 13.1 From the International Brigade Memorial Archive, Marx Memorial Library, London,
Box A-2, File D/59. Caption reads: 'Photograph taken in the Judicial Morgue on 31 October 1936.
It corresponds to Pedro Carrascal Puertobarrero, resident at la calle del Amparo, number 12, who
died as a consequence of the air raid of 30 October 1936.'

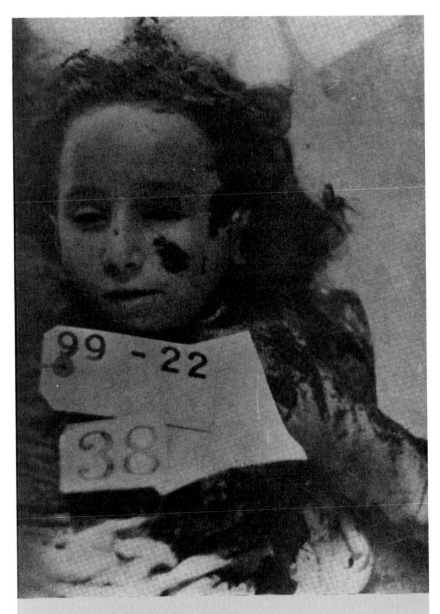

Fotografía obtenida en el Depósito Judicial el 31 de octubre de 1936.
Corresponde a CARMEN GARCIA CISNEROS, domiciliada en la calle del Nuncio, núm. 9, que falleció a consecuencia del bombardeo aéreo efectuado el 30 de octubre de 1936.

Plate 13.2 From the International Brigade Memorial Archive, Marx Memorial Library, London, Box A-2, File D/63. Caption reads: 'Photograph taken in the Judicial Morgue on 31 October 1936. It corresponds to Carmen Garcia Cisneros, resident at la calle del Nuncio, number 9, who died as a consequence of the air raid of 30 October 1936.'

The linguistic response to the power of the photographs is here portrayed as the emergence of an impoverished language that is presented as the most adequate reaction to their emotional impact. Words and images seem to be occupying the two pans of a scale that cannot be balanced, so that the more powerful is the impact of the photographs, the less effective language becomes in conveying it.

The failure of language, its inadequacy when faced with the enormity and monstrosity of war, is a leitmotif in *Three Guineas*, which is consistently struggling with the need to find 'new words' (TG, p. 265–7), to discard 'old, vicious and corrupt' ones (TG, p. 302), or to redefine overused and worn-out phrases. (TG, p. 285) It lies at the roots of the politics of 'secrecy' (TG, p. 330) embodied in the idea of a Society of Outsiders, which the essay promulgates as a sort of underground organisation with the potential to undermine war and the patriarchal system that supports it. It also explains the multiplication of voices and 'veils' (TG, p. 331) behind which the narrator feels the need to hide in order to speak her mind. Finally, this mistrust in the ability of language to communicate effectively is the very *raison d'être* of the form of *Three Guineas*, which, as a letter, is meant to cross the gulf of silence separating its writer from her correspondent. Yet, like all letters that have been too late coming, it finds itself repeatedly backtracking to the reasons for the delay in a manner which postpones the formulation of the reply even further.

Against this background of suspicion about language, the use of photographs in *Three Guineas* takes on an ambiguous character. On the one hand, as 'statement[s] of fact addressed to the eye' (TG, p. 164), photographs are endowed with an objectivity that language can never equal or rival. The Spanish pictures are thus presented as a neutral and impartial record of the reality of war which stands in sharp contrast to the partisan character of linguistic statements expressing different opinions about the value of war. On the other, the objectivity of these photographs is given as the necessary precondition for the construction of a consensus which reconciles different viewpoints and is perceived to be the foundation for the very possibility of communication. Even if the transparency of the photograph as a 'statement of fact' is initially established through its opposition to the potentially manipulative power of language, it is then reclaimed to stem the haemorrhage of linguistic credibility threatening to undermine the very existence of the essay.

The ambivalence that regulates the position of the photograph within the discourse of *Three Guineas* in its turn signals a slippage between two different conceptions of objectivity. In the first, objectivity is taken to rest on a direct and positive correspondence between the photograph and the reality it portrays which cannot be questioned or doubted. This positivistic conception of objectivity is then used as the foundation for a more rhetorical understanding which stresses the role played by the photograph in the formation of consensus. In this second sense, the objectivity of the photograph is identified with its ability to evoke identical responses from entirely different people, which is to say that it rests on the relationship between picture and viewer rather than on that between picture and event portrayed. The implication of this slippage is that the rhetorical or consensual aspect of the photograph as the producer of a unified language can exist only because the photograph itself is seen to lie beyond the realm of rhetoric, in a space where the correspondence between an object and its representation cannot be doubted or questioned.

This shift from epistemological objectivity to consensus is most clearly realised as the argument of *Three Guineas* moves from a consideration of the horrors of war to a detailed analysis of the rituals and customs enshrined in British institutions. The five plates inserted within the essay are collectively captioned as 'a crudely coloured photograph'. As photographs, they are endowed with the primary objectivity that is ascribed to the Spanish pictures, offering a true-to-life representation of their subject, the veracity of which cannot be doubted. This remains, though, a kind of borrowed objectivity, which is exploited by the narrator of *Three Guineas* to lend legitimacy to what is a very partial vision of the world inhabited by her male correspondent. As she concedes, the plates offer a representation of the sphere of public affairs and institutions 'as it appears to us who see it from the threshold of the private house, through the shadow of the veil that St Paul still lays upon our eyes; from the bridge which connects the private house with the world of public life'. (TG, p. 176)

In the terms set out by her earlier discussion of the Spanish pictures, these plates are presented therefore as occupying a mid-way position between the two poles of objective statement and rhetorical construct. Unlike the photographs from Spain, they are susceptible of multiple and contrasting interpretations, which in their turn illustrate the interests, traditions and education of their viewers. The first of the plates, for example, is of an elderly general covered in decorations and may be read according to two codes proposed in the text. The first is the conventional one, whereby the general's uniform and decorations are seen as outward symbols of the military virtues that are meant to 'impress the beholder with the majesty of the military office' and 'through their vanity to induce young men to become soldiers'. (TG, p. 180) This reading, which is a consensual one, is then disrupted by the intervention of the dissenting voices of those daughters of educated men who are excluded from practising the military profession. In the eyes of these outsiders, the display of military virtues 'by wearing pieces of metal, or ribbon' (TG, p. 179) is turned from 'a pleasing or an impressive spectacle' (TG, p. 180) to 'a barbarity which deserves the ridicule which we bestow upon the rites of savages'. (TG, p. 179)

The second reading of the general's picture suggests an alternative vision of imperial history which becomes fully articulated when the five photographic plates are read not as individual images, but rather as a continuum, as a narrative that is suspended between the condition of photography and that of the silent movie. This narrative traces back the internal fracture or divergence of views exemplified in the reading of the general's picture to the difference in educational opportunities enjoyed by the men and women of the educated class that is symbolised by the third plate. The photograph of the university procession is placed next to Mary Kingsley's recurring lament: "'I don't know if I ever revealed to you the fact that being allowed to learn German was all the paid-for education I ever had ...'" (TG, p. 155) Her comments on the disparity of educational provisions between herself and her brother form the 'angle' from which the photograph of the university procession is observed, revealing 'a world so remote, so formidable, so intricate in its ceremonies and traditions that any criticism or comment may well seem futile'. (TG, p. 183)

This characterisation of the world of the university as impermeable by and incomprehensible to those who have been excluded from it signals that the status of the photograph has undergone a significant transformation in the passage from the Spanish pictures to those of the march of the professions. Rather than being a transparent signifier capable of revealing those truths about historical events which writing cannot speak, these photographs become opaque representations which need the intervention of the text to yield their intended meaning(s). This transformation is especially evident when *Three Guineas* comes to discuss the opening up of the professions to women, a historical event which might have led to a radical change in the shape and direction of the march of the professions which in the essay symbolises the course of patriarchal history. The Sex Disqualification Removal Act of 1919 is taken to mark a potentially momentous change in the history of women's perception of this procession, which stops being 'a sight merely, a photograph, or fresco scrawled upon the walls of time, at which we can look with merely an aesthetic appreciation' (TG, p. 241), and becomes instead a movement which they may join, if they so wish.

This notion of transformation, though, is counteracted by the image of a judge in full dress presented by the fourth plate. In his opulence of flesh as well as of dress, from the tip of his wig to the bottom of his buckled shoes, this judge is offered as indisputable evidence of the connection between privilege and access to justice that the narrator claims is still preventing women from reaching the highest ranks of the professions. The resistance to change symbolised by the judge is confirmed by the data collected in *Whitaker's Almanac,* which offer ample evidence of the discrimination suffered by women within the Civil Service. Through this interplay between commentary and photograph, the initial interpretation of the 1919 Act as a moment of change in the history of women's exclusion from public life is revealed to be the result of an optical illusion, a distortion of perception that the photograph of the judge intervenes to correct.

This deployment of the photograph as evidence of a version of events that conflicts with that given in the text indicates a different use of the gap between language and photographic representation that had first been opened up in the description of the photographs from Spain. In the earlier instance that gap had worked both to underline the inadequacy of language as an instrument of communication and to establish the foundations for a consensus around the issue of war. But as Woolf's argument moves from the need to condemn war to an analysis of British patriarchal institutions, the distance that separates writing and photography stops functioning as a facilitator of consensus and becomes instead a space for the articulation of dissent. In this different use of the gap, the commentary exposes what we might call with Walter Benjamin the 'optical unconscious' of the images to which it relates.[22] The march of patriarchal history is thus broken up into a sequence of still photographs that capture the smaller movements and moments which would otherwise not be perceivable to the human eye.

In Benjamin's account of the history of photography, the revelation of the optical unconscious represents the specific contribution made by the new visual medium to European culture. Woolf's appropriation for writing of the function Benjamin ascribes to photography indicates both her recognition of the very specific quality of the power yielded by the medium and her anxiety about language's ability to withstand the challenge brought by photography. This anxiety is part of a wider concern expressed by Woolf in relation to the field of visual representation, which she feared might have been better positioned than writing to stand as a space of experimentation with new forms.[23] Her use of photographs in *Three Guineas*, both of the fictionalised pictures from Spain and of the actual plates, aims to set up an integrated system of representation where writing can take on the appearance of photography while photographs become densely textured artefacts in need of interpretation.

This exchange of functions between writing and photography is essential to establishing a central claim of the essay: the existence of a causal link between Fascism abroad and patriarchy at home, between the fictional pictures from Spain and the real plates from Britain. As writing and photography switch their respective positions, the distance between the two sets of photographs, one existing only in writing, the other reproduced as pictures, is shortened, with an effect of superimposition that brings to light the relation of one to the other. In this way *Three Guineas* manages to institute a linear connection between what can be seen, and therefore photographed, and what remains invisible but might nevertheless find some kind of articulation through language. This means that the type of irrefutable proof which the essay sets out to find is ultimately provided not by its photographs, but by language itself in its capacity to contain and control what photography is allowed to say.[24]

Notes

1. Throughout this chapter I refer to *Three Guineas* as an essay not in the broader sense of the term, but in a strictly generic one. This is meant to foreground the issue of genre in relation to Woolf's political writings and to reflect *Three Guineas*'s genealogy in her experiments with the mixed form of the 'novel-essay' from which *The Years* will also emerge. For an account of that genealogy, see Mitchell A. Leaska's introduction to *The Pargiters: The Novel-Essay Portion of* The Years (London: Hogarth, 1978), pp. ix–xxvii.

2. *Times Literary Supplement*, 4 June 1938. See also Anne Olivier Bell and Andrew McNeillie (eds), *The Diary of Virginia Woolf*, vol. 5 (1984; Harmondsworth: Penguin, 1985), p. 148 (3 June 1938), hereafter *Diary*, 5.

3. For a sample of readings celebrating Woolf's foresight in her analysis of the connections that link patriarchy and Fascism see Jane Marcus, *Art and Anger: Reading Like a Woman* (Columbus: Ohio State University Press, 1988), pp. 101–21; Brenda Silver, 'The Authority of Anger: *Three Guineas* as Case-Study', *Signs* 16.2 (1991), pp. 340–70; Susan Squier, *Virginia Woolf and London: The Sexual Politics of the City* (Chapel Hill: University of North Carolina Press, 1985), pp. 180–89. Michèle Barrett's introduction to *A Room of One's Own* and *Three Guineas* is at odds with these readings, stressing the ambivalent character of Woolf's political and feminist statements in the later essay (Harmondsworth: Penguin, 1993), pp. ix–liii. For a balanced analysis of the anti-Fascism of *Three Guineas* see Maroula Joannou, *'Ladies, Please Don't Smash These Windows': Women's Writing, Feminist Consciousness and Social Change 1918–1938* (Oxford, Berg, 1995), pp. 159–90. To my knowledge, there are only two readings of *Three Guineas* that mention the role played by the photograph in the overall economy of its arguments: see Patricia Laurence, 'The Facts and Fugue of War: From *Three Guineas* to *Between the Acts*', in Mark Hussey (ed.), *Virginia Woolf and War: Fiction, Reality, Myth* (New York: Syracuse University Press, 1991), pp. 225–45, and

Leila Brosnan, *Reading Virginia Woolf's Essays and Journalism* (Edinburgh: Edinburgh University Press, 1997), pp. 129–31.

4. Virginia Woolf, *Three Guineas* (London: Hogarth, 1938, where the plates are located opposite pp. 37, 39, 43, 113, 220.

5. For the reference to Frau Pommer see Morag Shiach (ed. and introduction), *Three Guineas* (Oxford: Oxford University Press, 1992), p. 395, n. 39. Subsequent references to this edition are incorporated into the main text as, for example, TG, p. 395, n. 39.

6. Monks House Papers Archive, University of Sussex Library, catalogue number B. 16f (hereafter MHP B. 16f); this particular page can be found in vol. 2 of the scrapbooks, p. 20 (in Woolf's own numbering). Both the cutting on Frau Pommer and the one reporting Hitler's speech are reprinted in Appendix I, pp. 350–53 of the Penguin edition, edited and introduction by Michèle Barrett. A full description of the contents of the scrapbooks is given in Brenda Silver, *Virginia Woolf's Reading Notebooks* (Princeton: Princeton University Press, 1983), pp. 255–314.

7. MHP B. 16f, vol. 2, p. 45.

8. MHP B. 16f, vol. 2, p. 46

9. MHP B. 16f, vol. 2, p. 44

10. MHP B. 16f, vol. 3, p. 61.

11. Nigel Nicolson and Joanne Trautmann (eds), *The Letters of Virginia Woolf*, vol. 6 (London: Hogarth Press, 1980), p. 85; hereafter *Letters*, 6.

12. See Arturo Barea's autobiography, *The Forging of a Rebel*, tr. Ilsa Barea (1941–6; London: Davis-Poynter, 1972), p. 585. I am extremely grateful to Rob Stradling of the University of Cardiff for alerting me to this passage in Barea and connecting the pictures from Getafe to those mentioned by Woolf in her letter.

13. Barea, *The Forging of a Rebel*, p. 596.

14. Caroline Brothers, *War and Photography: A Cultural History* (London: Routledge, 1997), p. 176, for the quotation and discussion of the *Daily Worker* page, which is reprinted in Brothers on p. 177.

15. See 'Why Art Today Follows Politics', in Rachel Bowlby (ed. and introduction), *The Crowded Dance of Modern Life* (Harmondsworth: Penguin, 1993), pp. 133–6.

16. *Diary*, 5, p. 32.

17. *Diary*, 5, p. 35.

18. Silver, *Virginia Woolf's Reading Notebooks*, p. 252.

19. MHP B. 16b, page unnumbered. Many thanks to Bet Inglis of the University of Sussex Library for her help with the scrapbooks and in deciphering Woolf's handwriting.

20. For Woolf's comments on having written *Three Guineas* as an argument with Bell see *Letters*, 6, p. 159 (17 August 1937); *Diary*, 5, pp. 111 (12 September 1937), 148 (3 June 1938).

21. On the birdcage as cliché see Claud Cockburn, *In Time of Trouble: An Autobiography* (London: Readers Union–Rupert Hart-Davis, 1957), p. 116, where he tells an anecdote of the Spanish War when one of his colleagues 'was sharply rebuked for mentioning a canary as the only living creature in one of the bombed houses of a village' and had to remove the remark even if it was factually accurate. Many thanks to Janet Montefiore for alerting me to this passage.

22. Walter Benjamin, 'A Small History of Photography' (1931), in *One-way Street and Other Writings*, tr. Edmund Jephcott and Kingsley Shorter (London: NLB, 1979), p. 243. Rachel Bowlby has also found echoes of Benjamin's notion in Woolf's essay on the cinema; see her introduction to *Crowded Dance*, pp. xx–xxiii.

23. See, for instance, 'Walter Sickert: A Conversation' (1934), in Leonard Woolf (ed.), *Collected Essays*, vol. 2 (London: Hogarth, 1966–7), pp. 233–44, and 'Foreword to Recent Paintings by Vanessa Bell' (1930), in *Crowded Dance*, pp. 97–100.

24. For Susan Sontag's famous dictum that 'as Wittgenstein argued for words, that the meaning *is* the use – so for each photograph', see *On Photography* (1973; London: Allen Lane, 1978), p. 106. In an extension of Sontag's proposition Mary Price has recently argued that the meaning of a photograph is always overdetermined by the verbal descriptions that accompany it; see *The Photograph: A Strange Confined Space* (Stanford: Stanford University Press, 1994).

14

Hyams Place: *The Years*, the Jews and the British Union of Fascists

David Bradshaw

Although 'The Jewish Question' formed no part of British Union of Fascists (BUF) policy when Oswald Mosley launched his organisation on 1 October 1932, anti-Semitism quickly gained a foothold in the BUF and by June 1934 it had become a key component of Mosley's demagogy. As he put it four years later in *Tomorrow We Live*, the Jew 'comes from the Orient and physically, mentally and spiritually, is more alien to us than any Western nation'.[1] Mosley expressed such sentiments on numerous occasions in the 1930s, especially in the period 1934–8, and if it had won power the BUF would have forcibly expelled British Jews deemed to be enemies of the Fascist state, while those allowed to remain in Britain would have been deprived of their citizenship.[2]

By the mid-1930s, of course, the persecution of Jews in the Third Reich was both well advanced and well documented. When Leonard and Virginia Woolf toured Germany in 1935 they saw banners in Bonn which proclaimed 'The Jew is our enemy' and 'There is no place for Jews in …'[3] The twofold argument of this essay is that Woolf's first-hand experience of German anti-Semitism, coupled with her exposure to newspaper coverage of the BUF's verbal and physical attacks on Jews, prompted her to link two kinds of anti-Semitism in *The Years*, while at the same time stressing the rightful 'place' of Jews in Britain both through the imaginary names of two important locations in the novel and through periodic references to the 'Jewish' colours blue and white. A number of critics have recognised that in her penultimate novel Woolf anatomises the 'deformed'[4] culture of which she was both a product and a victim, a civilisation disfigured by patriarchy, imperialism, militarism, homophobia, class prejudice and xenophobia. But Woolf's critical alignment of the BUF's and the Pargiters' anti-Semitism in *The Years*, and the way in which she inscribes her resistance to such bigotry, has not been examined hitherto.

Examples of anti-Semitism appear to be carefully spaced in *The Years*. In the first chapter, Eleanor Pargiter tells one of her sisters about a Jewish tenant named Mrs Levy and her family. '"Jews?" said Milly. She seemed to consider the taste of the Jews; and then to dismiss it'. (p. 30) Further on in the '1880' chapter, the ambitious Edward Pargiter weighs up the threat posed to his advancement at Oxford by a 'clever little Jew-boy from Birmingham'. (p. 48) Shortly afterwards the rain is said to have 'splayed out of the laughing mouths of gargoyles', and to have 'smeared the window where the Jew-boy from Birmingham sat mugging up Greek with a wet towel round his head' (p. 61), descriptive phrases which both confer a kind of institutional sanction on Edward Pargiter's contempt for his fellow undergraduate, and which anticipate, respectively, Sara and North Pargiter's grotesque anti-Semitic exchange in the 'Present Day' chapter and the chalking of BUF graffiti on the windows and doors of Jewish houses which the reader encounters just before it.

It is likely that the man addressing the crowd at Speakers' Corner in the '1914' chapter is another of the novel's anti-Semites. His point appears to be that Jews are conspicuous aliens in London whereas he is indigenous. 'Do I look like a Jew?' he asks his audience, while simultaneously holding up what is most probably a hideous caricature of one for contrast. (p. 228) Mrs Treyer, a guest at Kitty Lasswade's party in the same chapter, is described as 'an Oriental-looking woman, with a feather floating back from her head in harmony with her nose, which was Jewish'. (p. 245) Martin Pargiter feels he has 'nothing to say to that Oriental-looking harpy' whom he regards as one of Kitty's 'less desirable friends'. (p. 251) The Pargiters seem to be 'Spinners and sitters in the sun ... tolerant, assured' (p. 389), but their civilised comportment merely pargets over their racial intolerance and their more general obnoxiousness.

However, as mentioned above, the anti-Semitism of the Pargiters is nowhere more shockingly exposed than in the 'Present Day' chapter when Sara and North vilify a Jewish tallow-trade worker. North is reciting Marvell's 'The Garden' when Sara raises her hand:

> Her eyes were on the door.
> 'The Jew,' she murmured.
> 'The Jew?' he said ...

'The Jew having a bath,' she said.

'The Jew having a bath?' he repeated.

'And tomorrow there'll be a line of grease round the bath,' she said.

'Damn the Jew!' he exclaimed. The thought of a line of grease from a strange man's body on the bath next door disgusted him.

'Go on –' said Sara: 'Society is all but rude,' she repeated the last lines, 'to this delicious solitude.'

'No,' he said.

They listened to the water running. The man was coughing and clearing his throat as he sponged.

'Who is this Jew?' he asked. (p. 322)

Sara tells him that he is called Abrahamson and that 'he leaves hairs in the bath'. (p. 323) This makes North 'shiver' with revulsion:

'D'you share a bath with him?' he asked.

She nodded.

He made a noise like 'Pah!'

'"Pah." That's what I said,' she laughed ... "Pah!" – she threw her hand out – "Pah!"' (p. 323)

Sara informs North that following one of Abrahamson's previous visits to the bathroom she had rushed to a bridge over the Thames and asked the crowd flowing over it why she should '"join [their] conspiracy? ... all because of a Jew in my bath, all because of a Jew?"' (p. 323) She recalls that she had then dashed round to the office of a newspaper editor to report the presence of a Jew in her bath (Sara's account of her meeting with him is as incoherent as her description of the meeting she is taken to by Rose (pp. 178–9) earlier in the novel). North and Sara are brought back to the present when they 'hear the Jew thudding in the bathroom; he seemed to stagger from foot to foot as he dried himself. Now he unlocked the door, and they heard him go upstairs. The pipes began to give forth hollow gurgling sounds' (pp. 324–5), as if in mockery of Abrahamson's throat-clearing. The lodging-house plumbing is as collusive as the Oxford rain.

Discussing the holograph version of this passage, Grace Radin has commented: 'The disgust Elvira [who becomes Sara in *The Years*] expresses at sharing a bath with a greasy Jew sounds anti-Semitic. Such an attitude would not be uncommon among women of Elvira's background, and it may well have been Virginia Stephen's own attitude before she came to know Jews like Leonard Woolf and S. S. Koteliansky.'[5]

This last point is controversial, but it is widely accepted that anti-Semitism was not uncommon in upper-middle-class circles in the period covered by *The Years*,[6] and the question of how near Woolf's own attitudes were to those of her characters (if they were near at all) continues to be raised. Phyllis Lassner, for instance, is one of a number of critics who have interrogated Woolf's 'ideological assumptions' in *The Years*, *Three Guineas* and 'The Duchess and the Jeweller'.[7] In her discussion of *The Years*, Lassner focuses on the Abrahamson passage and quotes Freema Gottleib's observation that it '"savour[s] of the genteel antisemitism which afflicted Chamberlain's England in the years immediately preceding the Second World War"'. (p. 134)[8] But while Lassner rightly argues that Sara and North's 'discourse affirms the view that Woolf represents her characters' prejudices rather than her own' (p. 135), she goes on to ask: 'Where does [Woolf] position herself as "outsider" when, on the one hand, there is no positive identification with that other outsider, the Jew, and no narrative distance from the "sinister implications" of his portrait?' (p. 135)[9] Lassner emphasises what she sees as Woolf's 'ambivalence' towards Jews and contends that in *The Years* 'the question remains one of literary representation and its impact on readers, especially those concerned with her moral and political vision', before concluding her remarks on the Abrahamson passage with the comment that:

> In the 'sordid' history of how two characters in England between the wars perceive the Jew, the modernist moment fails to distinguish between 'genteel anti-semitism', Nazi racial policy, the plight of an impoverished and handicapped woman, and that of a Jew in 1936. (p. 136)

It seems clear to me, however, that the novel does draw such distinctions (albeit in a typically oblique fashion), and that in a text which is fundamentally concerned with deformation, pollution (p. 323), smeared things (for example, p. 140) and stains (for example, p. 298), Woolf does take care to positively identify with Jews and to provide a precise historical context for Sara's smear on Abrahamson which leaves the reader in no doubt as to the heinousness of her outburst.

Unlike the 'chalk cages' of the hopscotch games which children play on the pavements outside the houses of Mira (p. 9), Maggie and Sara (p. 165) and Delia (p. 111); 'the chalk marks which decorate academic lintels' (p. 55) at Edward Pargiter's college; and the words 'God is love' which have been scrawled in pink chalk on the gates of Apsley House (pp. 215, 147), the chalk symbols which deface the houses in the East End street which North passes along in the neighbourhood of Sara's house signify oppression. 'Somebody had chalked a circle on the wall with a jagged line in it' North observes. 'He looked down the long vista. Door after door, window after window repeated the same pattern'. (p. 294) In her specific description of what has been daubed on the houses, Woolf makes it quite plain that this graffiti is the work of the BUF and its supporters. 'This is our modern symbol which belongs exclusively to British Fascism' Mosley wrote. 'It portrays the flash of action in the circle of unity'.[10] On 4 September 1935, the day she decided to call her novel *The Years* and the day following the League of Nations' last-ditch attempt to defuse the build-up of tension which followed the clash between Italian and Ethiopian troops at the Walwal oasis on 5 December 1934, Woolf wrote in her diary:

> The most critical day since Aug 4th 1914. So the papers say. In London yesterday. Writings chalked up all over the walls. 'Don't fight for foreigners. Briton should mind her own business.' Then a circle with a symbol in it. Fascist propaganda, L. said. Mosley active again.[11]

The modern history of the Jews in Britain begins with 'the waves of immigration of Jews from Russia and eastern Europe that beat upon the shores of Britain in the quarter century following the assassination of Tsar Alexander II [in 1881]'.[12] The vast majority of these immigrants settled in the East End of London, with the result that before the BUF had even been founded the area had become a place 'where cultural tensions existed in certain parts between sections of the non-Jewish population and Jewish residents, in the sense that not all the former had reconciled themselves to that "piece of Jewish East Europe" which had been "torn up and put down again in the middle of East London"'.[13] On 28 October 1934 Mosley launched a vehement attack on Jews during a BUF rally at the Royal Albert Hall – 'It was, in effect, a declaration of war upon the Jewish community in Britain' one commentator has observed[14] – and from now on Fascist activity in the East End intensified.

Sara lives 'near the Prison Tower' (p. 293) (i.e., near the Tower of London) and so not far from the scene of the infamous 'Battle of Cable Street', the bloody climax of two years of almost continuous disorder involving Fascists and Jews in the East End, when, according to the BUF's version of events, 'the alien underworld of London rioted against a proposed march of British Blackshirts through British streets' on 4 October 1936.[15] In *Three Guineas* Woolf writes about the barriers which in her eyes made Oxford and Cambridge 'such uneasy dwelling-places – cities of strife ... where nobody can walk freely or talk freely for fear of transgressing some chalk mark ...' (p. 63) Further on in *Three Guineas* she writes of a 'monstrous male, loud of voice, hard of fist, childishly intent upon scoring the floor of the earth with chalk marks, within whose mystic boundaries human beings are penned, rigidly, separately, artificially'. (p. 191) Similarly, in the East End section of the 'Present Day' chapter, Woolf asks her readers to reflect on the oppressed and 'uneasy dwelling-place' which the area was for Jews during the stormy days of the BUF's East End campaign in 1935–7, and to take on board the appalling closeness of Sara's anti-Jewish invective to the rabble-rousing rhetoric of Mosley and his followers. Lewis notes that the BUF organised many street meetings in the East End, 'which on occasions could exceed 200 in a single month' and which were intended to terrorise Jews. He also reveals that the Battle of Cable Street was followed by what 'amounted to a virtual pogrom in the Mile End Road in October 1936'.[16]

Woolf followed the activities of the BUF with consternation. 'Leonard is caballing with the Labour Party as usual,' she told Quentin Bell on 24 January 1934. 'They think Mosley is getting supporters. If so, I shall emigrate'.[17] The following month she saw in the Fascist coup d'état which destabilised Austria 'the beginning of the end. We are to have Mosley within five years'.[18] Just under a year later, though, she was able to record in her diary that 'Mosley has no chance in the North ... He has had to shut down several branches',[19] but the Fascist threat was no less visible in London, where she not only observed BUF slogans and insignia scrawled on walls but also, in November 1936, on the front page of the *Blackshirt*, the BUF's newspaper.[20]

In the context of the BUF's anti-Semitic activity in the East End, therefore, Sara Pargiter's comments on the poor hygiene of Abrahamson, and her repugnance at the mere thought of him, assume a dreadful significance. 'In the holograph,' Radin informs us, 'Elvira will decide to remain in her apartment and learn to live with her Jew ... on even more intimate terms' (note, p. 95), and she also records that in a passage added to the party scene towards the end of the holograph Elvira concedes 'that perhaps the Jew is not such a bad fellow after all'. (p. 102) But Sara shows no sign of such open-mindedness in *The Years*, and even her gestures in her East End room bear a disquieting resemblance to those of the Fascists in the streets outside it. When waiting for Abel Pargiter to speak, Sara's mother is said to have 'raised her hand as if in expectation' (p. 115), and elsewhere her sister Maggie also 'raise[s] her hand with a curious gesture to her face'. (p. 162) A little further on in the novel Maggie again 'raise[s] her arms as if to ward off some implacable destiny' (p. 181), while Eleanor, too, has a proclivity to raise her hand in this way. (p. 411) So Sara's tendency to do the same thing is probably no more than a hereditary mannerism which symbolises the Pargiter women's need to defend themselves from the abuses of the patriarchal system; at one point in the '1917' chapter Sara 'raise[s] her hand to her head as if in salute' (p. 271) when describing her meeting with North on the day he leaves for the Front.

But while the most obvious explanation for Sara holding up her hand when North enters her room is that she is on the telephone (p. 295) – she is signalling to him that she cannot speak at that moment – when she raises her hand again as Abrahamson approaches the bathroom, and flings it out twice more when she tells her story of rushing to the Thames and the newspaper office (p. 323), her actions look more sinister. It would be going too far to suggest that Sara is actually saluting (either in earnest or in jest) in the Fascist manner, but such a reading would only be consistent with her almost ideological distaste for Abrahamson. As a girl, Sara's 'crooked[ness]' (p. 306) is mocked by North and Peggy and she is deprived of fatherly love (pp. 117, 122, 138); it is obvious that her deformed shoulder is just as much a token of her marred experience of life as a manifestation of her warped response to it. But these factors fail to explain the virulence of Sara's reaction to Abrahamson. The contrast with Eleanor's admiration for and work on behalf of the 'dear old Levys' (pp. 17, 29–30) could not be more striking – a point which is heightened by Woolf's changing of this character's name from Elvira to Sara. Sara, of course, was the wife of Abraham, and Woolf stresses the unnaturalness of Sara's almost pathological aversion to Abrahamson by emphasising her 'motherly' kinship with him; he is, in a nominal sense, her 'son' as well as Abraham's. In denigrating a figurative scion of the first Hebrew patriarch, Sara defames all Jews, and in her treatment of this character Woolf cautions that a room of one's own may just as easily become a site of evil and complicity as the drawing room of a Victorian family house. She registers her acknowledgment that the 'Outsider' is just as susceptible to bigotry as those who have excluded her. It is even possible that this was the 'point' which Woolf said she had in mind when she wrote the novel.[21] Sara is undoubtedly 'an odd customer' (p. 166), as a Holborn violet-seller recognises at one point in the novel, but at some stage Woolf seems to have decided to use her to represent the malignancy of 'Hitler in England'.[22]

Nicholas Pomjalowsky, who according to Radin is described as being 'half-Jewish' in the holograph (p. 95), tells Sara she is 'Prejudiced, narrow, unfair ...' (p. 272) – and with good reason, since the Pargiters' inveterate bigotry may well be evident in their nickname for him. They know Pomjalowsky is homosexual as early as 1918, but they do not call him Brown at that stage. In the 'Present Day' chapter, however, the Pargiters call Pomjalowsky 'Brown for short'. (p. 290) 'Why Brown if he's a foreigner, [North] wondered'. (p. 293) Perhaps because by the 1930s 'brown hat' was upper-middle-class slang for a homosexual, and Woolf wishes to call attention to the way in which the Pargiters cannot override their generic distaste for homosexuals even though they like Pomjalowsky as an individual.[23]

But Woolf does more than draw a parallel between the anti-Semitism of her own class and the BUF in *The Years*. Encoded within the novel is a complementary narrative in which a sequence of references to blue-and-white things emphasises the long history and legitimate place of the Jews in Britain. These blue-and-white markers appear to be spaced with the same care as the examples of anti-Semitism in *The Years*. Blue and white are the traditional colours of the tallith, the Jewish prayer shawl,[24] and they had been chosen as the colours of the Zionist flag as early as 1891. 'In 1933', however, 'the 18th Zionist Congress decided at its meeting [in Prague] that "by long tradition the blue-and-white flag is the flag of the Zionist Organisation *and the Jewish people*"'.[25] In the Pargiters' house in Abercorn Terrace there is a 'Dutch cabinet with blue china on the shelves' which is mentioned on four occasions (pp. 10, 11, 71, 148) – and no doubt the 'willow-pattern plates' (pp. 299, 304) in Sara's East End sitting room are from this set, one of many examples in the novel of the theme of inheritance. The Pargiter women wear 'dresses of blue and white sprigged muslin' (p. 34) in the '1880' chapter, and Edward recalls that when he last dined with Kitty Malone she wore a 'white and blue dress'. (p. 50) At the house of Lucy Craddock, Kitty's tutor, there is a bowl of flowers containing 'wild flowers, blue and white, stuck into a cushion of wet green moss' (p. 63) and further on in the novel, when Kitty (now Lady Lasswade) arrives back in Yorkshire, she comes across 'blue flowers and white flowers, trembling on cushions of green moss' (p. 264) while walking in her grounds. One way of understanding this repeated image is to read it as symbolic of the rootedness of Jews in England's legendarily 'green and pleasant land'. Again, in '1910', Rose watches Maggie place some flowers in a vase. '[Maggie] reminded Rose, as she watched her, of [her father] Digby ... as if to arrange flowers, to put the white by the blue, were the most important thing in the world' (p. 160) and one sentence later we read: 'Maggie took a blue flower and placed it beside a white flower'. Edward Pargiter wears a 'new blue suit with white stripes on it' (p. 149) in '1908' and in '1911' Edward VII is said to have been taken to his final resting place, highly eccentrically, 'under a white and blue Union Jack'. (p. 183) In that Woolf could hardly have been ignorant of the colours of her national flag, this strange statement must carry some other significance. It is probable that Woolf makes no reference to the Union Jack's red as a way of alluding to Edward VII's philo-Semitic reputation, the fact that, as André Maurois put it in 1933, he 'liked the society ... of Jews'.[26] E. F. Benson, in his own biography of Edward VII, also published in 1933, wrote of Edward when Prince of Wales:

> There was something about Jews that suited him: he like staying at their houses ... Great was the effect of the Prince's influence and example, and English homes which had been impregnable to the 'bright children of the sun,' as Disraeli gaily called his compatriots, were flung open when Prince Hal made them welcome.[27]

Further on in '1911', Eleanor stands in 'the Blue room' at Wittering in her white petticoat (p. 188), while in the most curious example of all, Sara arrives at Delia's party 'with one stocking that is white and one stocking that is blue'. (p. 351) Grace Radin has argued that Woolf has Sara appear at the party '[d]ressed as a fool, she retains her right to ridicule and mock, to be different' (p. 99), and this reading is not implausible. But Sara's strange stockings may be looked at in a different way. They are the last blue-and-white things in the novel, and as such it is deeply ironic that Sara turns up at Delia's party, hotfoot from her anti-Semitic rant, dressed in the colours of 'the Jewish people'.

The names of two imaginary London thoroughfares in *The Years* provide further evidence that Woolf was anxious to record, subtly but unmistakably, her abhorrence of, and resistance to, the harassment of Jews in London and beyond. First, in the '1910' chapter, Sara and Maggie live in a fictional Southwark street named Hyams Place. On her way to visit her cousins Rose wonders 'Who was Hyam?' (p. 155), unaware that 'Hyam' comes from 'the Hebrew word *hayyim* meaning life'.[28] Woolf's choice of street name expresses both her sense of the 'life' of the capital in general and, more specifically, the contribution of Jews to that life.

The connotations of the imaginary 'Milton Street' (p. 293), where Sara lives in the 'Present Day' chapter, are even more noteworthy. It seems certain that Woolf invents this street in order to recall the moment in English history when the Jews were formally readmitted into this country after an enforced absence of nearly four hundred years. Woolf would have been familiar with Leslie Stephen's essay on Milton in the *Dictionary of National Biography*, in which her father records that after the poet had lost his sight, 'the Bible was read to him in Hebrew' every morning before breakfast, and in which Stephen acknowledges in a note that 'Everything knowable about Milton has been given, with careful references to original sources, in Professor Masson's *Life of John Milton* ...'[29] In his fifth volume, Masson pauses to describe Cromwell's 'attempt to obtain an open toleration for the Jews in England':

> Since the year 1290, when they had been banished in a body out of the kingdom under Edward I, there had been only isolated and furtive instances of visits to England or residence in England by persons of the proscribed race. Of late, however, a certain Manasseh Ben Israel, an able and earnest Portuguese Jew ... had conceived the idea that, in the new age of liberty and other great things in England, there might be a permission for the Jews to return and live and trade freely ... Cromwell was thoroughly in favour of the proposal and let the fact be known ... In effect the readmission of the Jews into England dates from Cromwell's Protectorate.[30]

In that he was Cromwell's Latin Secretary, one of Milton's more recent biographers has argued that 'it must have been he who negotiated with the famed Rabbi Menasseh ben Israel for the readmission of the Jews to London' towards the end of 1655.[31] While the historian David Katz provides no evidence to support this claim in either of his standard books on the subject, it does seem possible that Woolf may have had Masson's passage on Cromwell and the readmission of the Jews in mind when she conceived the Abrahamson scene. But whether she did or did not, the crucial point is that Sara and North revile a Jew in a street bearing the name of the poet and libertarian whose works contain, as Woolf knew, 'an unusual concentration of biblical and Judaic sentiments ... [and whose] knowledge of Hebrew and Aramaic was sufficient to enable him in later years to read the Hebrew Bible and probably also the classical Hebrew commentators'.[32] In a manner which is characteristically indirect, Woolf challenges the BUF's declared policy of extirpating what it regarded as 'alien' elements from British society by evoking the 'new age of liberty' when Jews ceased to be a proscribed race and began to live freely in England once more.

In this respect it is also important to note that Abrahamson is 'Engaged to a pretty girl in a tailor's shop'. (p. 322) In the '1880' chapter, the daughter of Mrs Levy 'was working for a tailor' (p. 29) and, while it would be rather unusual if this same woman were also Abrahamson's fiancée, this is another detail in the novel which emphasises the continuous modern history of the Jews of London. In contrast, the 'Present Day' is a 'here and now' (p. 406) peopled by the blackshirts of the BUF and the greenshirts of John Hargrave's Anti-Semitic Social Credit Party of Great Britain. (p. 389)[33] Evening papers carry 'the usual ... blurred picture of a fat man gesticulating' (p. 313) and Pomjalowsky's broken wine glass (p. 405) is a portent of the shattered buildings and shattered lives which aerial bombardment will shortly bring to London.[34] In the last paragraph of the novel the morning sky wears 'an air of extraordinary beauty, simplicity and peace', but it is deeply deceptive, like the Pargiters' civilised polish.

The textual history of *The Years* shows that Woolf moved on from her idea of interlarding fiction and didactic essays soon after starting her penultimate novel. Nevertheless, Avrom Fleishman has written about how a reader of the novel might still pick up 'the impression that [it] ... is not an authentic product of the Woolfian imagination'. 'Yet, with sustained attention,' he continues, '*The Years*, composed with many of the same techniques, will be found to express its meaning in much the same terms as the greater members of the canon'.[35] As critics continue to prove Fleishman right, revealing how *The Years* 'shows the links among various exclusions: of women, homosexuals, servants, and colonized people', it is time to add Jews to that list.[36]

Notes

1. Oswald Mosley, *Tomorrow We Live*, 2nd edn. (London: BUF, 1938), p. 59. Ominously, the last section of this chapter on 'The Jewish Question' is headed 'The Final Solution', in which Mosley argues that a 'National Jewish State' should be created in one of the 'waste places of the earth'. (p. 60)

2. For detailed studies of the BUF, and more specifically its anti-Semitism, see Robert Benewick, *The Fascist Movement in Britain* (London: Allen Lane and The Penguin Press, 1972), especially pp. 217–34; Stephen Cullen, 'The Development of the Ideas and Policy of the British Union of Fascists, 1932–40', in *Journal of Contemporary History*, vol. 22, no. 1, January 1987, pp. 115–136; Colin Holmes, 'Anti-semitism and the British Union of Fascists', in Kenneth Lunn and Richard C. Thurlow (eds), *British Fascism: Essays on the Radical Right in Inter-War Britain* (London: Croom Helm, 1980), pp. 114–134; D. S. Lewis, *Illusions of Grandeur: Mosley, Fascism and British Society, 1931–81* (Manchester: Manchester University Press, 1987), especially pp. 90–113; Thomas P. Lineham, *East London for Mosley: The British Union of Fascists in East London and South-West Essex 1933–40* (London and Portland, Oregon: Frank Cass, 1998); W. F. Mandle, *Anti-Semitism and the British Union of Fascists* (London: Longman, 1968); Robert Skidelsky, *Oswald Mosley*, 3rd edn. (London and Basingstoke: Papermac, 1990), especially pp. 353–421; Leslie Susser, *Fascist*

and Anti-Fascist Attitudes in Britain Between the Wars (unpublished thesis, University of Oxford, 1989: MS DPhil c. 7624).

3. Anne Olivier Bell and Andrew McNeillie (eds), *The Diary of Virginia Woolf*, vol. 4, 1931–5 (London: Hogarth Press, 1982). p. 311.

4. Hermione Lee (ed.), *The Years* (Oxford: Oxford World's Classics, 1992), p. 361. Further references are to this edition and page numbers are given in the body of the text.

5. Grace Radin, *Virginia Woolf's 'The Years': The Evolution of a Novel* (Knoxville: University of Tennessee Press, 1981), p. 94. Further references are to this edition and page numbers are given in the body of the text.

6. See, for example, Hilary Spurling, *Ivy: The Life of Ivy Compton-Burnett* (London: Richard Cohen Books, 1995), pp. 277–8, 309.

7. Phyllis Lassner, '"The Milk of Our Mother's Kindness Has Ceased to Flow": Virginia Woolf, Stevie Smith, and the Representation of the Jew', in Bryan Cheyette (ed.), *Between 'Race' and Culture: Representations of 'The Jew' in English and American Literature* (Stanford: Stanford University Press, 1996), pp. 129–144. Quote from p. 129. Further references are to this edition and page numbers are given in the body of the text.

8. In a note on p. 207, Lassner draws further on Freema Gottlieb's 'Leonard Woolf's Attitude to his Jewish Background and to Judaism', in *Transactions of the Jewish Historical Society of England, 1973–75*, pp. 25–38, and shows how Sara's representation of Abrahamson 'coincides with a "Nazi typology," which justified closing swimming pools to Jews in 1933 because, as Sartre showed in his study of antisemitism, "the body of the Jew would render the bath wholly unclean"'. (p. 29)

9. For Woolf's projection of her 'Outsiders' Society' see *Three Guineas* (London: Hogarth Press, 1938), p. 193. Further references are to this edition and page numbers are given in the body of the text.

10. Oswald Mosley, *Fascism: 100 Questions Asked and Answered* (London: BUF Publications, 1936), n.p., from the Answer to Question 6.

11. *Diary*, 4, p. 337.

12. Geoffrey Alderman, *Modern British Jewry* (Oxford: Clarendon Press, 1992), especially pp. 102–151. Quote from p. 102. See also David Feldman, *Englishmen and Jews: Social Relations and Political Culture 1840–1914* (New Haven and London: Yale University Press, 1994) and V. D. Lipman *A History of the Jews in Britain Since 1858* (Leicester: Leicester University Press, 1990), especially pp. 43–117.

13. Holmes, 'Anti-semitism and the BUF'. Quote from p. 120.

14. Lewis, *Illusions of Grandeur*, p. 95. See also Mandle, *Anti-Semitism and the BUF*, pp. 10–12.

15. 'October 4th, 1936', in *British Union: Pictorial Record, 1932–1937* ([London]: BUF, [1938]), n.p. See also Benewick, *The Fascist Movement in Britain*, pp. 225–31; Lewis, *Illusions of Grandeur*, pp. 106–7, 124; and Mandle, *Anti-Semitism and the BUF*, pp. 53–6.

16. Lewis, *Illusions of Grandeur*, p. 106.

17. Nigel Nicolson and Joanne Trautmann (eds), *The Sickle Side of the Moon. The Letters of Virginia Woolf*, vol. 5, 1932–5 (London: Hogarth Press, 1979), p. 273; hereafter *Letters*, 5.

18. *Letters*, 5, p. 277.

19. *Diary*, 4, p. 280.

20. Anne Olivier Bell and Andrew McNeillie (eds), *The Diary of Virginia Woolf*, vol. 5, 1936–41 (London: Hogarth Press, 1984), p. 36; hereafter *Diary*, 5. The *Blackshirt: The Patriotic Worker's Paper* was published weekly. On the front page of the 21 November 1936 issue, Woolf would have noticed an anti-Semitic cartoon and this bold caption: 'Mosley Speaks in Bow [in London's East End]'.

21. *Diary*, 5, p. 70.

22. *Diary*, 5, p. 142.

23. On 23 July 1929, Brian Howard and Diana Guinness organised a widely reported hoax exhibition of paintings by the German abstract painter 'Bruno Hat' – an obvious calque on 'brown hat'. Lytton Strachey, one of many visitors to be taken in by Hat's specious genius, bought one of his works. See Marie-Jacqueline Lancaster, *Brian Howard: Portrait of a Failure* (London: Anthony Blond, 1968), pp. 272–5.

24. *Encyclopaedia Judaica* (Jerusalem: Keter, 1971), vol. 15, p. 743.

25. *Encyclopaedia Judaica*, vol. 6, p. 1338. Emphasis added.

26. André Maurois, *King Edward and his Times*, tr. Hamish Miles (London: Cassell, 1933), p. 281.

27. E. F. Benson, *King Edward VII: An Appreciation* (London: Longman, Green and Co., 1933), pp. 152–3. This aspect of Edward VII has been the subject of a recent book-length study: Anthony Allfrey, *Edward VII and his Jewish Court* (London: Weidenfeld and Nicolson, 1991).

28. Patrick Hanks and Flavia Hodges, *A Dictionary of First Names* (Oxford and New York: Oxford University Press, 1990), p. 160.

29. Leslie Stephen, 'John Milton', in *Dictionary of National Biography*, vol. xiii.

30. David Masson, *The Life of John Milton: Narrated in Connexion with the Political, Ecclesiastical, and Literary History of his Time*, 6 vols. (London: Macmillan, 1871–94), vol. 5 (1654–60), pp. 71–2. For a more up-to-date and authoritative account of the readmission of the Jews, and a discussion of the roles which the early sixteenth-century revival of Hebrew studies and millenarianism played in the success of ben Israel's mission to Cromwell, see David S. Katz, *The Jews in the History of England 1485–1850* (Oxford: Clarendon Press, 1994), pp. 107–44, and David S. Katz, *Philo-Semitism and the Readmission of the Jews to England 1603–1655* (Oxford: Clarendon Press, 1982).

31. A. N. Wilson, *The Life of John Milton* (Oxford: Oxford University Press, 1983), p. 250.

32. 'John Milton', in *Encyclopaedia Judaica*, vol. 11, p. 1587. For a fuller account of this aspect of Milton see Harris Francis Fletcher, *Milton's Semitic Studies: And Some Manifestations of them in his Poetry* (Chicago: University of Chicago Press, 1926) and Harris Francis Fletcher, *The Intellectual Development of John Milton*, vol. ii, 'The Cambridge University Period 1625–32' (Urbana, IL: University of Illinois Press, 1961), pp. 289–99.

33. See David Bradshaw, 'T. S. Eliot and the Major: Sources of Literary Anti-Semitism in the 1930s', in *Times Literary Supplement*, no. 4866, 5 July 1996, pp. 14–16.

34. As Radin notes, however, this moment may be interpreted more optimistically. 'Nicholas is reasserting his belief in human evolution and in the potential of the new generation; when he puts his glass down it shatters, as in the Jewish marriage ritual that symbolises fertility'. (p. 108)

35. Avrom Fleishman, *Virginia Woolf: A Critical Study* (Baltimore and London: Johns Hopkins University Press, 1975) p. 172.

36. Kathy J. Phillips, *Virginia Woolf Against Empire* (Knoxville, TN: University of Tennessee Press, 1994), p. 28.

15

No Longer a View: Virginia Woolf in the 1930s and the 1930s in Virginia Woolf

Linden Peach

As Kathy Phillips has pointed out, only recently has Virginia Woolf 'been recognised as a social thinker, let alone as someone with a sophisticated grasp of complex ideologies'.[1] Even in 1986, Alex Zwerdling could ask: 'Why has Woolf's strong interest in realism, history and the social matrix been largely ignored? Why has it taken us so long to understand the importance of these elements in her work?'[2] Perhaps the answers to Zwerdling's questions are partly in the nature of the engagement with historical and contemporary events in Woolf's fiction and partly in the critical assumptions with which Thirties writing is often approached.

Ten years on from Zwerdling's ground-breaking study, the central issue is not the long neglect of Woolf's interest in history and politics but the kind of critical approach her work requires, given that many events traditionally recognised as the linchpins of history are either treated obliquely in her fiction or ignored altogether. Although *The Years* (1937), for example, is a historical novel covering the period from 1880–1937, as one reviewer pointed out, the major happenings of those years are barely touched upon.[3] Thus the novel marginalises and/ or approaches obliquely the Boer War, the death of Queen Victoria, the First World War (to which only one page is devoted), the rise of the Labour Party, the demise of the Liberals, the suffragettes, the General Strike, the Wall Street Crash and the British Union of Fascists.

Although many reviewers drew attention to Woolf's oblique treatment of contemporary events in *The Years*, the cryptic nature of Woolf's work has not been adequately theorised even in recent scholarship. For example, Phillips argues convincingly that the various cultural fragments of Woolf's fiction do trace a coherent though non-linear pattern, but she theorises this by invoking and taking issue with a tired argument – George Lukács' view that Modernists jumble 'naturalistic' elements at random.[4]

Reading Woolf as a political novelist requires an approach posited on her oblique use of historical and contemporary events. The approach to Woolf's Thirties' fiction which I recommend in this essay, and illustrate with reference to the demise of the British Empire in *The Waves* (1931) and *The Years* (1937), I would describe as cryptanalytical. 'Cryptanalysis' is a mode of reading that focuses upon what is concealed or almost concealed in a text. The roots of the word are in the Latin 'crypta' – usually taken as referring to any vaulted building partially or entirely below ground level – and 'analýein' meaning to loosen or untie.[5]

Two frameworks of analysis confront us in this approach: Woolf's own cryptographic approach to history and politics in her fiction and her concomitant interest in historical events as cultural texts which can be read as such. Acknowledging that Woolf writes cryptically of political events poses ethical and epistemological problems for the reader. What purpose is served by so complicating the interpretative process and what does this reveal about Woolf's attitude to the subject matter? However, the encrypting of political events in Woolf's fiction is not intended to preserve the writing for a singular, private purpose. It is closely tied to her reading of cultural texts and expands our thinking about them.

There are suggestions throughout her diaries, essays and fiction that Woolf saw 'reality' as a codified, symbolic environment that has to be deciphered before it can be reinterpreted. For example, in her review of Kipling's *Letters of Travel, 1892–1913* she compares railway advertising posters to Kipling's depiction of the colonies: 'Just as the railway companies have a motive in hanging their stations with seductive pictures of Ilfracombe and Blackpool Bay, so Kipling's pictures of places are painted to display the splendours of Empire and to induce young men to lay down their lives on her behalf'.[6]

Critics have generally acknowledged that Woolf uses external description to illuminate psychic processes, but she also employs external description to illuminate the 'character' of a milieu, the codified nature of reality. Her fiction explores how the distorted and distorting social narratives that impinge on and determine individual lives are embedded in, and legitimated by, the codified nature of the social and cultural environment. In *The Waves* and *The Years*, Woolf is not only offering a critique of patriarchy, Englishness (as it is associated with a particular class) and Empire but pursuing the interest which pervades her work in how these concepts are constructed in the individual consciousness. In an early story, 'Phyllis and Rosamond', Woolf observes:

> For a study of history and biography convinces any right minded person that these obscure figures occupy a place not unlike that of the showman's hand in the dance of the marionettes; and the finger is laid upon the heart. It is true that our simple eyes believed for many that the figures danced of their own accord, and cut what steps they chose; and the partial light which novelists and historians have begun to cast upon that dark and crowded place behind the scenes has done little as yet but show us how many wires there are, held in obscure hands, upon whose jerk or twist the whole figure of the dance depends.[7]

Woolf's interest in the 'many wires … held in obscure hands, upon whose jerk or twist the whole figure … depends' might profitably be seen in terms of Michel Foucault's concept of 'archaeology' and the related concepts of the 'historical *a priori*' and 'archive'. In *The Archaeology of Knowledge* (1969), Foucault argues that meaning can only be understood in relation to the discursive system as a whole. While initially he argued for an objective rather than an interpretative account of discourse, he revised this view out of growing recognition of the interconnectedness of discourse and power. Foucault came to think of the discursive system as consisting of a 'discursive formation', in which certain statements are granted a force and legitimacy denied others that are excluded from it, and 'discursive events', in which an utterance changes the configuration of statements that operates in a 'discursive formation'.

Although discourses in Foucault's view are precarious ensembles, 'conditions of existence' can be elicited from them by the 'archaeologist'. Foucault defines 'archaeology' as a practice that, like much of Woolf's writing, 'questions the already-said at the level of its existence'.[8] While this may sound initially applicable to the work of any writer, Woolf anticipates Foucault in her understanding of 'the already-said' as a discursive formation related to wider systems of power. Thus reading historical and political events cryptanalytically, Woolf is interested in the 'formal identities, thematic continuities, translations of concepts, and polemical interchanges' in the fields of, for example, Englishness, imperialism, patriarchy and the family.[9] In questioning 'the already-said' and what is permitted to be said within dominant social discourses,

Woolf's fiction bears out two of Foucault's salient assumptions about what he calls the 'archive' – the domain of statements – articulated in the culture of post-war Britain: that it cannot be completely uncovered and that it emerges in fragments and at different levels.[10]

In many respects, criticism that tries to anchor the later fiction in a traditional form of verisimilitude misses the point of Woolf's work. I would suggest that even the later fiction is more accurately seen in terms of Foucault's concept of 'archaeology' than social realism. Woolf's primary aim is not that of the social realists, to define the thoughts, representations, images and preoccupations that are concealed and revealed in discourses. From *Jacob's Room* to *Between the Acts*, Woolf's fiction is concerned, as Foucault says of the 'archaeologist', with how knowledge is diffused; with how it gives rise to concepts, and takes form in cultural texts; with how notions and themes migrate from the field (of statements) in which they originated to another; with how the 'historical *a priori*' relates to institutions, social customs, private and public behaviours, or political discourses.[11]

One of the current issues in post-colonial theory is the anxiety over the way in which much post-colonial criticism has over-emphasised actual, significant historical events. It is now recognised that such an emphasis displaces awareness of the multivalent cultural processes at work.[12] Here, I am afraid I am going to have recourse to what has become a fashionable trope in recent Woolf criticism: that in focusing on the multivalent processes at work in the cultural interpretation of events, Woolf was ahead of her time and only recently has criticism began to catch up with her.

According to Valentine Cunningham, two frames of analysis under-pin many approaches to the Thirties: a literary-historical frame that 'involves a sort of knee-jerk division between Modernism and the Thirties' and a cultural-historical frame that denies anything written in the 1930s 'the highest *literary* merit'.[13] Both of these have adversely affected critical responses to Woolf's Thirties fiction. Although critical interpretations – or reinterpretations – of her works written in the 1930s have played an important part in revealing Woolf as a complex political thinker, the overview of her Thirties work has remained somewhat skewed.

The Waves, dominated by the voices of six rather generalised char-acters between which the boundaries are somewhat fluid, is generally seen as a work of 'High Modernism', a novel of the Thirties that is not a Thirties novel. Eric Warner, for example, insists that it is 'the final fruit of Woolf's great decade, 1920–1930'.[14] Many reviewers thought of it in Modernist terms and usually as a poem rather than a novel. Frank Swinnerton considered it 'a series of rhapsodies', Louis Kronenberger believed it to be 'a kind of symphonic poem ... in prose' and an anonymous reviewer in the *Times Literary Supplement* argued that it was 'a poetic novel'.[15] But, as John Mepham has pointed out, Woolf was not satisfied with its reception. We know from her diary that she wanted reviewers to recognise 'that [the novel] is solid & means something'.[16]

Eric Warner's association of *The Waves* with the Modernism of the Twenties also exemplifies the cultural-historical approach to Thirties writing that Cunningham identifies. Implicit in Warner's argument is the assumption that work of the Twenties is of more value in artistic terms than that of the Thirties:

> Indeed as the Thirties were to change radically the tone and temper of the time, it is hardly going too far to see *The Waves* as one of the last fruits of modernism itself ... Her subsequent novel, *The Years*, was an ill-fated attempt to adapt to these changes; but the work was ground out in a long, tortuous and painful struggle ...[17]

The Years, unlike *The Waves*, is at least included in Alex Zwerdling's canon of Woolf's fiction 'deeply engaged by the question of how people are shaped (or deformed) by their social environment' and by historical forces.[18] However, even here it does not receive as much attention as the later novel *Between the Acts*, in which Woolf is said to be most 'conscious of and responsive to contemporary events'.[19]

Critics have generally ignored the fact that before completing the first draft of *The Waves*, Woolf had published *Orlando* (1928). A novel about the unfreezing of history, *Orlando* mounted a challenge to monological narratives of gender and national identity and sought to defamiliarise history in order to question habitual ideas about cultural identity in Britain after the First World War. It is also based on Woolf's view that English history as it is traditionally written is posited on a narrative of conquest and violence.

The imagery of the italicised interludes in *The Waves* concerns the 'shadow' side of Englishness and Empire. The sun that rises in the second interlude in *The Waves* may be the old sun of Empire but it exposes the savagery of the oppressors and, in the images of the 'poisoned assegais' and the 'turbaned warriors', the violence with which the Empire threatens to strike back: 'The wind rose. The waves drummed on the shore, like turbaned warriors, like turbaned men with poisoned assegais who, whirling their arms on high, advance upon the feeding flocks, the white sheep'.[20]

Jane Marcus points out that *The Waves* draws attention to the part played by the Stephen family in constructing cultural hegemony in nineteenth-century India. Kathy Phillips sees the turbaned warriors of the second interlude as an allusion to the Sepoy Mutiny of 1857.[21] But neither Marcus, who actually challenges ahistorical interpretations of the novel, nor Phillips sees the novel as engaging with the events of the years 1919–30 even though they were among the most turbulent as far as British relationships with India were concerned. This may be because neither really develops a cryptanalytical reading of the novel which links it to Woolf's reading of contemporary and historical events as cultural texts.

It would be difficult to imagine any author writing a novel in the period 1928–30 concerning the fusion of religious, military and imperialist elements in the English national identity, and including the subject of English involvement with India, not being influenced by the events of the 1920s. The Government of India Act of 1919, when India was denied Dominion Status, had provided that a Commission be set up after ten years to examine the possibility of further advance for India. However, in response to the Congress Movement's demand for complete independence, the Simon Commission was appointed two years earlier in 1927. But when the Congress Movement realised that Dominion Status would not in fact be granted, the Commission's report in June 1930 was received amidst widespread disorder in India itself that led to the arrests of Mahatma Gandhi and Jawaharlal Nehru. At the end of October, Lord Irwin, the Viceroy, announced the decision to grant India Dominion Status. While retaining a Viceroy appointed from London, India would be ruled by Indians at both national and local levels.

The agreement between the government and shadow cabinet over India had important consequences for the public mood and for domestic politics in Britain. It led eventually to the much-publicised split between Stanley Baldwin and Winston Churchill whose evocation of the 'warrior races' when he took up the cause of the Indian princes in 1930, attacking the conciliation of Indian nationalism, mirrors Woolf's image of the 'turbaned warriors' and their assegais. In an article in the *Daily Mail*, Churchill stressed the Hindu contempt for the millions of Untouchables and that Dominion Status could not be obtained by those who treated their 'fellow human beings, toiling at their side' so badly.[22] He resigned from the shadow cabinet because of what he saw as the frightful prospect of losing India.

Whereas I agree with Marcus and Phillips that there is a strong elegiac element in *The Waves* – there are frequent references to elegies that are meant to be taken as the elegy for Empire – there is also the 'frightfulness' of the prospect of the end of Empire. It is this perceived 'frightfulness' that is the basis of Woolf's approach to the events of 1919–30. The critique of Empire in *Jacob's Room* and *Orlando* exposes the homosocial and patriarchal bonds within the upper class that support imperialism. *The Waves* and *The Years*, however, concern the effect of the prospect of the end of Empire on members of that class. Jane Marcus and Kathy Phillips have focused upon how the individuals in *The Waves* have been influenced by ideologies of Empire and imperialism. I would argue that the individual voices and the interludes also reflect the anxieties of the late 1920s over the demise of the Empire in India.

The death in India of Percival, who is a stereotypical product of the English public school system and the Arthurian Knight Parsifal transferred to the early twentieth century, can be read as analogous of the demise of the British in India. But his death focuses not so much on the demise itself as on the anxiety over Britain's involvement in India. This anxiety is heightened rather than alleviated by the various intellectual and cultural frameworks that confronted anyone in the Thirties who was engaging with Anglo-India. The predominant anti-imperialist literary modes of the Thirties were irony and parody. The demise of the Anglo-Indian Empire may easily have been incorporated in a less speculative text than *The Waves* in a way that had become commonplace. But in encrypting the collapse of the British Empire in *The Waves*, Woolf provides fresh critical depth.

Bernard's elegies to Percival invoke the use of India in popular romance where loved ones or brothers meet their death, while the intertext in the details of Percival's death – he is thrown from a flea-bitten mare – is the absurd figure of Don Quixote which undermines both the romance and the heroism in Britain's imperialist project. Bernard's assessment that in righting a bullock cart, Percival solved the Oriental problem is not only absurd but, read within the context of the parliamentary debates at the time Woolf was working on the novel, caustically ironic. Bernard's references to half-naked Indians only able to 'swarm' and 'chatter' and to an old man only able 'to contemplate his navel'[23] express both the arrogance of his class towards the peoples of the Empire, in this case India, and its view of the Indians as unable to assume responsibility for their own government. As soon as he envisages India, Bernard sees 'crenellated buildings which have an air of fragility and decay'.[24] At one level this may prefigure the demise of the British Empire in India but it also reflects Bernard's view of India as a social and political economy. The bullock cart travelling along the sun-baked road may be read cryptanalytically as India under Dominion Status. The cart 'sways incompetently from side to side' – the use of the word 'incompetently' is particularly provocative and clearly invokes more than just how a cart is driven – and eventually, almost predictably, it becomes stuck in a rut.[25] Percival is envisaged as solving the problem by 'applying the standards of the West' and by 'using the violent language that is natural to him', a fusion that demonstrates Woolf's Foucaultian interest in how traditional concepts and thematic continuities are transferred from one domain to another; in this case, from the language of the public school to the application of British standards of progress and behaviour in the administration of Empire.

The Waves puts at least as much emphasis upon the reactions of Percival's friends to his death as upon the education system and the social forces which shaped him as a particular type of English hero. Percival's death inaugurates the second half of their day, the declining sun analogous of the declining Empire. But once again the focus is upon the intellectual anxiety created by the prospect of the loss of Empire. The waves in the penultimate interlude, having lost their light – a cryptic allusion perhaps to Enlightenment notions of history and progress – now fall 'in one long concussion'.[26] The image of former cornfields evokes a traditional, rural Englishness with which notions of Empire were bound: 'Now the corn was cut. Now only a brisk stubble was left of all its flowing and waving'.[27] The cut corn clearly signifies the physical end of Empire but 'waving' – evoking the celebration of nation through the waving of flags – also suggests that equally importantly the psychological Empire has come to an end. Although the effect of patriotic flag-waving in countries where the radical left had acquired an anti-colonial tradition is complicated, colonial exhibitions, military parades, jubilees and state occasions encouraged the people to identify with the nation and the imperial state.

The interlude is as much prophetic as descriptive: 'The tree, that had burnt foxy red in spring and in midsummer bent pliant leaves to the south wind, was now black as iron ...'[28] The seasonal changes in the tree suggest the stages of Empire, the colonisers bending to the needs and demands of the colonised Indians, but also betray anxiety over what kind of India will emerge under Dominion Status: not only 'black' but defiant. The next line – 'The land was so distant ...' –

encapsulates anxieties about Britain's removal from the region's affairs; distanced physically, historically, economically and culturally.

The sense of youth and endless possibility focused on Percival in the first part of the novel, analogous of that enshrined in the Empire, are replaced by anxiety, sober reflection and even pessimism: 'The door will not open; [Percival] will not come. And we are laden'.[29] Percival, like the Empire of which he is analogous, served as a binding power for his friends who belong to or have affiliations with the social class in whom cultural and economic power resides. Despite the last-ditch defiance in the final section of the novel by Bernard who is writing about Percival, we are left with the dominant impression of the six friends fragmenting and with a dwindling sense of possibility.

After his death, what Percival's friends imagine he might have accomplished in India becomes, as Phillips points out, increasingly grandiose.[30] But this argument can be taken further. Bernard believes that Percival would have protected people dying of famine and disease and would have done justice to the Empire. These views of him seem analogous of the defence of Empire in the light of fears as to how the period of British rule would come to be viewed after Indian independence.

The anxiety that all Percival's friends suffer after his death is exacerbated because they are unable to imagine an alternative to the interconnection of English national identity and Empire with which they have all grown up. Louis, the son of an Australian banker, was so desperate to be accepted by his English upper-class friends that he fabricated a past with roots in Ancient Egypt. As a reflection of Woolf's cryptic reading of the events of 1919–30, this is doubly ironic because Egypt was taken under British control to facilitate trade with India. Even Rhoda's exotic fantasies, through which she seeks to escape from the discomforts of school, are shaped by the ideologies of Empire. The white petals that at one point she floats in a brown basin are inflated to become ships and then an armada. While the sinking of her armada anticipates her suicide – as a female she is never able to realise her dreams like Louis – it also anticipates Percival's death and the loss of India. But Rhoda also prefigures, like Louis, the failure of England to envisage an alternative identity for itself, to free itself from the concepts and ideologies of Empire.

The expulsion of England from India, although it could never – can never – be complete, is a worrying prospect for those of Bernard's generation and class. It signifies the demise of what has impelled the development of England as an imperialist power. Empire is fraught not only with the weight of its burden, but with the anxiety of its loss.

In *The Years* Woolf filters occluded or marginalised historical discourses through a revision of a familiar genre previously marked by the authority and certainty of conventional historicism. In this case, it is the traditional family saga. In contrast to the conventional family sagas, *The Years* presents a sustained focus on marginalised women within an upper-middle-class family who are relatively impoverished and further marginalised by their father's failure to provide for them after his death. Although eventually Eleanor becomes a charity worker, Rose becomes involved in political work and Peggy becomes a doctor, the men fare better, becoming university teachers, lawyers or colonial administrators.

Woolf had originally conceived of *The Years* as a 'novel essay' – like *The Pargiters* or *Here and Now*. Between episodes dramatising the fictional lives of her characters, she had intended to place socio-historical essays. The chapters themselves were to be grounded in social realism in a far less opaque way than Woolf's novels to date and to an extent that seemed to represent, in John Mepham's words, an 'astonishing turnabout' in her views of the novel.[31] For the first time since *Night and Day* Woolf returned to employing an impersonal narrator and a point of view external to her characters while rewriting in other ways the traditional family saga genre. Her own comments on the novel and her revisions to the various drafts – conversations between the characters are more revealing and politically explicit than in the final novel[32] – suggest that she found the novel becoming too polemic.

However, despite the fact that the novel is closer to traditional realist writing than her previous works, and thereby more overtly political, Woolf still seems to have wanted to approach historical and political events cryptographically. As in her earlier work, her primary interest is the 'discursive formations' which may be extrapolated from the way in which political actions and events are interpreted. Pamela Hansford Johnson recognised this in her review when she argued that 'each member of the Pargiter family is strengthened or devitalised, as the case may be, by the influence of externals hardly realised subjectively'.[33] The novel might be said to lose sight of its representation of the Victorian family as an oppressive patriarchal institution and to eschew the delineation of women as active agents in society in favour of its concern with family conversations. But it is commensurate with Woolf's interest in the codified nature of 'reality' that social change is obliquely hinted at while the focus is placed on the 'discursive formations' that are revealed in social intercourse.

Kathy Phillips points out that the empty English values with which *The Years* presents us are constantly connected to notions of Empire and that the novel undercuts the glory of Empire every time colonisation is mentioned.[34] But *The Years*, too, is a novel which bears the stamp of Woolf's cryptanalytical reading of the events of the Thirties. Like *The Waves*, the novel looks back on Empire through a post-Empire lens.

The Years begins, for example, with Colonel Abel Pargiter and his friends at their club in 1880 recalling stories of India, Africa and Egypt. His eyes are 'screwed up, as if the glare of the East were still in them'.[35] The cigar that he holds suspended in his hand cryptically suggests not only the suspended nature of his life but of his class in the wake of the demise of the British Empire. Outside in the traffic-filled street everyone seems to have a goal in mind. But when Pargiter turns his back for a moment his friends disperse. The group is described ambivalently as having 'broken up'. The empty chairs to which he returns are analogous of the end of Empire – the void that *The Waves* anticipates and with which England is to have to come to terms. Sir William's later description of himself as looking a 'bally ass' in front of the Indians who humble themselves before him again reflects fears in parliament and the press during the Thirties as to how history would regard the English colonisers.

Much later in the novel, it is no coincidence that North is invited by Sara to a meal of mutton. For he has made his money as a sheep farmer in East Africa where the native rulers were generally swindled out of the best grazing land. But the meal is not what he expected: there is a yellowed stain on the table cloth, the undercooked mutton runs with blood, the yellow potatoes look hard and the 'slabbed-down mass of cabbage' is 'oozing green water'.[36] As in the details of Percival's death in *The Waves*, there is a carnivalesque element here that undermines the mythical dignity of Englishness. The references to an excess of blood and water suggest the impurities, orifices and leakages of the lower body excluded from the classical ideal body while the colours – red, yellow, green – are those which signify bodily infection and disease. Every aspect of the meal, including the behaviour of the skivvy who acts as a maid, brings to the fore what the traditional rituals of upper-class English life kept at a distance.

The previous occasion on which a meal as ruined as this was served in the novel was when Mrs Pargiter was dying; there the dried-up meat mirrored her exhausted life. Here the mutton reflects the anxiety in the Thirties over Empire. The reality of butchery, revealed in the undercooked joint, disturbs (the) North; suggesting the return of what has been repressed in the narratives of Empire in Africa (and, of course, India) – the blood of the indigenous population as well as of the sheep. North and Sara watch the ominous red trickle running down into the well of the dish – a cryptic allusion to the history of Empire that leads into an undefined future for colonisers and colonised alike. Here Woolf appears to be looking back to Leonard's *Empire and Africa*, in which he warned:

> Europe is certainly strong enough to fasten its landlordism and capitalism securely and permanently upon Africa; but if it does, while a few men reap a fine harvest of profits, the world as a whole will reap a finer harvest of misery and degradation.[37]

The conversation is interrupted by the noise of lorries which pass outside, but, unlike, the traffic watched by Colonel Pargiter at the beginning of the novel, they make the floors and the walls, the basic structure of Sara's home, 'tremble'. Outside the new jazz music played on a trombone is 'wailing' and 'doleful' and, like their conversation itself, highlights that they are at the end of something. The anxiety over what will be left in the place of the Empire is underscored here by the remains of the joint: a 'disagreeable object ... daubed with gory streaks'.[38]

While, at one level, Woolf may be accused in *The Years* and in *The Waves* of not making sufficient distinction between the different ethnic populations of the British Empire, she pursues the concerns of her Twenties fiction with how the 'othering' of Empire is an essential part of a mythical, homogeneous English identity. But the Thirties was a period of much intellectual and political anxiety over Empire, and of debates in parliament and the press over Dominion Status for India. Behind Woolf's cryptic concern with these anxieties in her fiction, requiring a cryptanalytical approach to her texts, lies her concern with the multivalent cultural processes that can be extrapolated from the way events are interpreted and constructed.

Notes

1. Kathy J. Phillips, *Virginia Woolf Against Empire* (Knoxville, TN: The University of Tennessee Press, 1994), p. xi.
2. Alex Zwerdling, *Virginia Woolf and the Real World* (Los Angeles and London: University of California Press, 1986), p. 15.
3. Pamela Hansford Johnson, review, *English Review*, April 1937, pp. 508–9. Reprinted in Robin Majumdar and Allen McLaurin (eds), *Virginia Woolf: The Critical Heritage* (London and Boston: Routledge and Kegan Paul, 1975), p. 388 [388–9].
4. Phillips, *Virginia Woolf Against Empire*, p. xiv.
5. The Oxford English Dictionary defines cryptanalysis as 'the art of deciphering a cryptogram by analysis'. Susan Stanford Friedman in recommending a geopolitical approach to Woolf's work is the only critic to suggest, albeit in passing, that Woolf's fiction be read in this way.

She uses the word 'cryptographic' which means 'to write' rather than 'to read or analyse' what is hidden. Cryptography and cryptanalysis are the two aspects of what is called cryptology. 'Uncommon Readings: Seeking the Geopolitical Woolf', in *The South Carolina Review*, vol. 29, no. 1 (fall, 1996), p. 35 [24–44]. The increasingly wider adoption of the term 'cryptanalysis' is perhaps signified by its inclusion as a category in the European Society for the Study of English Conference at Debrecen, Hungary, in 1997.

6. Virginia Woolf, review of Rudyard Kipling, *Letters of Travel, 1892–1913*, in *Athenaeum*, 16 July 1920. Reprinted in Andrew McNeillie (ed.), *The Essays of Virginia Woolf*, vol. III (London: The Hogarth Press, 1988), p. 240 [238–241].
7. Susan Dick (ed.), *The Complete Shorter Fiction of Virginia Woolf* (London: The Hogarth Press, 1985), p. 17.
8. Michel Foucault, *The Archaeology of Knowledge* (1969; tr. 1972, reprinted London and New York: Routledge, 1994), p. 131.
9. Foucault, *The Archaeology of Knowledge*, p. 127.
10. Foucault, *The Archaeology of Knowledge*, pp. 130, 131.
11. Foucault, *The Archaeology of Knowledge*, pp. 137–140.
12. Stephen Slemon, 'The Scramble for Post-Colonialism' in Chris Tiffin and Alan Lawson (eds), *De-Scribing Empire: Post-colonialism and Textuality* (London and New York: Routledge, 1994), pp. 15–32.
13. Valentine Cunnigham, 'The Age of Anxiety and Influence; or, Tradition and the Thirties Talents', in Keith Williams and Steven Mathews (eds), *Rewriting the Thirties* (London and New York: Longman, 1997), pp. 5–6.
14. Eric Warner, *Virginia Woolf, The Waves* (Cambridge: Cambridge University Press, 1978), p. 15.
15. Frank Swinnerton, review, *Evening News*, 9 October 1931, p. 8; Louis Kronenberger, review, *New York Times Book Review*, 25 October 1931, p. 5; *Times Literary Supplement*, 8 October 1931, p. 773. Reprinted in Majumdar and McLaurin (eds), *Virginia Woolf: The Critical Heritage*, p. 268 [267–268]; p. 274 [273–5]; pp. 264–5 [263–5].
16. John Mepham, *Virginia Woolf: A Literary Life* (Basingstoke: Macmillan, 1991), p. 143.
17. Warner, *Virginia Woolf, The Waves*, p. 16.
18. Zwerdling, *Virginia Woolf and the Real World*, pp. 13–14.
19. Zwerdling, *Virginia Woolf and the Real World*, p. 302.
20. Gillian Beer (ed.), Virginia Woolf, *The Waves* (Oxford: Oxford University Press, 1992), p. 60.
21. Jane Marcus, 'Britannia Rules *The Waves*' in Karen Lawrence (ed.), *Decolonising Tradition: New Views of Twentieth-Century 'British' Literary Canons* (Urbana, IL: University of Illinois Press, 1988), pp. 136–162 and Phillips, *Woolf Against Empire*, p. 181.
22. Martin Gilbert, *Churchill: A Life* (London: Mandarin, 1993), p. 335.
23. Woolf, *The Waves*, p. 111.
24. Woolf, *The Waves*, p. 111.
25. Woolf, *The Waves*, p. 111.
26. Woolf, *The Waves*, p. 173.
27. Woolf, *The Waves*, p. 173.
28. Woolf, *The Waves*, p. 174.
29. Woolf, *The Waves*, p. 176.
30. Phillips, *Virginia Woolf Against Empire*, p. 154.
31. Mepham, *Virginia Woolf: A Literary Life*, p. 151.
32. I am indebted here to Grace Radin, *Virginia Woolf's* The Years: *The Evolution of a Novel* (Knoxville, TN: The University of Tennessee Press, 1981).
33. Pamela Hansford Johnson, review, *English Review*, April 1937, pp. 508–9. Reprinted in Majumdar and McLaurin (eds), *Virginia Woolf: The Critical Heritage*, p. 388 [388–9].
34. Phillips, *Virginia Woolf Against Empire*, p. 36.
35. Hermione Lee (ed.), Virginia Woolf, *The Years* (Oxford: Oxford University Press, 1992), p. 5.
36. Woolf, *The Years*, p. 302.
37. Leonard Woolf, *Empire and Commerce in Africa; A Study in Economic Imperialism* (London: The Labour Research Department and George Allen and Unwin, 1920), p. 363.
38. Woolf, *The Years*, p. 304.

16

Come in from the Cold War: Rebecca West and Storm Jameson in 1930s Europe

Joanna Labon

The most striking anomaly of the Cold War was the existence of a divided Europe, within which there resided a divided Germany, within which there lay a divided Berlin ... an arrangement, so at odds with all previous standards of geopolitical logic ... Still the passage of time can make even the oddest of situations seem ordinary.[1]

A round white Easter egg, rolling across Europe, left on the roads traces of blood: Warsaw Berlin Vienna Budapest. Rome Prague tomorrow. To be devoured with the mind's salt.[2]

To look afresh at the 1930s, we have to think beyond the Cold War. It is in the way. The habit of mind which divided Europe in two halves persists (the Germans called it 'mauer im kopf' – a Berlin Wall in our heads). In 1997 the historian John Lewis Gaddis looked back on a divided Europe as 'the oddest of situations'. In 1940, before this odd situation had ever come about, Storm Jameson imagined Fascism as a lethal rolling egg, and listed the European cities of 'Warsaw Berlin Vienna Budapest. Rome Prague tomorrow' (EL, p. 258) – with barely a comma to separate them. In the 1930s Europe had no division between east and west, yet for those of us who are writing about literature in the 1930s, such a division is still, a decade after the changes of 1989, a habit of mind, and consequently Eastern Europe in our literary landscape has remained distant and unexplored, 'failed' by the red decade.[3] It is my intention in this essay to suggest ways in which we might redress this.

Storm Jameson's novel *Europe to Let* and Rebecca West's book *Black Lamb and Grey Falcon: A Journey through Yugoslavia in 1937*[4] are key texts which reveal much of interest to the study of gender, politics and history of the 1930s. Both were published just as the Second World War was beginning (1940 and 1941, respectively) and evince the last moments of the 'pre-Cold War'. These moments beg examination from a post-Cold War perspective. Post-1989, and more particularly at the beginning of a new century, it might be rewarding to redraw our map of 1930s Europe. Central Europe, then as now, offered a potent mix of art and politics, and its volatility then can be considered in the light of the Yugoslav conflict of our own era. Terry Eagleton recently praised Slavoj Zizek, writing: 'It is hardly surprising that a psychoanalytic theorist of such virtuosity should have emerged from the ethnic conflicts of former Yugoslavia, just as Europe's previous most fruitful encounter between Marx and Freud was the product of the Frankfurt School on the run from Nazi anti-semitism'.[5] True: miserable and ruptured as the history of Eastern Europe is, it has provided the 'fruitful encounter'. Storm Jameson and Rebecca West represent an alternate view of the 1930s to that of young men going off to fight in Spain and write poetry. These two women were by the late 1930s middle-aged, public figures with much work behind them. Although both vigorously supported the Spanish Republican Government in print, neither of them joined the International Brigade, yet each made travel part of their intellectual fight against Fascism. These mature women went to Eastern Europe and wrote prose.

Both writers have been eclipsed or marginalised to different degrees by literary history. Both had high public profiles in the 1930s, and had already achieved outstanding bodies of work, yet do not feature greatly in critical accounts of the period. Storm Jameson is almost forgotten. This raises certain questions. They are both disqualified for inclusion in the 'Auden generation' by age and gender,[6] yet Storm Jameson's efforts on behalf of European Jews at PEN were arguably more effective than the visits of Auden, Orwell or Spender to Spain. Without wishing to underplay the importance of the Spanish Civil War to the literature of the 1930s, or its iconic value to the left, we must recognise, as West and Jameson did, that it was Hitler's Germany and not Franco's Spain which posed the greater threat to Europe – and, indeed, to civilisation. West and Jameson, in travelling through Hungary, Czechoslovakia and Yugoslavia in the late 1930s, looked into the belly of the beast. Yet perhaps because their journeys extended to countries which later became part of the Eastern Bloc, their work lost its relevance to critics living in a Cold War culture.

In *The Morning After: Sexual Politics After the Cold War*, Cynthia

Enloe sounds a note of caution. 'It doesn't seem quite time yet to pronounce that the Cold War is over' she writes. 'Not if by the Cold War one means a densely woven web of relationships and attitudes that have sustained not only large and lethal militaries but also ideas about enemies, about rivalries'.[7] Each side in the Cold War, Enloe argues, had to convince its people that the world was dangerous, that it needed protective weaponry, that women needed the protection of men. She calls this 'the gendered culture of danger'. (p. 15) Eastern Europe seemed dangerous, but gender binarism also typified the Cold War era, and it is perhaps not a coincidence that the 'third wave' of feminism, emphasising gender rather than separate spheres, coincided with the political changes of the late 1980s. Feminist literary criticism was affected by Cold War thinking in a number of ways which have led to the exclusion of some writers from the new, reconsidered canon. The North American feminist view of the 1930s emphasises Anglo-American over inter-European connections; thus, Bonnie Kime Scott's diagrams illustrate a particular set of literary connections.[8] Feminist criticism has also emphasised Modernist writers, and female networks, whereas many of Rebecca West's important friendships were with men, while Storm Jameson preferred the company of European exiles and a few close friends to London literary circles: 'I was born with a distaste for coteries', she claimed.[9] However, if we can set aside our Cold War Anglo-American Modernist bias, certain features of both writers (West's arguable un-feminism and Jameson's un-Modernism, as examples) may seem less 'problematic'. Such a redrawing of the literary map can be, in itself, part of the gradual ending of the Cold War.

The idea of 'Central Europe' was reinvented in the mid-1980s by Vaclav Havel in Prague, Adam Michnik in Warsaw and George Konrad in Budapest as a way of thinking beyond the Iron Curtain. Although at the time it seemed impossible to imagine Europe without an armed and guarded border separating its two halves, the idea recalled an earlier, integrated period where culture flourished despite and because of the Austro-Hungarian empire. With hindsight, the revival of the idea of Central Europe seems far from nostalgic, and rather prophetic. In the 1930s the idea of Europe (as found in its geographical centre) was treasured by Storm Jameson. She saw the need to preserve, in the face of Fascism, values such as civic humanism, a broad and multilingual culture, the toleration of national minorities and the open society (a concept originated by Henri Bergson who greatly influenced Rebecca West).[10] This is a very similar set of ideas to those cherished in the 1980s by groups of non-Communist

East European urban intellectuals (or, to give them their Cold War tag, 'dissidents') and retained as part of the democratisation programme post-1989, for example in the cultural and economic initiatives supported by George Soros.[11] Vaclav Havel writes about intellectual character in a way which concurs with what Jameson so admired: 'One idea is firmly rooted in our [Czech] common awareness: that the inability to risk, in extremis, even life itself to save what gives it meaning and a human dimension leads not only to the loss of meaning but finally and inevitably to the loss of life as well ... one must not tolerate violence in silence in the hope that it will simply run its course'.[12] The idea that 'one must not tolerate violence in silence' is very close to Jameson's credo. Thus *Europe to Let* gives models of a Central European ethos, one of the features of 'civilisation' (a keyword for Jameson), and pits it against the brutality and ignorance of nascent Fascism. The idea of Central Europe thus connects the pre- and post-Cold War periods very closely.

In considering two 'pre-Cold War' texts from a 'post-Cold War' perspective, I do not wish to construct a false picture. Firstly, I do not suggest that West and Jameson were part of an as yet undiscovered movement. Secondly, I would be wary of a new Orientalism which fetishises the East of Europe instead of the West. Thirdly, it would be wrong to give the impression that either author saw Central or Eastern Europe as a homogenous mass. On the contrary, both texts emphasise the differences between countries, or small states or even cities within those states. Each describes, and implicitly defends, a vibrant, heterogeneous (both multiracial and miscegenetic) and religiously diverse Europe, against the racially purifying forces of Fascism. As should become clear, West and Jameson have separate experiences in different countries and are fascinated by the diversity they find. The palimpsest of races and histories which characterises the region is also set against England.

Europe to Let's narrator, 'Esk', is from the North of England, and 'freed from it' (EL, p. 4) by having served as an officer in the First World War. He maintains an affiliation with the 'liberal ideals of 1890' (EL, p. 109) and as the novel unfolds he develops from an alienated somewhat cynical drifter, to an active participant in history, by working to preserve an independent Czechoslovakia. Unlike D. H. Lawrence, who sought abroad a warm and exotic experience more sensuous than that available in dark, damp, sterile England, Esk has a harsher quest. He seeks 'truth', even if it is uncomfortable: 'This was 1923 – January. I was no longer a soldier. I was a writer, and I had chosen to come to Germany because I thought that Germany, starving, bankrupt, must have removed some, at least of its filthy rags from truth'. (EL, p. 4) Jameson said of the novel in her memoirs, 'It was about Europe – portraits of Europe seen in this and that light, from this and that angle, as a painter might go on trying to get at the truth of a man or woman, looking for it both in himself and his model ... For once I was too sure of the probity of what I was writing to feel either bored or impatient'. (JN 2, p. 13) Her assessment is characteristically spare (and self-critical), but Jameson offers a useful point: that the novel was a conscious effort to understand Europe, to explain and present it. Which cities does she use to 'get at the truth' of Europe? Prague, Budapest, Vienna and Berlin, with only a brief sketch of Paris, just as it is being turned over to the Nazis. Esk's visits take him through Europe – Prague, Vienna, Budapest – over the years, ending when he witnesses at close hand the Munich crisis and the hand-over of Czechoslovakia to Hitler in October 1938. Jameson took the same route as her narrator through Europe in 1938 as newly appointed President of International PEN and, as so often in Jameson's work, her own experiences are worked into fiction, giving the novel a disturbing keenness. In a Europe heading for war, Jameson's sense of impending tragedy heightened her experience: 'The mortal certainty that we were seeing France for the last time heightened every colour, every image, every sensation', she wrote in 1939. (JN 2, p. 16) Esk finds Czechoslovakia to be a small, proud nation threatened with its very existence by Germany. In Prague (which is west of Vienna), he finds 'a distinct race of Europeans' (EL, p. 113), among them General Stehlik and his assistant Hana, who are working to preserve their democratic nation-state against Nazi homogeneity. The traditions and ideals of civilisation are at stake: 'In Czechoslovakia the *idea* of Europe lived as it lives nowhere else' (EL, p. 134), just as 'In Prague the Seventeenth century is still alive'. (EL, p. 132) In Central Europe, intellectual life is central, and the character of Hana, 'Believing that a good Czech ought before everything to be a European, she studied at the Sorbonne and in Munich, Geneva and London: she had so little money that the days when she treated herself to bread with her midday soup she did without supper'. (EL, p. 137) This picture of the life of the mind taking priority over material comfort also describes Jameson's own student days.

In *Europe to Let*, the small, cultured nation battling to preserve itself against brute force is contrasted by Jameson with a particular view of England. Seen from Europe, England is callous, distant, naive, self-important: fattened by its own empire to the point of bloated delusion. Several remarks like, 'the English never know anything' (EL, p. 66) indicate that for Europeans the English, because of their power and their island geography, cannot understand the threat which Hitler poses. The accusation is made explicit in an explosive speech by General Stehlik:

> The whole English nation is mad. Except poor ignorant devils. You talk about fixations while in Germany you are laughed at, despised, robbed, insulted. Why doesn't your government speak out? What are they telling the Nazis behind your backs? Behind Benes's back! You encourage us to think of ourselves as the out-post of western democracy; the defence of civilised people against tyranny. Is that how you really think of us? Or are we becoming useless to you, rubbish you're going to throw into Hitler's hands to keep him busy for a week or two?' (EL, pp. 125–6)

Esk's reaction is one of shame, which the reader is asked to share, and it marks his turn against England in order to 'become' European:

> A sterile anger filled me. Why in God's name have the old men who rule England let things reach this stage, where the choice is between surrender to rascals who torture their opponents and a second more unspeakable war? (EL, p. 132)

Esk's progressive alienation from England reflects Jameson's own anti-patriotic pacifism which was born of the bitterness of the First World War and bred by the disappointing sight of Europe's inter-war decline. Despite the positive model of Czechoslovakia, it is near-Fascist Hungary, where the novel ends, which seems to represent the immediate future.

East of Vienna, as Jameson recorded in her memoirs, she felt unsafe: 'Vienna is as far east as an Englishman can go without losing touch completely with a tradition, only part Christian, which holds in one and the same hand even countries hostile to each other'. (JN 1, p. 405) She found Budapest claustrophobic: 'too many wires, laid under-ground, cross here' (EL, pp. 236–7); its only channel is a dark, sensual, Conradian river: 'a black sinuous line which was the Danube'. (JN 1, p. 388) Esk in *Europe to Let* senses a geographical vulnerability to invasion:

> Romans, Germans, Mongols, Turks, have all squatted in it. Sauntering along the embankment, I know that I have reached

the end of the navel cord tying me to my past. Farther east than this I should be in a new country. (EL, p. 228)

Esk's olfactory disgust contains an anti-Semitic complicity:

> The foreign tourists and the Jews. One steps out of the streets of Jewish business houses and shops in which the tourists fumble for their money and you are in a street like a drain. It gives off a heavy pungent smell – earth, sweat, oil. Perhaps it is the river, seeping under the foundations of the houses, that one smells. (EL, pp. 228–9)

In her memoirs too, Jameson described the degeneration of the city, and how the Jews of Pest were disliked, yet her conscience drew her to take their side. In the novel Esk visits Budapest in July 1936, June 1937 and July 1938. He befriends a bedraggled Jewish journalist, whose position worsens progressively as his work is disabled by anti-Jewish laws. There are threats on his life and finally even his articles for the British press are rejected. His hospitality to Esk becomes tinged with need, and his tourist guide's patter tainted with menace and sad irony: 'Andràssy Street, behind you, is the finest street in Europe,' he tells Esk. 'It will be to let when they have got rid of the dirty Jews.' (EL, p. 232) Tihaneth's gloomy fatefulness indicates the cycle of cruelty which seems to beset Eastern Europe. A recurrent fascination for Jameson was 'the mystery which has haunted my life, and haunts it – the mystery of cruelty' (JN 1, p. 92), and it is not surprising to learn that she wrote the introduction to the first edition of the diary of Anne Frank, who became a symbol of the tragic collision of innocence and brutality.[13]

Although she certainly sided with the victims of cruelty, Jameson also attempts to show the mentality of Fascists. Esk meets a pair of young Hungarians who are brother and sister. The young man asks:

> Why doesn't your country make friends with the Germans? ... You won't be able to do anything against them. How could you? They're all marvellous – like lions. Majestic fellows. That man Hitler is like God, he makes men. The German air force is absolutely magnificent ... With these hands ... I am going to chuck in the Danube every Jew I meet. On the right day...' (EL, p. 256)

Even his kinder sister justifies Hungary's allegiance with Nazi Germany on the grounds of self-preservation: 'Our only chance is to march *with* them. If we don't, they'll squeeze us to death'. (EL, p. 257). *Europe to*

Let presents in fiction the dangerous cocktail of fear and frustration which will lead to War.

In terms of real politics the message from *Europe to Let* is clear: appeasement will not work and Hitler must be fought. The form this message takes, namely the realist novel, is useful to Jameson to present the English reading public with events and situations very close to those occurring in Europe, but which were not being covered by the broadcast media, and I have suggested elsewhere that Jameson at times used fiction deliberately in order to evade press censorship.[14] Jameson also made her case in *The End of This War*.[15] Similarly, Rebecca West's *Black Lamb and Grey Falcon* is above all an argument against appeasement, although it is a more complex text which contains history, literary criticism, philosophy, psychology, fiction, art history, anthropology and theology. Moreover, as has been observed, it is as long as the Old Testament. Like Jameson, West *is* offering testimony, to a way of life which is under threat. The book's hybrid form allows her in the epilogue to make explicit her argument that Britain must to go to war against Hitler. The direct political engagement of these texts, each rooted in an experience of Eastern Europe, casts a new light on a version of the 1930s where, after the failure of the Spanish Civil War, writers gave up on politics, dismissed the decade as low and dishonest, and emigrated to America. Eastern Europe was crucial to the mental geographies of both West and Jameson, even as war broke out.

West's journey to Yugoslavia had a spiritual purpose as well as a literary one. Just as James Frazer and Jessie Weston's anthropological writings had inspired 1920s Modernists to find metaphors in past cultures for the crisis in contemporary culture, so West was able to mould the experience of Yugoslavia to her literary and political purpose. Yugoslavia was exotic. It was the source of experiences unavailable in England. Yet it was within easy reach; H. G. Wells and George Bernard Shaw also visited Dubrovnik, for example. West's Yugoslav diary records how she left London after lunch on 23 March and was in Zagreb by midnight of the 26th.[16] Her train journey meant an easy and gradual transition, one quite different from the six days in an ocean liner then necessary to reach New York. En route to Zagreb, West and her husband rest up at hotels, lunch with British acquaintances, shop and stroll around three cities – Berlin, Munich and Salzburg. Instead of the total institution of the sealed vessel the route to Yugoslavia is narrative, episodic, unpredictable, and each leg of the journey allows West to observe atmosphere ('No sign of Nazis in Berlin. Lovely golden day.' RW *Diary 1*, 24 March, f. 1), architecture and human behaviour.

West possessed an unusual ability to integrate herself into other cultures – she felt akin to the Jews, for example – and found much in Greek Orthodox ceremonies which she took part in, particularly in Macedonia, fulfilling. West originally trained as an actress (the church services are viewed theatrically), and she enjoyed the possibilities offered by acting a part, disguise and pseudonyms. Her many names sometimes come from animals (as lovers, she and H. G. Wells were 'Panther' and 'Jaguar' to one another) and she is frequently intrigued by animal metaphor. Yugoslavia, as it were, offered her a menagerie of images with which to express herself. West selects these images, and weighs them for usefulness. Her Yugoslav notebooks became repositories of potentially useful images. In the museum at Struga, for example, West saw a stuffed calf with two heads, and noted it as a 'superb analogy'. (RW *Diary*, 7 May, f. 100) In *Black Lamb and Grey Falcon* she elaborates, recounting the story of a peasant who brought the calf to the museum saying that with one head the calf drank milk, while the other spat it out, so the calf died after a few days. West makes this symbolic of the way in which human beings often discard what is good for them, and so suffer. In doing so, she makes the head which drank 'lovely' and the other 'hideous' (BL, p. 732) – an embroidery on the truth (I have seen the calf in Struga Museum and in fact the two heads are very similar), but a useful one for her view of the human condition.

West's technique in making a political argument draws on Lawrence, Bergson, St Augustine, Henry James and Proust, among others (unfortunately space does not permit full discussion here). It also uses theatrical device. West makes herself the main character of the book, and at the apotheosis of the drama the great plain of Kossovo provides the backdrop for her key monologue:

> I said to myself, 'if it be a law that those who are born into the world with a preference for the agreeable over the disagreeable are born also with an impulse towards defeat, then the whole world is a vast Kossovo, an abominable blood-logged plain ...' I began to weep, for the Left Wing people among whom I had lived all my life had in their attitude to foreign politics achieved such a betrayal. They were always right, they never imposed their rightness. (BL, p. 913)

Through the poem about the grey falcon of Kossovo Plain and the self-imposed defeat of Tsar Lazar, Rebecca West is 'shown' something about her own past and about the failure of the British Left. An inherent impulse towards defeat has prevailed among those she describes as 'I and my kind, the Liberals of Western Europe' (BL, p. 915), 'We Westerners' (BL, p. 917) as well as 'Left Wing people among whom I had lived all my life'. (BL, p. 913) Their 'attitude to foreign politics' has resulted, we can guess, in failing first Spain, then France, then Germany, then Czechoslovakia, now Yugoslavia, by refusing to mobilise Britain into war. They will also fail England. In *Black Lamb and Grey Falcon*, West is taking up a position on her role as a writer in politics.[17] West has been described as 'a Nietzschean Socialist Feminist',[18] but she can also be seen as a proto-existentialist as she charges the left with timidity. Rebecca West's Kossovo experience results in her separation from the left, from pacifism, and from the impulse to defeat. West's process of receptivity, observation, contemplation and lastly interpretation is presented openly. Following this, the reader is transferred from a primitive ritual in Kossovo to the problematic condition of England. Yugoslavia 'writes obscure things plain', and 'furnishes symbols for what the intellect has not yet formulated'. (BL, p. 914)

Yugoslavia may be exotic and primitive, but, as West puts it, 'the primitive mind is the foundation on which the modern mind is built'. (BL, p. 914) West was of the generation whose universe spanned Frazer, Weston, Freud and even Madame Blavatsky. Her artistic process was exploratory: 'I really write,' she said, 'to find out what I know about something and what is to be known'.[19] In several intense, contemplative passages of *Black Lamb and Grey Falcon*, she thinks deeply, often having dislocated herself in order to 'learn something more'. (BL, p. 914) This sometimes leads her to a disturbing realisation, or to conclusions which are 'discreditable to myself' (BL, p. 914) such as the realisation that Western Liberalism is deeply flawed. The words 'learned ... recognised ... felt ... thought longer' (BL, p. 914) remind the reader of the mental effort that is going on on just one level of the experience which is being replayed. She draws the reader in to this process of accumulating knowledge or wisdom.

> I had sinned in the same way, I and my kind, the Liberals of Western Europe. We had regarded ourselves as far holier than our Tory opponents because we had exchanged the role of priest for the role of lamb, and therefore we forgot that we were not performing the chief moral obligation of humanity, which is to protect the works of love. (BL, p. 915)

To reach the point of realisation through the process described, West needs a place which is at sufficient distance from England to allow her the mental freedom to become receptive, and which will furnish her with symbols and analogies, yet which is not too distant from her own culture. Yugoslavia offers an 'in-between' position for West. It is an outer fringe, an exotic but accessible 'wonderland'.[20] Imagining Europe in the 1930s without the block of Cold War separation, we can approach more closely West's vision, both of Yugoslavia and of the condition of England. Yet even by the time her book was published, the barriers of silence had begun to go up. Vinaver, West's friend and guide in Yugoslavia, never saw a copy of the book in which he 'plays' the main character of Constantine: communication was severed, and West drew a line under the Europe she had known with her epigraph to *Black Lamb and Grey Falcon*, 'to my friends in Yugoslavia who are now all dead or enslaved'.

At the end of the 1930s, both Rebecca West and Storm Jameson shared a sense that something was wrong with England, but also, after witnessing Europe, discovered that there was also much worth saving. In writing *Black Lamb and Grey Falcon* and *Europe to Let* both contributed to the debate against appeasement. Neither lived to see the end of the Cold War (they died in 1983 and 1986, respectively). Their political engagement as writers perhaps owes something to the mix of politics and culture which they experienced abroad, and their books allow us access to the gender, politics and history of the 1930s in exciting ways, particularly by rereading them as part of 'coming in' from the Cold War.

Notes

1. John Lewis Gaddis, *We Now Know: Rethinking Cold War History* (Oxford: Clarendon Press, 1997), p. 115.
2. Storm Jameson, *Europe to Let: The Memoirs of an Obscure Man* (London: Macmillan, 1940), p. 258. All further references to EL are to this edition and page numbers are given in the main body of the text.
3. See Arthur Koestler, Ignazio Silone, André Gide presented by Enid Starkie, Richard Wright, Louis Fischer, Stephen Spender, *The God That Failed: Six Studies in Communism* with an introduction by Richard Crossman, MP (London: Hamish Hamilton, 1950). The book looks back on 1930s Communism as the youthful folly of idealistic young men.
4. Rebecca West, *Black Lamb and Grey Falcon: A Journey Through Yugoslavia in 1937* (1941; London: Macmillan, 1984). All further references to BL are to this edition and page numbers are given in the main body of the text.
5. Terry Eagleton, 'Enjoy!', a review of *The Indivisible Remainder*, *The Abyss of Freedom* and *The Plague of Fantasies* by Slavoj Zizek, in *London Review of Books*, 27 November 1997, pp. 7–9.
6. The phrase coined by Samuel Hynes, *The Auden Generation: Literature and Politics in the 1930s* (London: Bodley Head, 1976).
7. Cynthia Enloe, *The Morning After: Sexual Politics After the Cold War* (London: University of California Press, 1993), p. 7.
8. Bonnie Kime Scott, *Refiguring Modernism Volume 1: The Women of 1928* (Bloomington: Indiana University Press, 1995). See Fig. 1, 'A Tangled Mesh of Modernists', p. xxiii and Fig. 2, 'A Triple Web of Attachments', p. xxv.

9. Storm Jameson, Autobiography of Storm Jameson: *Journey from the North*, 2 vols (1970; London: Virago, 1984), vol. 2, p. 153. Further references to JN 1 and JN 2 are to this edition and page numbers are given in the body of the text.

10. Much could be said about the Bergsonian nature of *Black Lamb and Grey Falcon*. West's guide in Yugoslavia, the poet Stanislav Vinaver, had been a student of Bergson in Paris.

11. An excellent discussion of Central Europe is to be found in George Schöpflin and Nancy Wood (eds), *In Search of Central Europe* (London: Polity, 1989).

12. Vaclav Havel, 'An Anatomy of Reticence', in *Living in Truth* (London: Faber, 1989), pp. 183–4.

13. Anne Frank, *Diary of a Young Girl* (London: Constellation Books, 1952), with an introduction by Storm Jameson.

14. See Joanna Labon, 'Tracing Storm Jameson', in *Women: A Cultural Review*, vol. 8, no. 1, Spring 1997, pp. 33–47.

15. Storm Jameson, *The End of This War* (London: Allen and Unwin, 1941).

16. The notebook labelled 'Diary of 2nd Yugoslav Trip' (vols 1 and 2) is in the Rebecca West archive, Beineke Rare Book and Manuscript, Yale University. Further references to RW *Diary* are given by page number in the body of the text. These references are RW *Diary* 1, ff. 1–7. I wish to thank London University Central Research Fund for their grant which gave me access to the Rebecca West archive.

17. This debate was fuelled by Julien Benda in *Le trahison des clercs* (1927); *The Great Betrayal*, tr. Richard Aldington (London: Routledge, 1928) which accused intellectuals of betraying their role as scholars by becoming involved in politics.

18. John Stokes, '"A Woman of Genius": Rebecca West at the Theatre', in Michael R. Booth and Joel H. Kaplan (eds), *The Edwardian Theatre* (Cambridge: Cambridge University Press, 1995), p. 194.

19. Interview with Rebecca West, by Marina Warner in George Simpson and Frank Kermode (eds), *Writers at Work: The Paris Review Interviews* (London: Secker, 1985), p. 18.

20. The phrase is from H. G. Wells, who said, 'Rebecca wanted history to be full of wonderlands', *H. G. Wells in Love* (London: Faber, 1984), p. 100.

The Contributors

Gillian Beer is King Edward VII Professor of English at Cambridge University and President of Clare Hall, Cambridge. Her numerous publications include *Darwin's Plots: Evolutionary Narrative in Darwin, George Eliot and Nineteenth-Century Fiction* (1983), *George Eliot* (1986), *Arguing with the Past* (1989), *Open Fields: Science and Cultural Encounter* (1986), and *Virginia Woolf: The Common Ground* (1996).

David Bradshaw is Hawthornden Fellow and Tutor in English at Worcester College, Oxford University, and a University Lecturer in English. Editor of *The Hidden Huxley* and *Brave New World* (both 1994), and Oxford World's Classics editions of *The White Peacock* (1997) and *Women in Love* (1988). He has published articles on Bloomsbury, Conrad, T. S. Eliot, Huxley, Woolf and Yeats.

Jane Dowson is a Senior Lecturer in English and Cultural Studies at De Montfort University. Her publications include *Women's Poetry of the 1930s: A Critical Anthology* and *The Selected Poems of Frances Cornford*. She is currently writing about Modern, Modernist and contemporary women poets.

Elena Gualtieri is a Lecturer in English at the University of Sussex. She has published in *Textual Practice* and is writing a book on Virginia Woolf's essays, feminism and history, to be published by Macmillan.

Alison Hennegan was literary editor of *Gay News* from 1977–83 and editor of the Women's Press Book Club from 1984–92. She created the Lesbian Landmarks series for Virago, providing introductions for that series and a wide range of other reprinted editions of twentieth-century women writers. She is a member of the English Faculty of the University of Cambridge.

Maroula Joannou is a Senior Lecturer in English and Co-ordinator of the MA in Women's Studies at the University of Eastern England in Cambridge and Chelmsford. She obtained her Ph.D from Cambridge

University as a mature student and is the author of *'Ladies, Please Don't Smash these Windows': Women's Writing, Feminist Consciousness and Social Change 1918–38*, and co-editor with David Margolies of a book of essays in memory of Margot Heinemann and another with June Purvis on the women's suffrage movement.

Joanna Labon is a postgraduate student at Birkbeck College, University of London. Her Ph.D, 'Europe to Let. Rebecca West and Storm Jameson: English Literary Responses to Fascism c. 1940', is supervised by Tom Healy. Previously a publisher (at Faber and Faber and Jonathan Cape), and Consultant on Eastern Europe at ICA Talks, she has edited a literary magazine, *Storm: New Writings from East and West*, from 1990–94 and *Balkan Blues: Writing Out of Yugoslavia*, 1995.

Elizabeth Maslen is a Senior Lecturer in English at Queen Mary and Westfield College, University of London. She has published several articles on women writers of the 1930s and is the author of a recent study of Doris Lessing in the series *Writers and their Work*. She is currently working on a book about the politics of fiction written by women between 1928 and 1968.

Janet Montefiore is a Senior Lecturer at the University of Kent where she teaches English and Women's Studies. She is the author of *Feminism and Poetry* and *Men and Women Writers of the 1930s* and has published numerous articles and reviews on women's poetry, feminist theory, and a wide range of twentieth-century literature. She is currently researching the life of Nancy Cunard.

Linden Peach is a Reader in English at Loughborough University. He has previously taught at Bretton Hall, the University of Leeds and Goldsmiths College, University of London. His recent publications include *Toni Morrison, English as a Creative Art* (with Angela Burton), *Angela Carter and Toni Morrison: New Casebook*. He is currently completing a study of Virginia Woolf in her historical context.

Wendy Pollard is a mature student completing a Ph.D on the literary reception of the work of Rosamond Lehmann, at Lucy Cavendish College, University of Cambridge under the supervision of Alison Hennegan.

Jean Radford is a Senior Lecturer in English at Goldsmiths College, University of London and is the author of *Dorothy Richardson*, Harvester Key Women Writers, 1991. Her recent publishers include 'The Women and the Jew: Sex and Modernity', in Bryan Cheyette and

Laura Marcus (eds), *Modernity, Culture and 'the Jew'*, Polity, 1997. She is currently writing a book entitled *The Other Side of Modernity: Modernism Revisited* for Edinburgh University Press.

Sylvia Vance has a Ph.D from Oxford University on the rise of Fascism and the parallel interest in pacifism in the 1930s and its influence on women writers of the decade including Storm Jameson. In Canada she co-edited an anthology of writings by native women, *Writing the Circle*. She is a Lecturer at St Edmund's Hall, Oxford University.

Diana Wallace is a Lecturer in English at the University of Glamorgan. She obtained her Ph.D for a thesis on inter-war women's writing, which is to be published as a book by Macmillan's at Loughborough University. She was Research Assistant to Professor Marion Shaw. She has also taught at Nottingham Trent University and has contributed to Marion Shaw (ed.), *An Introduction to Women's Writing from the Middle Ages to the Present Day*.

Keith Williams is a Lecturer in English at the University of Dundee and has previously taught at the Universities of Leeds and Exeter. He is the author of *British Writers and the Media 1930–45* and has just edited a collection of essays with Steven Matthews, *Rewriting the Thirties: Modernism and After*. He is currently writing studies of Modernism and the movies and inter-war reportage.

Tory Young teaches part-time at the University of Eastern England and for the Open University. She has a Ph.D on Modernism and the visual arts obtained from Newcastle University and is currently researching the representation of Nancy Cunard.

Index

INDEX

INDEX

St. Louis Community College
at Meramec
Library